THE FUTURES OF LEGAL E
LEGAL PROF

We are currently witnessing an unprecede..... ..a.. siormation in the legal profession and legal education. The Legal Services Act 2007 and the Legal Aid, Sentencing and Punishment of Offenders Act 2012 have both enabled and necessitated dramatic structural changes to the profession, as well as impacting on its ethos and ethicality. The recent Legal Education and Training Review (LETR) promises similarly dramatic change to the provision of legal education, reflecting the shifting landscape of both the legal professional market and higher education in general. These transformative changes bring both exciting opportunities and challenges with which everyone involved in the law—from university lecturers, to senior partners in leading law firms, to the judiciary—must grapple. This edited collection comprises a selection of papers presented at the second conference of CEPLER, Birmingham Law School's Centre for Professional Legal Education and Research. The aim of the conference, and thus this collection, was to bring together leading academic scholars, senior figures from professional practice, policymakers, and representatives of the regulatory authorities, to reflect on the key issues arising from this transformative moment. As such, this volume of essays covers diverse ground, from curriculum development to professional theory, enriched and enhanced by the range of backgrounds and perspectives of its contributors.

The Futures of Legal Education and the Legal Profession

Edited by

Hilary Sommerlad
Sonia Harris-Short
Steven Vaughan
and
Richard Young

·HART·
PUBLISHING

OXFORD AND PORTLAND, OREGON
2015

Published in the United Kingdom by Hart Publishing Ltd
16C Worcester Place, Oxford, OX1 2JW
Telephone: +44 (0)1865 517530
Fax: +44 (0)1865 510710
E-mail: mail@hartpub.co.uk
Website: http://www.hartpub.co.uk

Published in North America (US and Canada) by
Hart Publishing
c/o International Specialized Book Services
920 NE 58th Avenue, Suite 300
Portland, OR 97213-3786
USA
Tel: +1 503 287 3093 or toll-free: (1) 800 944 6190
Fax: +1 503 280 8832
E-mail: orders@isbs.com
Website: http://www.isbs.com

Hart Publishing is an imprint of Bloomsbury Publishing plc.

British Library Cataloguing in Publication Data
Data Available

ISBN: 978-1-84946-655-4

Typeset by Compuscript Ltd, Shannon
Printed and bound in Great Britain by
CPI Group (UK) Ltd, Croydon CR0 4YY

Foreword

In 1988 Richard Abel produced the first ever compendium of statistics on the legal profession and legal education and training in England and Wales.[1] The figures ended in December 1985. They represent the start of a genuinely evidence-based approach to these subjects, replacing a long tradition of continuing controversies based largely on speculation, opinion, or self-interest. About two or three years later a leading barrister is reputed to have said in effect: 'A magnificent achievement. Is it not a pity that the history of the legal profession started in 1986?'

That statement is now out of date. There are now so many legal professions and 'professions' that commentators cannot agree how many there were in 2013; some talk as if the history of modern legal services in England and Wales begins with the Legal Services Act 2007; there is no consensus on whether the Legal Education and Training Review represents a fresh start or merely the continuation of a series of periodic reports that date back at least as far as the Ormrod report of 1970. Nearly all are agreed that legal services are in a continuing process of complex changes that is far from over and quite unpredictable. Accordingly it was brave of the organisers of this symposium to produce a book that interprets the current situation. Although it cannot help to be more than an album of snapshots of the situation in 2013–14 from a variety of angles and perspectives, it is still welcome as a very well-informed and helpful starting point for trying to make sense of a complex situation in flux. It is written by leading experts and activists in the field and it marks a growing recognition of the academic and practical importance of two new areas of expertise—the legal education professional and the scholar of legal services.

The acronyms scattered through this book are evidence of growth of special expertise in these two overlapping fields: LSA, LSB, SRA, CILEX, LET, LETR, ASBs, QASA, BTS, QLTS have joined those of longer standing such as ACLEC, CPD, QLD, BVC and TFRG. However, the issues are not solely matters for specialists. Any legal practitioner or academic lawyer who wishes to try to understand the current situation and likely new directions will find this book an indispensable guide.

William Twining, Emeritus Quain Professor of Jurisprudence
University College London
August 2014

---

[1] R Abel, *The English Legal Profession* (Oxford, Blackwell, 1988).

Acknowledgements

This volume of essays was birthed at the second conference of Birmingham Law School's Centre for Professional Legal Education and Research (CEPLER), held in October 2013. Established in 2012, CEPLER aims to promote professional legal education at both undergraduate and graduate level, and to foster research opportunities on legal education and the legal profession. Our thanks go to all the speakers at the second CEPLER conference and to those in the audience who asked probing questions. We would also like to thank Lesley Griffiths for her assistance with the conference organisation, Tina Martin for her careful editing of this volume and Rachel Turner from Hart Publishing for her guidance and support.

Table of Contents

Contributors

Editors

Hilary Sommerlad is Professor of Law and Research Director of the Centre for Professional Legal Education and Research (CEPLER) at Birmingham Law School.

Sonia Harris-Short is former Professor of Family Law and Policy at Birmingham Law School and the former Head of CEPLER.

Steven Vaughan is a Lecturer at Birmingham Law School and Education Director of CEPLER.

Richard Young is Professor of Law and Policy at the University of Birmingham.

Author Biographies (in alphabetical order)

Richard L Abel is the Michael J Connell Distinguished Professor of Law Emeritus at UCLA School of Law, California. He is a leading global scholar on the legal profession whose publications include the seminal text *English Lawyers between Market and State* (Oxford, Oxford University Press 2003).

Julia Evetts is a Professor Emeritus in the School of Sociology and Social Policy at Nottingham University. She has published widely on professions and occupations, including women's and men's careers in law, teaching, banking, and science and engineering in industrial organisations.

James R Faulconbridge is a Professor at the Lancaster University Management School. His work covers globalisation and professional service firms; knowledge, learning and innovation; and mobility in everyday and business life.

Rosemary Hunter is Professor of Law at Kent Law School. A feminist legal scholar, her research spans family law, access to justice, domestic violence, women's employment (including women in the legal profession and women judges), anti-discrimination law and dispute resolution.

Tony King is the Director of the Clifford Chance Academy at the international law firm Clifford Chance LLP. After qualifying as a solicitor and a period teaching at the then College of Law, he has been involved in education, training and professional development at Clifford Chance since 1988.

Mavis Maclean is joint Director of the Oxford Centre for Family Law and Policy at Oxford University and a Senior Research Fellow in the Faculty of Law. She has carried out socio-legal research since 1974.

Daniel Muzio is Professor of Professions and Organization at Newcastle University Business School. His research focuses on professions and knowledge workers, their work, management and organisation.

Alex Roy was Head of Development and Research at the Legal Services Board till April 2014, when he left to take up a post as Manager (Pensions and Investments) at the Financial Conduct Authority.

Andrew Sanders is Professor of Criminal Law and Criminology at the University of Birmingham, where he is Head of the School of Law. He is a board member of the Bar Standards Board and former Chair of the Committee of Heads of University Law Schools in England and Wales.

Julian Webb is Professor of Legal Education at the Law School, Warwick University. His research interests focus on legal education policy and theory, the ethics and professional regulation of lawyers, social and legal theory, and the ethics of socio-legal research. He was one of the project leads on the *Legal Education and Training Review*.

1

The Futures of Legal Education and the Legal Profession

HILARY SOMMERLAD, RICHARD YOUNG,
STEVEN VAUGHAN AND SONIA HARRIS-SHORT

W E ARE CURRENTLY witnessing an unprecedented transformation in the legal profession and legal education. The Legal Services Act 2007 (LSA) and the Legal Aid, Sentencing and Punishment of Offenders Act 2012 (LASPO) have both enabled and necessitated dramatic structural changes to the profession, as well as impacting on its ethos and ethicality. The recent Legal Education and Training Review (LETR) promises similarly dramatic change to the provision of legal education, reflecting the shifting landscape of both the legal professional market and higher education in general. These transformative developments bring both exciting opportunities and challenges with which everyone involved in the law—from university lecturers, to senior partners in leading law firms, to the judiciary—must grapple.

This edited collection comprises a selection of the papers presented at the second conference of Birmingham Law School's Centre for Professional Legal Education and Research (CEPLER), held in October 2013. The aim of the conference, and thus this collection, was to bring together leading academic scholars, senior figures from professional practice, policymakers and representatives of the regulatory authorities, to reflect on the key issues arising from this transformative moment. The conference therefore covered diverse ground, from curriculum development to professional theory, enriched and enhanced by the range of backgrounds and perspectives of its contributors. This breadth was a key strength of the conference, as it is of this collection. How a person will experience and respond to recent developments in legal education and the legal profession, and that person's take on the futures of the legal profession and legal education, will inevitably be shaped by their position in the field. The book therefore presents a range of perspectives on these issues by including chapters which are wholly theoretical, others which are empirically grounded, one which presents the regulator's view, one written by a practitioner and finally, one written by an external observer who is nevertheless an expert academic commentator on the English legal profession. Thus, its contents do not only provide a timely account of where we are in terms of the legal profession and legal education but, more importantly, set out a series of visions of the futures of the legal profession and legal education.

CEPLER has the twin aims of promoting in undergraduate and graduate legal education an enhanced awareness of professional culture, values and practices, and fostering cutting edge research on the legal profession and legal education. The conference theme of 'The Futures of the Legal Profession and Legal Education' was therefore extremely apt. Here, 'futures' is intentionally plural, as the possibility of there being but one future for the legal profession or for legal education is low. This collection is far from representing mere speculation, however. While the direction and nature of social change is perhaps always more uncertain than post-hoc analysis allows, there are nonetheless clear turning or tipping points, and that is certainly true in this field. First, we appear to have reached a pivotal moment in the process of change which has transformed the legal profession over the course of the last three decades. The developments in the solicitors' branch are particularly striking: the provisions in the LSA which enable law firms to become Alternative Business Structures in partnership with other occupations marks the end of the distinctiveness of legal services and the profession, while the cuts to the scope of legal aid implemented under LASPO will dramatically erode the 'social service' arm of the legal profession.[1] Second, as the recent institution of the LETR indicates, the level of change across the justice system has profound implications for the thousands of people graduating from degree programmes and professional training courses in law every year.

The dramatic change in the demographic profile of the law student body is itself a major factor in this process of transformation. As one of the paradigmatic 'classical' professions, it was until the mid-1980s overwhelmingly male, white and middle class;[2] however, since 1989 female trainee lawyers have outnumbered males,[3] and the proportion of Black, Asian and Minority Ethnic (BAME) trainees has risen significantly in the last decade.[4] This diversification of the profession has extended to both the types and

---

[1] S Brint, *In an Age of Experts: The Changing Role of Professionals in Politics and Public Life* (Princeton, Princeton University Press, 1994); HW Arthurs, 'The State We're In: Legal Education in Canada's New Political Economy' (2001) 20 *Windsor Yearbook of Access to Justice* 35.
[2] As well as being heterosexual and able-bodied—though the data on all the protected characteristics other than gender, age and ethnicity are thin.
[3] Law Society, 'Annual Statistical Report 2000' (Law Society, 2000) para 9.7.
[4] Black Solicitors Network, 'Diversity League Table 2013' (BSN, Law Society and Bar Council, 2013).

sites of practice: the once numerically small and relatively homogenous guild-like institution[5] is today a large[6] and fragmented occupational field which contains both increasingly impoverished organisations and also one of the most profitable sectors of the UK economy.[7] The field encompasses regulated and unregulated entities, qualified and unqualified law workers, claims management companies, conveyancing firms, high street practices, global corporate firms and new multidisciplinary practices, to name just some of the varieties of practitioners and sites. These changes in the profession's composition and size have generated further transformations, for instance in its traditional values and the sorts of skills, attributes and forms of knowledge entailed in legal work.[8] Above all, they are part of a deeper transformation from a pre-capitalist craft occupation,[9] which was self-regulated through the mechanism of collegiality and in which, in the solicitors' branch, every practitioner could in theory become a partner,[10] into a capitalist service industry in which the majority of lawyers are employees.

Before considering these transformations in more detail, it is worth reminding ourselves that they are linked with, and prompted by, broader socio-economic changes, such as the decline of the Keynsian interventionist state.[11] Many of the developments are the result of the well-documented

---

[5] EA Krause, *Death of the Guilds: Professions, States, and the Advance of Capitalism, 1930 to the Present* (New Haven, Yale University Press, 1996).

[6] The solicitors' profession grew by over 200% between 1981 and 2013—Law Society, 'Trends in the Solicitors Profession: Annual Statistical Report 2013' (Law Society, 2013).

[7] Turnover in the UK legal services sector grew by 60% between 1995 and 2003, to a total of £19bn. By 2010, despite downturns in performance, it had grown by another 35% to reach £25.6bn—Legal Education and Training Review, 'Setting Standards: The Future of Legal Services Education and Training Regulation in England and Wales' (SRA, BSB and CILEX, 2013) 77, available at: www.letr.org.uk.

[8] The literature on this change is vast, but see for instance the chapters by Evetts (ch 2); Faulconbridge and Muzio (ch 3); and Webb (ch 6) in this volume; also C Glasser, 'The Legal Profession in the 1990s: Images of Change (1990) 10 *Legal Studies* 1; G Hanlon, 'Professionalism as Enterprise: Service Class Politics and the Redefinition of Professionalism' (1998) 32 *Sociology* 43; H Sommerlad, 'The Implementation of Quality Initiatives and the New Public Management in the Legal Aid Sector in England and Wales: Bureaucratisation, Stratification and Surveillance' (1999) 6 *International Journal of the Legal Profession* 311; H Sommerlad and P Sanderson, 'Exploring the Limits to the Standardization of the Expert Knowledge of Lawyers: Quality and Legal Aid in the United Kingdom' (2002) 54 *Syracuse Law Review* 987; J Hagan and F Kay, *Gender in Practice: A Study of Lawyers' Lives* (New York, Oxford University Press, 1995).

[9] See for instance H Sommerlad, 'Managerialism and the Legal Professional: A New Professional Paradigm' (1995) 2 *International Journal of the Legal Profession* 159, for discussion of the modernisation of working processes within law firms so that they became capitalist entities increasingly involved in the mass production of a 'legal product', rather than individualised services run as partnerships.

[10] Traditional law firms and barristers' chambers are therefore likened to 'kinship' networks; see M Burrage, 'From a Gentleman's to a Public Profession—Status and Politics in the History of English Solicitors' (1996) 3 *International Journal of the Legal Profession* 45.

[11] Also referred to as the welfare state—that is the state that emerged as a consequence of the experience of the Great Depression, two world wars and political struggles for a more

hegemony of neo-liberal thinking about the relationship between the public and private sectors, the benefits of applying the logics of the market to wider and wider spheres of human activity and transferring responsibility for the resolution of social problems from the state to the individual.[12] For instance, for over a decade the state has been reducing its responsibility for the provision of dispute resolution—a function identified by Weber as basic to its role.[13] Other developments arise from the way in which, in the corporate sphere, the generation of profit has come to be seen as the primary metric for success. Free market ideologies have transformed the profession into one that is thoroughly commercial and market driven, eroding justice and rights in the public discourse of law so that it has become a commodity much like any other. The LSA exemplifies and accelerates this development. Such free market ideologies are also seen in higher education: the rise in student fees; and, for law in particular, the tensions between employability/ vocationality and a liberal arts education.

The dominance of market-based rationality together with the erosion of the self-employed practitioner model have in turn generated fundamental shifts in the technologies of production of legal services of the kind that labour process theorists[14] concerned with divisions of labour would recognise: 'unbundling',[15] web-based provision and the redistribution of tasks down a hierarchy of employees. On the supply side, these structural changes have been facilitated by higher education's dramatic expansion and, as noted above, its diversification which has provided the profession with a supply of practitioners whose 'difference' justifies their confinement to subordinate roles (including that of the salaried partner)[16] and hence both its stratification and commercialisation.[17]

---

socially just society, achieved through the application of the new Keynesian economic paradigm which proposed government intervention to create employment and redistribute wealth.

[12] The term neo-liberal is problematic, apparently oversimplifying a complex, contingent range of phenomena. However, there are sufficient common features to give it conceptual validity. For Stuart Hall, one of its primary threads is 'possessive individualism' and consequent anti-statism: S Hall, 'The Neo-Liberal Revolution' (2011) 48 *Soundings* 10–11. See too, C Crouch, *The Strange Non Death of Neo-Liberalism* (Cambridge, Polity Press, 2011). In her chapter in this volume, Evetts refers to the phenomenon as economic liberalism.

[13] M Weber, *Economy and Society*, vol II (Berkeley, University of California Press, 1978) 905.

[14] H Braverman, *Labour and Monopoly Capital: The Degradation of Work in the Twentieth Century* (New York, Monthly Review Press, 1998).

[15] R Susskind, *The End of Lawyers?* (Oxford, Oxford University Press, 2008).

[16] As Faulconbridge and Muzio show in their chapter in this collection, the creation and increasing use of the salaried partner position is intimately linked with increased leverage in firms; it is also a position which is disproportionately filled by women.

[17] This commercialisation, or increased focus on and achievement of profitability, has been widely discussed and charted; see, eg, R Suddaby and T Viale, 'Professionals and Field-Level Change: Institutional Work and the Professional Project' (2011) 59 *Current Sociology* 423, and also, in this volume, Evetts (ch 2) and also Faulconbridge and Muzio (ch 3).

This collection explores each of these driving forces, and our reflections on them here provide an important backdrop since they underline the fact that the profession is embedded in and therefore contingent on the wider social structure. The term 'profession' is consequently fluid, making it important to consider how it has been and is currently conceptualised.

I. CONCEPTUALISATIONS OF THE PROFESSION

The meaning of the term 'profession' has long been contested, even within the Anglo-American field where its distinctiveness from other occupational categories has been primarily asserted,[18] and this debate underscores the profession's historical contingency. Thus, the classical view, following Emile Durkheim,[19] is of an institution which fulfilled a key social function as an intermediary between individuals and the state and the market—a function which it was able to perform because of its (interlinked) 'traits', in particular its autonomy, distinctive ethicality and specialist expertise.[20] This functionalist conception, which corresponded to the profession's self-representation, is therefore associated with a particular historical era: the profession's pivotal role in the development of modernity was made possible by its unique moral and intellectual authority,[21] and was the basis for the special relationship with the state which it developed in the nineteenth century.

The macro-level social changes touched on above therefore did not only begin to transform the role of law and the profession, but also stimulated new theorisations, this time following Max Weber,[22] which have themselves

[18] M Saks, 'Defining a Profession: The Role of Knowledge and Expertise' (2012) 2 *Professions & Professionalism* 1; MS Larson, *The Rise of Professionalism: A Sociological Analysis* (Berkeley, University of California Press, 1977).

[19] E Durkheim, *The Division of Labour in Society*, G Simpson trans (New York, The Free Press, 1964); Durkheim's view that the division of labour and occupational groups represented the moral basis for modern society led him to focus on professions as entities which embodied functional social forces and would be able to act as integrative and adaptive institutions which could save modern society. This view influenced a range of sociologists writing in the middle of the twentieth century including Talcott Parsons who wrote of the professions' 'collectivity orientation': T Parsons, 'Professions and Social Structure' in T Parsons (ed), *Essays in Sociological Theory* (Glencoe, The Free Press, 1954).

[20] AM Carr-Saunders and PA Wilson, *The Professions* (Gloucestershire, Clarendon Press, 1933); this book exemplified the uncritical, functionalist/trait theory approach to the professions.

[21] D Sugarman, 'Blurred Boundaries: The Overlapping Worlds of Law, Business and Politics' in M Cain and C Harrington (eds), *Lawyers in a Postmodern World: Translation and Transgression* (Buckingham, Open University Press, 1994) 105.

[22] M Weber, *Economy and Society* (London, University of California Press, 1978) 220–22. Weber's legacy to subsequent (neo-Weberian) theorists of the professions was his focus on professionals' technical qualifications, and his view of classes as status groups which are communities based on ideas of proper lifestyles and the honour accorded them by others, and who therefore practise closure against outsiders. Key neo-Weberians included T Johnson,

been drivers of further change. For instance, the challenge posed to the established social order by a range of developments such as the civil rights movements, the erosion of deference to traditional authority and the collapse of manufacturing is reflected in a growing cynicism about the profession, discrediting functionalist/trait theory. By the late 1960s, this benign conceptualisation had been largely displaced by the neo-Weberian perspective which viewed professions as middle class projects to win exclusive rights to practise in specified occupational fields and thereby achieve high social status and enhanced income ('monopoly rents').[23] In this interpretation the claim to special traits and consequently to market shelters was realised and retained through social closure.[24] This entails building a 'monopoly of expertise' by making 'theoretically inexhaustible knowledge resources ... socially finite',[25] which serves both to frustrate attempted encroachments on a profession's market by other occupations and to restrict entry to those who it deems fit and proper persons: 'a restricted number of eligibles'.[26] And as feminist neo-Weberians point out, the location of these projects within 'the structural and historical parameters of patriarchal-capitalism' of the nineteenth century meant that only white males could be eligible.[27]

Social closure in the sense of outright exclusion from the profession was therefore undermined by social modernisation (in particular the mass entry of women into higher education) and the need for workers who, as a result of their 'non-normativity',[28] could be constituted as 'non-partner material'. At the same time, the profession's legitimacy was eroded by a body of empirical work grounded in the neo-Weberian perspective which, inter alia, critiqued the unrepresentative nature of the profession's social

Professions and Power (London, Macmillan, 1972); Larson, *The Rise of Professionalism* (n 18); and RL Abel, 'Comparative Sociology of Legal Professions' in RL Abel and PSC Lewis (eds), *Lawyers in Society Volume 3: Comparative Theories* (Berkeley, University of California Press, 1989) 80.

[23] That is, the returns associated with professions' monopolies and their capacity to raise these returns by limiting their membership (closure)—the term 'monopoly rents' is therefore associated with neo-Weberian interpretations of professionalism as a project to raise income and status through 'social closure'; see J Berlant, *Profession and Monopoly: A Study of Medicine in the United States and Great Britain* (Berkeley, University of California Press, 1975); and E Freidson, *Professional Dominance: The Social Structure of Medical Care* (New York, Transaction Books, 1970).

[24] Larson, *The Rise of Professionalism* (n 18).

[25] ibid, 223.

[26] F Parkin, *The Social Analysis of Class Structure* (London, Tavistock Publications, 1974) 44.

[27] A Witz, 'Patriarchy and Professions: The Gendered Politics of Occupational Closure' (1990) 24 *Sociology* 675.

[28] Finding an appropriate term to describe individuals who do not belong to the majority group which does not either essentialise or pathologise the lower status group is problematic. In addition to 'non-normative', 'non-traditional' is also used. Devon Carbado and Mitu Gulati speak of outsiders, which captures the closure tactics used by 'insiders'. See DW Carbado and M Gulati, 'Working Identity' (2000) 85 *Cornell Law Review* 1259, 1267. We and our contributors have used a variety of terms as seems appropriate to the context.

base and found that the profession exploited its exclusive practice rights by charging excessive fees and giving poor quality service, while its disciplinary bodies were seen to be complacent and lax.[29] The resulting decline in public support for the practice and administration of law,[30] generated pressure for what Alan Paterson summarises as the renegotiation of the profession's 'social contract',[31] which took the form of a range of regulatory changes.

II. REGULATORY CHANGE, MARKETISATION AND ENTERPRISE

In the last four decades we have seen a series of regulatory reviews and legislative changes to the control and ordering of the legal profession, many of which have sought to open up legal services to greater competition (from both internal and external sources).[32] Sir David Clementi's report in 2004, perhaps the most significant and far reaching of these reviews, paved the way for the LSA and the regulatory settlement which ended lawyers' powers of self-regulation, created an independent legal complaints scheme and

[29] This body of empirical work is vast and extends to all sectors of the profession, and in most jurisdictions; see, eg, AS Blumberg, 'The Practice of Law as Confidence Game: Organizational Co-Optation of the Profession' (1967) 1 *Law & Society Review* 15; P Fennell, 'Solicitors, their Markets and their "Ignorant Public": The Crisis of the Professional Ideal' in Z Bankowski and G Mungham (eds), *Essays in Law and Society* (London, Routledge, 1980); P Fennell, 'Advertising: Professional Ethics and the Public Interest' in PA Thomas (ed), *Law in the Balance: Legal Services in the Eighties* (Oxford, Martin Robertson, 1982); M McConville et al, *Standing Accused: The Organisation of Practices of Criminal Defence Lawyers in Britain* (Oxford, Clarendon Press, 1994); H Cousy, PT Fenn and R Van den Burgh, 'Introduction: Issues in Law and Economics' (1998) 87 *The Geneva Papers in Risk and Insurance* 147; A Sherr et al, *Lawyers: The Quality Agenda Volume I: Assessing and Developing Competence and Quality in Legal Aid: The Report of the Birmingham Franchising Pilot* (London, HMSO/ The Legal Aid Board, 1994); M Seneviratne, 'Consumer Complaints and the Legal Profession: Making Self-Regulation Work?' (2000) 7 *International Journal of the Legal Profession* 39; LM Mather, CA McEwen and RJ Maiman, *Divorce Lawyers at Work: Varieties of Professionalism in Practice* (New York, Oxford University Press, 2001); RA Chandler and N Fry, 'Regulating a Reluctant Profession: Holding Solicitors to Account' (2008) 32 *Accounting Forum* 303.

[30] Including scathing critical reports from the Consumers' Association persisting into the twenty-first century; see: 'Solicitors Savage Consumers Group for Critical Reports' *Law Society Gazette* (2 November 2001), available at: www.lawgazette.co.uk/35407.article.

[31] In this Paterson follows the functionalist view of professions as key agents in fulfilling the functions necessary to social order. However, whereas classical functionalists described the relationship between the profession and wider society as a social bargain, Paterson prefers the term 'contract' since for him this better conveys its contingency and, consequently, the dynamic nature of the concept of legal professionalism which, 'being socially constructed ... evolves over time': A Paterson, *Lawyers and the Public Good* (Cambridge, Cambridge University Press, 2012) 16.

[32] On these reviews and reforms, see: M Zander, 'The Thatcher Government's Onslaught on the Lawyers: Who Won?' (1990) 24 *International Lawyer* 753; Legal Services Institute, 'The Legal Services Act 2007: An Act of Revolution for the Legal Profession?' (LSI, 2011), available at: www.thelegaleducationfoundation.org/the-legal-services-institute-downloads/the-legal-services-act-2007-an-act-of-revolution-for-the-legal-profession.

introduced non-lawyer owned providers of legal services.[33] Evidently, these regulatory reforms and the solvent effect of marketisation on the boundaries between professional groups and the increasing penetration of professional fields by non-professional discourses and forms of practice, such as 'Human Relations',[34] have further undermined classical professional ideology and accelerated the fragmentation of its organisational forms.

The chapter by Julia Evetts in this collection provides a theoretical overview from a distinguished sociologist of the professions and professionalism of the impact of some of these changes. She is sympathetic to the functionalist view of the professions, arguing that a distinctive ethicality is indeed inherent in the logic of 'classical' professionalism and sits alongside important ideological elements. She is therefore concerned with the relationship between this logic and that of the market and enterprise, focusing on how the latter has penetrated not only the corporate sector of the legal profession, but also, primarily as a result of the regulatory changes introduced by the neo-liberal strategy of New Public Management (NPM),[35] the public sector (including legal aid practices reliant on public funding). She shows how the discourse of enterprise, realised in the application of the NPM techniques of quasi-markets, audit modalities of accountability, and a model of quality based on consumer satisfaction, has eroded the autonomy and privileged relationship which the classical professions traditionally enjoyed with the state, and the way in which contemporary professionals are enmeshed in organisational systems which privilege managerial and accounting rationalities, and focus on output rather than processual expertise. As these rationalities become internalised by professional actors, traditional collegial values are replaced by an individuated and self-regulated governmentality, and professionals begin to embed managerialism in their career strategies. Nonetheless, Evetts also argues that the logics of enterprise and professionalism have the potential to produce hybrid forms in which professional collegiality is replaced by multidisciplinary teamworking, and managerial control operates more consensually. Her conclusion, however, is that there are risks implicit in this hybrid professionalism which include the unintended consequences of target driven cultures, and the bleaching out of professional values and ethics from relationships with clients/customers.

---

[33] D Clementi, 'Report of the Review of the Regulatory Framework for Legal Services in England and Wales' (MOJ, 2004), available at: webarchive.nationalarchives.gov.uk+; www.legal-services-review.org.uk/content/report/index.htm.

[34] A Abbott, *The System of Professions: An Essay on the Division of Expert Labour* (Chicago, University of Chicago Press, 1988).

[35] New Public Management (NPM) is the term coined to describe the range of disciplinary mechanisms introduced in the mid-1970s as part of the neo-liberal project to control public sector professionals. See, eg, C Hood, 'A Public Management for All Seasons?' (1991) 69 *Public Administration* 3.

III. THE CORPORATE SECTOR: FINANCIALISATION, RATIONALISATION AND 'PROLETARIANISATION'

The enrichment of corporate practice as a consequence of globalisation has fractured the homogeneity of the profession, and has in other ways been a significant factor in the erosion of classical professionalism. For instance, in the solicitors' branch it has shifted the locus of power from the professional association to individual firms, and as a result has similarly shifted attention away from the professional body to individual organisations. The coincidence between the expansion and diversification of the profession's supply base with the growth and capitalisation of this sector and consequent need for employee technicians has stimulated the horizontal and vertical rationalisation of labour within these firms.[36] In their contribution to this collection James Faulconbridge and Daniel Muzio reflect on the relationship between diversification and changes in the social organisation of labour. They begin by exploring in detail the penetration of corporate firms by the logic of the financial sector in which they are enmeshed, and the way in which this logic, through the proxy of metrics such as the profits per equity partner (PEP) ratio, has impacted on these firms' structure and organisation, workforce composition, work organisation and sense of mission. They then demonstrate that measuring a firm's success using these metrics (which are largely developed by external factors such as the trade press) has provided pressure to 'leverage' work to raise profit ratios, by increasing the proportion of both salaried partners (who are disproportionately non-normative) and law workers on lower salaries with intermediate or minimal qualifications, and the volume of work which can be 'produced' through document management systems. This process—which appears to vindicate predictions made in the 1980s that many practitioners would become proletarianised[37]—leads them to reflect on the threat that the prioritisation of profit poses to the service ethic and professional standards. Although their analysis of data gathered since the financial crisis indicates that this transformation may have been conjunctural rather than epochal, coinciding with the excessive leveraging in the financial sector which brought about the economic crash, they suggest that the opportunities provided by the LSA might yet facilitate an intensification of this process. Their chapter therefore reinforces Evetts's analysis of the tensions between the logics and culture of professionalism, expertise and service, and those of enterprise, profit, commercial success and organisational efficiency, and echoes her concerns about the threat the profession's marketisation and stratification pose to traditional professional values.

---

[36] Hagan and Kay, *Gender in Practice* (n 8).
[37] C Derber, *Professionals as Workers: Mental Labour in Advanced Capitalism* (Boston, GK Hall & Company, 1982).

IV. TRANSFORMATIONS ON THE HIGH STREET
AND IN THE COURTS

Parallel to the pressures generated by financialisation for cost reduction and rationalisation within corporate firms, there developed from the 1990s a concern with the 'excessive' cost of legal aid, leading to a series of reforms impacting most dramatically on the traditional high street law firm and the day to day work of the judiciary in the lower courts. Drawing on the neo-Weberian theorisation of professionalism as an exploitative monopoly project, neo-liberal discourse evoked a litigious legal aid litigant,[38] and her 'fat cat' lawyer, who required control through the NPM techniques[39] discussed by Evetts. The combined strategy of cost-capping and cost-control auditing, fixed fees and preferred supplier contracting concentrated legal aid practice in the hands of fewer and fewer providers. Simultaneously, the 1996 Woolf Report and subsequent Civil Procedure Act 1997 initiated an ongoing programme of cost reduction in the work of the courts, as an element in a strategy (ostensibly) designed to streamline procedure, and enhance access to the system and responsiveness to its users. The chapters by Mavis Maclean and Rosemary Hunter explore these facets of professional change.

Maclean is concerned with the delivery of family justice and how the NPM reforms of legal aid are impacting both on the legal profession and those seeking access to legal advice and support upon family breakdown. As with the changes to the profession generally, the transformation of the family law sector has been a lengthy and ongoing process, which Maclean has been researching for over 20 years. She draws on this experience to situate contemporary developments in the pressures which successive governments have placed on the system, as they have sought to move family disputes out of the hands of lawyers and the courts and into the hands of other often non-legally qualified professionals, principally mediators. This key policy objective has been justified by a discourse which is an extension of that of the 'fat cat lawyer', in which family lawyers are depicted as committed to the promotion of adversarial and lengthy proceedings in their own interest. Maclean uses the extensive research she has conducted, with colleagues such as John Eekelaar and Robert Dingwall, to show that this is a myth. This work indicates that the Family Law Practitioner Association (subsequently renamed Resolution) transformed the culture of family law

---

[38] A strong anti-legal aid discourse began in the early 1990s, which propagated an image of the vexatious client who pursued unmeritorious claims (at taxpayers' expense), exemplified by Gary Streeter, Conservative Under Secretary of State at the Lord Chancellor's Department, quoted in 'Streeter Confirms Legally Aided Litigants are Rottweillers' (1996) *New Law Journal* 1378.

[39] See Sommerlad, 'The Implementation of Quality Initiatives' (n 8), and H Sommerlad, 'Some Reflections on the Relationship between Citizenship, Access to Justice and the Reform of Legal Aid' (2004) 31 *Journal of Law and Society* 345.

practice into one that was non-adversarial and dedicated to negotiation and compromise and that, as a result, far from exacerbating conflict and litigation, practitioners worked effectively to achieve lasting agreement and settlement in the best interests of all parties. Further, the research found little evidence to support either the notion that mediation is any cheaper than the services of a solicitor, or the existence of significant levels of demand from parties to separation and divorce for alternative services.

Maclean goes on to detail the early findings from a new research project being conducted with Eekelaar which is examining how the legal profession has responded both to past pressures and those resulting from the government's recent austerity measures, including LASPO. There are positive findings. She describes how law firms have reacted with energy, vigour and determination, finding new, creative, more cost-efficient ways to continue to deliver key legal services to their clients. However, the results of a small survey of the fast emerging 'online divorce market' claiming to offer cost-effective access to information, advice and services on divorce raises a number of questions. The picture emerges of an unregulated and often confusing array of websites, offering different types of information, advice and services by variously qualified individuals in a manner which is likely to prove less than clear to the average consumer.

Most importantly, Maclean asks whether, as a result of these changes, we are seeing increasing inequalities between those who can afford to exercise autonomy and choice in the new and diverse legal services market and those who are constrained by limited resources to accept whatever the most 'cost efficient' option may be. Her chapter prompts us to further question whether the history of mediation and mediators she sets out is about to repeat itself with the current turn to McKenzie Friends as (supposedly) less costly, less formal sources of court support for litigants.

Hunter's chapter examines changes in judicial practices and subjectivities and reflects on the increasing presence of women on the bench, the extent to which the 'old judge'—male, white and middle class—has been supplanted, and the potential for achieving greater diversity and equality. She identifies three dynamic factors in the development of the new judiciary. The first of these is neo-liberal NPM, which has sought to rationalise case management in civil, criminal and family law, and to render the judge responsible for the process, implying the development of long-term relationships with parties to an action and their representatives. However, and as she notes, such continuity is prejudiced by other aspects of NPM, such as the increased reliance on part-time, fee-paid judges. Second, Hunter argues that judicial practice has become increasingly influenced by bio-politics, which requires the judiciary to acquire expertise in human behaviour and its management, leading to greater dependence on the 'psy' professions. She shows the impact of this on the process of managing cases, assessing evidence and making dispositions across the full range of courts. The growth in therapeutic courts and practices and the centrality of child welfare to the work of the Family and Youth courts are prime examples. The latter involve the judge working with a range of specialists, such as Cafcass officers,[40] psychiatrists and social workers. Echoing Maclean's concerns, Hunter identifies the way in which the emphasis on efficient case management and speedy resolution may be in danger of displacing child welfare as the primary goal of the Family Court system.

Hunter goes on to reflect on the significance of the new qualities and skills demanded by this transformed judging in terms of the opportunities they might seem to open up for women wishing to enter this traditionally male domain, and links her reflections with the third change factor: the equality and diversity agenda and its impact on judicial appointments. She notes that at the base of the recruitment pyramid, the Judicial Appointments Committee has devoted considerable energy towards encouraging applications from under-represented groups, but that positive engagement with the diversity agenda is attenuated the nearer one approaches the apex of the higher courts, where the performative requirements of the role are associated with the more traditional 'male' judicial characteristics, and it is harder for women to be recognised as merit worthy.

Further, these changes and their implications for greater diversity in the judiciary are not without their problems. The concentration of the 'new judge' in the lower courts continues to mark women and other outsiders as 'different' and may therefore do little to enable them to retain the respect and authority enjoyed by their 'old' male colleagues both within and outside the judiciary. At the higher levels of the judiciary, changes resulting from the pressures of neo-liberalism, bio-politics and the equality and diversity agenda are much less marked. Here the 'old (male) judge' remains very much in charge—the detached, authoritarian arbiter with the 'old' judicial (masculine) qualities of 'sound judgement', 'decisiveness' and 'objectivity'. Hunter's chapter therefore poses uncomfortable questions such as whether it is possible (and, if so, progressive or dangerous) to speak of gendered traits and characteristics. As she shows, the general view that they do exist makes it possible to justify the confinement of women to the lower (less valued and respected) therapeutic courtroom. So, as with the chapter by Evetts, the message to be taken from Hunter's contribution is nuanced: there is a positive side to some of the changes—but it appears that they carry a price in a range of ways, from their potential for sustaining gendered stereotypes to their impact on access to justice.

---

[40] Children and Family Court Advisory and Support Service—a non-departmental public body which represents children's interests in court proceedings.

V. LEGAL EDUCATION AND TRAINING

The themes discussed above in relation to the legal profession resonate with, and are inextricably linked to, legal education.[41] The transformed profession pushes and pulls on the legal education structures which help to shape it. Discourses of enterprise and financialisation are as relevant to legal education as they are to the profession, particularly in a world of higher student fees and uncapped intakes for law school. Unbundling and fragmentation are also equally relevant and raise questions about how we train the lawyers of the future; to give but two examples: (i) does, or should, a specialist road traffic accident personal injury claims handler need a separate, special accreditation or qualification scheme?; (ii) will, or should, the person providing online divorce support (as discussed by Maclean) need a law degree? Questions of diversity and social exclusion are often pushed by the profession back on to legal education providers, suggesting that it is an input problem of higher education. To address this, at least in part, legal apprenticeships are much in vogue: at individual law firms, through the qualifications frameworks of the Chartered Institute of Legal Executives;[42] and via government.[43] For law firms and legal services, the transformation of the profession presents, as well as challenges, opportunities that lead to innovation. However, it is debateable whether legal education providers are as willing, or as well prepared, to innovate.

It is evident that the implications of this complex of changes are not only that the profession requires a new approach to training, but also that the multiplicity of legal education pathways that lead to the profession also need serious review and rethinking. Law graduates seeking to enter the profession are not only facing a future very different from that which the previous generation could look forward to; in many ways they may be unclear about what the future holds at all.

However, despite the fact that the transformation of the last few decades undergone by the profession has also impacted on legal education, the changes here have been on a less revolutionary scale. It is true that curricula have been modified to take account of, for instance, the skills movement and the diversification of the student body—for instance there is more

---

[41] See H Sommerlad and P Sanderson, *Training and Regulating those Providing Publicly Funded Legal Advice Services: A Case Study of Civil Provision* (London, Ministry of Justice, 2009) for discussion of the relationship between training and professionalism, and in particular the implications for those practising legal aid law.

[42] Chartered Institute of Legal Executives, 'Apprenticeships in Legal Services' (CILEX, 2014), available at: www.cilex.org.uk/study/legal_apprenticeships.aspx.

[43] In England, the Department for Business, Innovation and Skills has its Trailblazer programme, see: www.gov.uk/government/consultations/future-of-apprenticeships-in-england-richard-review-next-steps; in Wales, legal apprenticeships are being developed by Skills for Justice, the Sector Skills Council: www.sfjuk.com/about/nations/justice-sector-in-wales/higher-apprenticeship-in-legal-services-wales.

'clinic' teaching and employability initiatives. The expansion of 'social' law has generated new modules, while the curriculum also reflects the dominance of the profession by the corporate sector.[44] A socio-legal approach has become important in some law schools, signalling the partial erosion of the received idea of law as a closed formal realm and explicitly embracing instead its embeddedness. But in essence the law school curriculum remains doctrinal and traditional. At the same time, it has become harder for law graduates to qualify as lawyers, as competition for pupillages and training contracts have intensified, producing a growing pool of paralegals.[45] These barriers which many (especially 'non-traditional') aspiring lawyers face, together with the sharp changes in the nature of professional organisation and legal practice, have for some time been generating calls for a radical overhaul of legal education, triggering a series of reviews. The latest of these is the LETR undertaken by the Solicitors Regulation Authority (SRA), the Bar Standards Board (BSB) and the Institute of Legal Executives Professional Standards (IPS).

VI. THE LETR

The LETR appears likely to shape the future of legal education and training for some time to come. Intended to be the most substantial review of legal education and training since the publication of the 1971 'Ormrod Report',[46] the LETR appointed an independent research team to make recommendations on the basis of the evidence it gathered. One of the lead researchers, Julian Webb, uses his chapter to set the review against a backdrop of a changing legal services market, shifting systems and values of professional regulation, and a growing international debate about the nature and functions of legal education. He thus provides a useful bridge between the issues raised in the chapters by Evetts, and by Faulconbridge and Muzio concerning the marketisation and financialisation of the legal profession, and the implications of these for legal education. For example, he notes that the demands of powerful commercial customers for cheaper and more focused legal services has led to the unbundling and routinisation of many legal tasks which in turn raises questions about the skills and ethical stances that educators should seek to inculcate in those non-lawyers or para-lawyers now operating at the lower reaches of the legal profession. Similarly, Webb echoes Evetts' point that the growing influence of

---

[44] An issue discussed by Andrew Sanders in ch 7 of this collection.

[45] H Sommerlad, 'The New "Professionalism" in England and Wales: Talent, Diversity, and a Legal Precariat' in S Headworth et al (eds), *Rhetoric and Reality* (forthcoming).

[46] Committee on Legal Education, *Report of the Committee on Legal Education* (Cmnd 4595, 1971) (Ormrod Report).

commercial logic within legal entities is producing hybrid forms of legal/ managerial workers. Not surprisingly, then, the LETR identifies a need for legal educators to inculcate greater 'commercial awareness' and managerial skills. More broadly, its implicit answer to the concern that market forces are driving out even the possibility of lawyers acting ethically in the public interest (rather than a narrowly conceived client interest) is a requirement that legal ethics, values and professionalism should be central throughout the continuum of education and training. Much will, of course, depend on the content that is poured into those concepts, the definition of which is inevitably subject to more powerful socio-political forces than the LETR itself constitutes.

Echoing our opening comments about the need to understand the profession as a socially embedded institution and hence the significance of the rise of neo-liberalism, Webb highlights how the regulatory revolution achieved by the LSA was inextricably linked to broader socio-political changes. He focuses in particular on the neo-liberal project of removing the 'dead hand of the state' as well as dismantling professional monopolies in favour of competition, assumed to be the best protector of both the consumer and public interest. Self-interested self-regulation was to be replaced with flexible and pluralistic 'outcomes-focused' regulation designed to ensure responsiveness to the market. As Webb notes, echoing Evetts' discussion, this contributes to a reworking of the meaning of professionalism in which competence is assured through heightened competition and limited bureaucratic oversight. Webb, like us, notes with concern that universities have not been immune to the neo-liberal agenda, with higher education itself now treated as a private economic good to be privatised and marketised, and educators under increased pressure to demonstrate student employability.

The headline conclusion of the LETR was that there was no evidence that the existing education and training system was not fit for purpose, but that there was a need to build on existing strengths as well as remedy key weaknesses. As a co-author of this report, Webb is able here to present a nuanced account of how and why the detailed recommendations designed to achieve this were fashioned as they were, and to identify progress (or lack thereof) that has been made on their implementation. It would be inappropriate to seek to summarise here all the many fascinating points Webb makes about the process, product and consequences of the LETR, not least because the chapter by Andrew Sanders itself presents something of a detailed critique of its stance on legal education.

Sanders' chapter builds on Webb's reflections, as he considers what should be the central elements of all law degrees in England and Wales, and what educational principles and values should underpin the education and training of entrants to the legal profession in that jurisdiction. While acknowledging the neo-liberal turn in society, education in general and legal education in particular, he nonetheless argues that the regulatory settlement created by the LSA both makes possible and even requires that undergraduate law students receive a broad intellectual education which equips them to operate as 'good citizens', self-reflectively aware of their capacity to shape law and society, rather than just as narrow technicians. This is so because the regulatory objectives laid down in the LSA include encouraging an independent, strong, diverse and effective legal profession, promoting the public interest, improving access to justice and supporting the rule of law.

For Sanders, inculcating in students an understanding of these objectives and how different ways of practising law might affect them, requires law schools to move away from their traditional focus on doctrinalism (studying the rules) and decisively towards socio-legalism (studying the socio-economic shaping, and impact, of law and lawyers). He notes, however, that the Legal Services Board (LSB) has chosen to emphasise other regulatory objectives laid down by the LSA, in particular promoting the interests of consumers and promoting competition in legal services. This has led to a focus on requiring no more from entrants to the legal profession than basic competence to be achieved through outcomes-focused regulation. He sees the LETR as falling into a kind of ideological trap created by the expressed views of the LSB and practitioners. Thus, Sanders argues that the LETR accepted the idea of outcomes-focused regulation (including the need for greater 'commercial awareness') without thinking through from first principles (as set out in the LSA) what those outcomes should be. Similarly, it uncritically reported its (unscientifically collected) findings that most practitioners regarded jurisprudence and socio-legal studies as the least relevant in the curriculum. The upshot could well be, warns Sanders, a continuing focus within law degrees on law and legal disputes relating primarily to corporations and the wealthy. Echoing Richard Abel's arguments (discussed below), Sanders makes a strong pitch for redirecting the student gaze to law that serves the poor and that seeks to hold state and private power to account.

A linked point is that the case for teaching 'social awareness' is as strong, if not stronger, as that for 'commercial awareness'—lawyers need to understand the complex problems of the poor and how these are rooted in power relations, together with the complex ways in which law can exacerbate or ameliorate these. Only then can they truly serve the public interest, access to justice and the rule of law. One of the 'outcomes' that legal services regulators should therefore encourage is a socio-legal understanding of law and power. As this is unlikely to be the focus of vocational legal education, it must be central to the law degree.

At root, Sanders' argument can be seen as predicated on the notion that there is still mileage in the classical vision of professionalism in which lawyers act in the public interest rather than purely for their own enrichment. Supposing there is support for his position, how might such a vision be secured? While Sanders is correct in arguing that the legal academy has far more flexibility and intellectual freedom than it currently exploits, the support of policymakers, regulators and the legal profession will surely be important to his proposed reorientation of legal education. There is little sign of such support at present, however.

It was very important to us that the CEPLER conference, and this volume, should include contributions from practitioners and policymakers. The chapters by Alex Roy and Tony King offer a diametrically opposed vision of the future of legal education from those articulated by Webb and Sanders. Roy's chapter gives the perspective of the regulator and sets out a vision of how the LSB sees the potential future of legal education. He asks probing questions about whether the current system of regulation of legal education and training acts as a proxy for, rather than a measure of, quality, and whether the current focus on broad-based training at the starting point of a lawyer's career is sufficiently targeted, or appropriate, for a career that may span a number of decades. How does a law degree, or vocational course, that most students finish in their early twenties relate to the competence required by a legal practitioner in their fifties or sixties? Roy also questions the fact that the current suite of regulations on education and training only targets a small proportion of those engaged in legal services (that is lawyers regulated by the LSB). This is particularly concerning given the moves towards fragmentation and unbundling in legal services (discussed above) where those involved in the field may be wholly outside the current legal education and training regulatory framework. The overarching theme from Roy's chapter is the need for, and possibilities of, flexibility in legal education, framed in terms of quality and affordability. Flexibility in regulatory design is also important, a point reinforced by Webb's argument for a meta-regulatory approach to legal education. Roy shows that this requires the regulator to have a varied toolbox, moving beyond conventional 'command and control' (hierarchical) and market (competition) regulation by emphasising the importance of 'community' (engaging stakeholders in deliberative regulatory procedures) and 'design' (getting the right organisational structures, tools, technologies and people in place). This strategy, borrowed from the financial services sector post the credit crunch,[47] certainly has much that is appealing, but the question of whether it will prove any better than previous regulatory approaches remains to be seen. It does, however (or, at least can) cohere with the 'outcomes focused' and risk-based regulatory approach currently taken by the SRA and BSB.

---

[47] C Scott, 'A Meta-Regulatory Turn? Control and Learning in Regulatory Governance' in S Muller et al (eds), *The Law of the Future and the Future of Law* (Brussels, Torkel Opsahl Academic EPublisher, 2012).

Looking to the future, Roy argues that regulators will have to focus more on risk and the range of interventions they can make to manage it where necessary. These include—but are not limited to—education and training requirements. This, Roy suggests, is likely to see providers of legal education rewarded with more freedom to innovate, and creating courses that better meet the needs of the market and individuals seeking to work in the market. If this happens, the marketisation of legal education will be in step with the wider financialisation of legal services. Whether this is a good thing in educational terms is debateable. As the chapter by Sanders indicates, there are clear dangers in shaping legal education and legal services around the demands of the market, where the rich and the powerful are likely to trump the concerns of the poor, the dispossessed, and other marginalised groups in society. Nor is the market, when left to its own devices, likely to advance the diversification of the profession.

The chapter by Tony King—Director of the Clifford Chance Academy at the international law firm Clifford Chance LLP—provides a fascinating insight into how someone steeped in the world of practice views the changes and challenges which confront the profession. Like Roy, King discusses the need for quality, but from a very different angle. Identifying the three main challenges facing legal services as regulatory, financial and organisational, King focuses on three matters which he considers require particular effort and thought in order to ensure that the sector, 'continues to go from strength to strength'. The first goes to the quality of entrants, which King suggests is an issue of communication, standards and access. In the context of communication, he argues that there needs to be a balance between the benefits and challenges of a career in law conveyed to would-be entrants in a manner which is objective, comprehensive and understandable, and which reaches as widely as possible. To achieve this will be no mean feat of course. As for standards and access, King tempers his argument about the need for access to and mobility within the profession with the need for quality. This is clearly incontrovertible: the public interest in the administration of justice and the rule of law do not require widening access and mobility at any cost, and King applauds the current work of the SRA in developing a competency-based framework as supporting the drive to maintain quality. However, it is interesting that King does not define quality: a highly fluid concept, it is rarely defined but regularly invoked by the profession to effect closure. King's second argument is that the training continuum should reflect the needs of the various parts of the sector. This entails, he argues, teaching institutions and legal employers communicating with each side so that they each know what the other needs and can deliver. This is, however, more easily said than done; as Webb notes, 'the lack of established structures for effective engagement between the professions and the academy has been a recurrent complaint of every review of legal education in England and Wales since 1934', and the LETR's recommendation that a Legal Education Council be set up in order to achieve a dialogue appears to have fallen on stony ground. King's third challenge for legal services and legal education concerns continuing competence. This, he argues, should be tailored to suit the needs of the different parts of the sector and, echoing Roy, he proposes that the academy, practitioners and regulators should work together to produce tailored and relevant solutions that will benefit all stakeholders.

The value of including a practitioner perspective is underlined by the way in which King's chapter exemplifies the argument made by Evetts, Faulconbridge and Muzio, and Webb, that competition in the economic and regulatory markets in which law firms operate acts as a major driver for change. In a granular account of the specifics of law firm market forces, he details how factors such as price sensitivity and pricing structures (including the controversial use of billable hours),[48] leverage within teams of lawyers, and the shift to commoditised legal services in some areas feed directly into competition between providers. This echoes the turn towards commodification and the increased leverage of employees in large law firms discussed by Faulconbridge and Muzio. It is striking too that both King and Maclean describe how legal services are being unbundled—but at opposite ends of the legal services spectrum: high street family law practices; and global commercial law firms.

The themes of the volume are drawn together in the final chapter which is based on the conference presentation given by our keynote speaker, Richard Abel, Connell Distinguished Professor of Law Emeritus and Distinguished Research Professor, UCLA. Abel, whose compendious output includes the seminal text 'English Lawyers between Market and State',[49] has, for several decades, been the leading scholar of the legal profession. His work has been grounded in the neo-Weberian critique of its traditional claims (and their academic counterpart, 'trait theory'). Like Magali Larson,[50] he therefore conceptualises professionalism as a project which aimed to control not only how many could enter, in order to achieve monopoly status and

---

[48] The ethicality of law firms billing clients in this way has been much debated in the last 3 to 5 years, as has the relative competitiveness of this model of billing. A number of firms are moving away from billable hours towards fixed fee costs for their clients: see, eg, Riverview Law: www.riverviewlaw.com. For a wider discussion of this issue, see the report prepared by Christine Parker and David Ruschena for the Legal Services Commission in Queensland, Australia: C Parker and D Ruschena, 'The Pressures of Billable Hours: Lessons from a Survey of Billing Practices Inside Law Firms' (2012) 9 *University of St Thomas Law Journal* 618, available at: www.lsc.qld.gov.au/__data/assets/pdf_file/0007/175480/The-pressures-of-billable-hours-Parker-and-Ruschena.pdf; and S Fortney, 'Soul for Sale: An Empirical Study of Associate Satisfaction, Law Firm Culture, and the Effects of Billable Hour Requirements' (2000) 69 *University of Missouri-Kansas Law Review* 239.

[49] RL Abel, *English Lawyers between Market and State: The Politics of Professionalism* (Oxford, Oxford University Press, 2003).

[50] Larson, *The Rise of Professionalism* (n 18).

the associated high income, but also 'who' could enter, so as to enhance lawyers' collective status. This perspective does not, of course, entail a denial of the central importance of law and the profession, but rather that the promise of ethicality and justice is regularly traduced and—echoing Sanders' concerns—he argues that law schools tend to be complicit in this process since they teach students to 'argue both sides of every case, approach law positivistically, as a set of constraints to be manipulated or evaded, followed grudgingly, only as required by the letter of the law, not its spirit'.[51]

The connections between legal education and professional ethicality implicit in this comment have been central to Abel's research, and underpin the themes he engages with in his chapter which include the close relationship between the legal profession and the socio-economic order. Despite his critique of the profession's exploitation of their market shelters, Abel, like Evetts, is concerned about its marketisation, arguing that this is bad for consumers since, when trading off the quality of legal services for lower prices, they confront acute problems of information asymmetry given their inability to evaluate which legal solutions they need or who is best placed to deliver them. He further argues that 'free' markets are bad for workers, as they make possible poorly paid, insecure working conditions, the most extreme of which are generally performed by marginalised groups, and points to the growing phenomenon in the United States of unemployed graduates, lower starting salaries, law firm layoffs and dissolutions and spiralling educational indebtedness—a picture we in the United Kingdom will all recognise. For Abel, however, the profession's location in the economy and society is also central to issues of ethicality and he addresses these in a discussion of the causes of lawyer misconduct and possible remedies. A further theme, which underlines the concerns raised by Maclean's discussion of LASPO and family law, is the chronic problem of unequal access to law— here Abel reflects on the potential for legal education to ameliorate this.

VII. CONCLUSION

Abel's concluding reflections on the rule of law, and the need to defend it at moments when national security is threatened, remind us that an independent legal profession is a critical component of the democratic social order. But the radical changes which have overtaken the profession raise the question of whether we still have an independent legal profession. And if we do, how can it be sustained, and what kind of education can support it? In order to engage with these questions on both a theoretical and practical

---

[51] RL Abel, 'What *Does* and *Should* Influence the Number of Lawyers?' (2012) 19 *International Journal of the Legal Profession* 131, 187.

level, we present in this collection a selection of chapters which range from academic discussions of theory to the briefer reflections of a policymaker and practitioner. Their contributions are particularly timely as the regulatory settlement created by the LSA is perhaps not so settled;[52] the futures of the legal profession and legal education are therefore uncertain and in need of steering. To chart and shape the possible futures, it is important to understand both the past and where current trajectories are likely to take us. This book thus forms part of a conversation that needs to take place between the state, the legal profession, legal educators, law students, users of legal services and all those who care about the future of democracy and the rule of law.

---

[52] See, eg, the 2013 consultation by the Ministry of Justice of the legal services statutory framework: www.redtapechallenge.cabinetoffice.gov.uk/moj-review-of-legal-services-regulation, and the June 2014 speech by the Lord Chancellor Chris Grayling to CILEX on reducing regulatory burdens in the legal profession: C Grayling, Lord Chancellor's Speech' (CILEX Presidential Dinner, London, 4 June 2014), available at: www.gov.uk/government/speeches/lord-chancellors-speech-at-cilex-presidential-dinner.

2

Professionalism, Enterprise and the Market: Contradictory or Complementary?

JULIA EVETTS

IS THERE ANY future for professions or are we witnessing the final demise of the guilds[1] and of guild-like social institutions? Following deregulation by state governments, can this privileged category of occupations, which have been called 'professions' in the Anglo-American world, continue to maintain their powerful social and economic positions? Threatened, as they are, by ideologies of managerialism, markets, enterprise and customer sovereignty, can the ideology of professionalism compete and survive?

Since the 1980s the concept of 'enterprise' has become dominant in political thought and practice. Enterprise has come to be associated with economic liberalism and its appeals to the efficiency of markets, the liberty of individuals, the sovereign consumer and a non-interventionist state. The idea of enterprise has strong links with the market and the controls of managerialism and rational organisations. The concept of 'professionalism' has had a different focus, however, with an emphasis more on occupational expertise, service work, knowledge and competence: the professional is first and foremost an expert. For a long time the sociological analysis of professional work differentiated professionalism as a special means of organising work and workers, contrasting this with the hierarchical, bureaucratic and managerial controls of industrial and commercial enterprising organisations. Professionalism had a different logic and a different culture.

The transformation of American lawyers from free professions into sellers of services in the market[2] may be dated from 1977 when the Supreme Court

---

[1] EA Krause, *Death of the Guilds: Professions, States, and the Advance of Capitalism, 1930 to the Present* (New Haven, Yale University Press, 1996).

[2] The term 'free profession' derives from the conceptualisation of the classical professions as characterised by a special ethicality and hence able to act as 'free', intermediary institutions, neither part of the market nor the state. This was essentially an Anglo-American characteristic

authorised them to advertise on television.[3] In England and Wales, legal marketing can be traced back to 1986 when the Law Society of England and Wales first permitted lawyers to advertise.[4] From the 1990s, other jurisdictions in Continental Europe (for instance, Spain, France, Germany and Italy) progressively opened the way for advertising. Traditionally, despite having always had one foot in the market, a primary characteristic of professionals has been their claim that they operate according to a general ethics based upon solidarity and citizenship. Their move into advertising can therefore be argued to place law more into the market and away from the ethics of a free profession.

So the question becomes whether it is possible to preserve, maintain and encourage professionalism in practitioners who work in service and knowledge-based occupations such as law, which are now thoroughly 'marketised' and consequently dominated by profit expectations. This chapter considers the extent to which the logics and culture of professionalism, expertise and service might be reconciled to and linked with the logics and culture of enterprise, profit, commercial success and organisational efficiency. It will ask if professionalism and enterprise are inevitably contradictory or whether, and under what circumstances and conditions, the two might be complementary. The first section of the chapter considers the arguments for seeing professionalism and enterprise as contradictory and as contrasting alternatives for organising work. The second section considers the arguments for seeing enterprise and professionalism as acting on one another to produce new hybrid forms of legal service, and in doing so explores the conditions under which the two might be complementary.

I. ENTERPRISE AND PROFESSIONALISM: THE CONTRADICTIONS

The state has always been perceived as a powerful actor in sociological theories of professions, but the promotion of an enterprise culture required a reduction in its powers: for almost three decades now the state has no longer been seen as a protector and organiser, but rather as a parasite and a straitjacket on the development of the economy.[5] Thus, its power had to be reduced by cutting taxes and social insurance and by deregulating business and industry. Market forces were proposed to substitute for state regulation.

---

and was not a feature of professions in Europe; see M Burrage and R Thorstendahl (eds), *Professions in Theory and History* (London, Sage Publications, 1990).

[3] A Rush, 'US District Court: Some Advertising Rules Unconstitutional' (2007) September/October *State Bar News* 4.

[4] D Sugarman, *A Brief History of the Law Society* (London, Law Society, 1994).

[5] M Albert, *Capitalisme contre Capitalisme* (Paris, Le Seuil, 1991) 53.

This change has been paralleled in the shift from so-called social service professionalism to commercialised professionalism in England.[6] The questioning of the importance of the professions from the 1980s onwards generated 'a real battle ... to determine who controls professions and professionals, how they are assessed, what their function is, how their services are to be delivered and paid for, and so on'.[7] This 'battle' was accompanied by a shift in social theorising about the professions. Professions were no longer interpreted as socially integrative; the emphasis was more on a neo-Weberian critique of professions as ideological.[8]

Welfare state professional occupations such as social work, nursing and teaching diverged considerably from the free profession model (exemplified by law and medicine). Over time, welfare professions had come to control growing resources and demand even more on behalf of public interests and disadvantaged individuals and groups, while also seeking to further their own interests. This expansion in the demands for services[9] appeared to have no limit, since they concerned human needs, difficult to assess and define as these are. The lobby for continued growth of the public sector was, however, not strong enough to oppose (in fact in many cases it supported) the new forces at hand in the era of the enterprise culture which set the agenda for much of the public discussion on professions and exploited the so-called New Public Management (NPM).[10]

Various forms of NPM led to the implementation of measures designed to promote a culture of enterprise in many Western countries. These measures included cutbacks in funding for the public sector and especially large areas such as education, health and social welfare and local governments; downsizing, starting on lower layers and continuing on management levels; flexible labour market strategies such as part-time work, externalising or outsourcing; changing certain public service provisions into private enterprises; divisions into purchasers and providers of services; introducing quasi-markets, accountability, and quality measurements.[11] It is important to note, however, that welfare state professional occupations and particularly health professions are crucially influenced by gender

---

[6] G Hanlon, *Lawyers, the State and the Market: Professionalism Revisited* (Basingstoke, Macmillan, 1999); *cf* C Pollitt and G Bouckaert, *Public Management Reform: A Comparative Analysis* (Oxford, Oxford University Press, 2000).

[7] Hanlon, *Lawyers* (n 6), 1; *cf*, E Freidson, *Professionalism: The Third Logic* (London, Polity Press, 2001).

[8] J Evetts, 'Professionalism: Value and Ideology' (2013) 61 *Current Sociology* 778.

[9] LG Svensson and J Evetts (eds), *Sociology of Professions: Continental and Anglo-Saxon Traditions* (Göteborg, Daidalos, 2010).

[10] J-E Lane, *New Public Management* (London, Routledge, 2000); Pollitt and Bouckaert, *Public Management Reform* (n 6); P Taylor-Gooby (ed), *Welfare States under Pressure* (London, Sage Publications, 2001).

[11] M Power, *The Audit Society: Rituals of Verification*, 2nd edn (Oxford, Oxford University Press, 1999).

differences. If traditional forms of professionalism (including high status, rewards and autonomous decision-making) are currently experiencing a decline, this is happening alongside other changes in some feminised health professions which are achieving re-formation, new controls over their work and upward social mobility.[12] There are then large variations in the consequences and effects for particular occupational groups.[13]

In terms of logics again, the following can be identified, starting first with 'the logic of enterprise, the market and consumerism'. Market-like forms or quasi-markets of control in public professional services have been implemented in many countries. These include: privatisation of service production to various degrees; divisions between politicians and executives as purchasers and professionals as providers of services; competition, bidding, contracting and marketing; payment by results; internal markets; accounting (often only in economic terms); and freedom of choice for clients, or rather customers.[14] These are the most prevalent forms of enterprise and market directions, creating new relationships between the government, the public and the professionals. Thus, market closure and occupational control tend to erode, and professionals are confronted with the logic of the market threatening to un-make the professions in several ways.[15]

Second, 'the logic of enterprise and management' has been emphasised. The importance of administrative management in contrast to professional discretion has been firmly emphasised in many areas and countries.[16] Thus, the role of managers and supervisors has been regarded as much more significant, and the strong tradition of recruiting managers in professional organisations from within the occupational group was broken. This went together with a decline in trust in professional workers[17] and an increased resort to litigation by client/customers.[18] The development of management (and particularly financial management) as a separate and distinctive category of work has tended to close practitioner career progression into management, with the result that the control of professional production is taken over by (financial) managers.[19] The bonds between the professional

---

[12] IL Bourgeault, C Benoit and R Davis-Floyd, *Reconceiving Midwifery* (Montreal, McGill-Queen's University Press, 2004); A Liljegren, 'Pragmatic Professionalism: Micro-Level Discourse in Social Work' (2012) 15 *European Journal of Social Work* 1.

[13] I Hellberg, M Saks and C Benoit (eds), *Professional Identities in Transition: Cross-Cultural Dimensions* (Göteborg, Almquist & Wikse, 1999); Freidson, *Professionalism* (n 7).

[14] P du Gay and G Salaman, 'The Cult[ure] of the Customer' (1992) 29 *Journal of Management Studies* 615.

[15] V Fournier, 'The Appeal to "Professionalism" as a Disciplinary Mechanism' (1999) 47 *Social Review* 280.

[16] Pollitt and Bouckaert, *Public Management Reform* (n 6).

[17] H Perkin, *The Rise of Professional Society* (London, Routledge, 1988); G di Luzio, 'A Sociological Concept of Client Trust' (2006) 54 *Current Sociology* 549.

[18] Svensson and Evetts, *Sociology of Professions* (n 9).

[19] MS Larson, *The Rise of Professionalism* (New Brunswick, Transaction Publishers, 2013).

group and the employment organisation in such cases will be different, as the collegial relationships between different layers in the organisation are replaced by more formal bureaucratic relationships. The management control models of audit and accounting have been replacing models of trust between managers and professionals.[20] What has been labelled 'hard managerialism' has displaced trust with various criteria of performance and indicators for review and accounting, based upon more explicit forms of rationality in management by objectives, target setting and evaluations.

Markets and managerialism have converged and increased the extent of formal organisational characteristics in professional work. One result is more focus and specialisation and hence more efficient work and service units in markets. Public service bureaucracies, however, have lacked many of the aspects of identity, hierarchy and rationality that have characterised formal and complete organisations (see further below). The entrepreneurial actors (usually found among private companies which are the prototype used in theories of organisations) are also lacking. An entrepreneurial organisational actor would have independence, autonomy and self-interested goals with rational means, commanding independent resources within clear boundaries.[21] In contrast, public administration involves agents fulfilling given tasks and often several inconsistent objectives, and following given rules, leaving little space for their own intentions and rationality. An organisation is lacking an essential unity when members are recruited, guided and controlled according to external rules, values, norms, standards and interests instead of an internal policy.[22] This is the case with many professional occupations for which professional institutes and associations provide the guiding principles and ways of working. Hospitals, universities and schools may, for example, be described as arenas, where the members have considerable autonomy towards local managers, as well as cultural authority and legitimacy, and are controlled by external parties such as professional associations and state regulatory authorities.

The reconstruction process now well underway in such arenas could be explained in different ways: as an intentional policy and strategy aimed at constructing complete organisations; or as a side effect of introducing markets into professional organisations, customers instead of clients, auditing instead of rules, and managers and expertise instead of orders and binding norms. All these factors can be both causes and effects in a dialectical relation—the discourse of enterprise reconstructing organisations and that

---

[20] Power, *The Audit Society* (n 11); D Jary, 'The Implications of the Audit Society? The Case of Higher Education' in M Dent, M O'Neill and C Bagley (eds), *Professions, New Public Management and the European Welfare State* (Stoke-on-Trent, Staffordshire University Press, 1999) 29.
[21] N Brunsson and K Sahlin-Andersson, 'Constructing Organizations: The Example of Public Sector Reform' (2000) 21 *Organization Studies* 731.
[22] Svensson and Evetts, *Sociology of Professions* (n 9).

discourse being reinforced by those changes.[23] Many of these reforms have met surprisingly little resistance from professionals in most parts of the Western world, and have been introduced at great speed by central and local governments of various political orientations.[24]

Organisations do require certain features in order to be 'complete'. First, to see something as an organisation means to endow it with identity. This in turn means emphasising autonomy and defining boundaries and collective resources. Many reforms represent an attempt to install or reinforce these features of identity in public services. For instance, local autonomy has been increased in hospitals throughout Europe,[25] and also in schools in many countries.[26] Deregulation and decentralisation of decision-making have also taken place. Staff are employed by the units, and the division of labour among professionals is determined locally by managers rather than by central or professional regulations. Single units have become economic entities with budgeting, resource allocation, local accounting and auditing. Boundaries to the environment have been constructed in policy documents, defining assets, members and results as external or internal. As already noted, providers of services have been separated from purchasers and customers. Public services have been more or less forced to formulate special profiles emphasising the differences from other similar service providers for their own marketing, contracting and auditing purposes.[27]

Second, a complete organisation coordinates objectives and activities, and coordination is achieved by an authoritative centre in a hierarchy, directing the actions of the members. Various reforms have tried to enforce coordination by, for example, creating local internal working teams, which should be guided by organisational policies and values rather than central rules or professional norms. New managerialism has defined executives as managers with freedom to manage rather than civil servants following and implementing central directives.[28] Leadership and management training have been the first priorities for further education of the personnel, which has been conspicuously evident in allocation of resources for competence development.[29]

---

[23] For examples of these processes in practice see E Kuhlmann, *Modernising Health Care: Reinventing Professions, the State and the Public* (Bristol, Policy Press, 2006) on health care; and S Gewirtz et al (eds), *Changing Teacher Professionalism: International Trends, Challenges and the Way Forward* (Abingdon, Routledge, 2009) on teaching.

[24] R Dingwall, *Essays on Professions* (Aldershot, Ashgate, 2008).

[25] M Dent, *Remodelling Hospitals and Health Professions in Europe* (Basingstoke, Palgrave Macmillan, 2003).

[26] Gewirtz et al, *Changing Teacher Professionalism* (n 23); SJ Ball, AG Dworkin and M Vryonides (eds), 'Education in a Globalised World' (2010) 58 *Current Sociology* Monograph 2.

[27] Svensson and Evetts, *Sociology of Professions* (n 9).

[28] J Webb, 'Work and the New Public Service Class?' (1999) 33 *Sociology* 747.

[29] Ball, Dworkin and Vryonides, 'Education in a Globalised World' (n 26).

Third, complete organisations are assumed to be rational in the sense that goals, preferences, alternatives and consequences should be systematically forecasted and evaluated. Management-by-objectives has replaced rules and directives. Various and inconsistent objectives have been subjected to attempts to simplify them and to make up hierarchies of goals. An alternative strategy has been to break down the service provider into smaller units in order to create clearer objectives; in the NHS, this has taken the form of inspection and service supplying units, or purchasing and providing units.[30] Organisations are expected to account for their actions, and to be efficient. A focus on results passes responsibility on to the local managers to decide upon the best way to organise work, and this freedom to choose makes managers responsible for the results of the choices made. Thus, the idea of accountable managers and professionals is promoted, which further constructs the idea of the rational organisation. In this way, output results have largely replaced organisation by rules and regulations;[31] professional competence is measured according to specific organisational goals of efficiency instead of professionally controlled credits, performances and values; and efficiency is linked to individual rewards and privileges in the context of the specific work organisation. Total quality management emphasises the demands and the satisfaction of customers rather than competence according to professional standards, and front line autonomy and discretion is controlled by work organisation managers.[32] Professional competence as standardised credentials before entry into professional work organisations has partly been replaced by control of results and a culture of performativity.[33]

All this produces a new quest for professionalism in the sense of self-regulated competence in autonomous individuals or teams. In so-called knowledge-based companies, the dependence on such individual or team competences is regarded as a crucial issue, and much effort is put into strategic recruitment and socialisation by culture and values, and other methods of binding those employees into the firm.[34] Many of these changes connect professionals with their work organisations rather than with their professional occupations and associations, and professional

---

[30] Dent, *Remodelling Hospitals* (n 25).

[31] See ch 3 by Faulconbridge and Muzio in this collection.

[32] S Frenkel et al, *On the Front-Line: Patterns of Service Work Organization in Comparative Perspective* (New York, Cornell University Press, 1999).

[33] SJ Ball, 'Professionalism, Managerialism and Performativity' in L Moos and J Krejsler (eds), *Professional Development and Educational Change: What Does it Mean to be Professional in Education?* (Copenhagen, Danmarks Paedagogiske Universitets Forlag, 2003) 23.

[34] KE Sveiby, *The New Organizational Wealth: Managing and Measuring Knowledge-Based Assets* (San Francisco, Berrett-Koehler, 1997); Frenkel et al, *On the Front-Line* (n 32).

work competence becomes primarily defined and assessed by the work organisation.

Through the establishment of quasi-markets and payment by results, and the development of professionalism as a discourse used by managers, the relationships between clients and professionals have in many areas turned into customer relations. The production, publication and diffusion of quality measurements thereby become crucial indicators for transforming welfare services into a market.[35] The relationships between consumers and professional producers are shaped by the interest of the consumers in the product or the service provided. The service product is specialised and focused, making it possible to compare one service with that offered by other producers. The marketing of an occupational group and its service is expected to be more closely related to work organisations, and to the needs of the potential group of clients or customers, rather than to the competence of the professionals in relation to regulations and standards managed by professional associations and state authorities. Entrepreneurial forms individualise work relations, making rules and regulations less determining, and informal networks, personal qualities and negotiating skills more important.[36] This entails an increase in the responsibility of the individual clients or customers to estimate the quality of the services and the competence of the professionals, which partly solves the old problem of professional hegemony and paternalism, but to the possible disadvantage of professional occupations and their exclusive control of certain bodies of knowledge and values.

The following chain of reasons and causes is a summary of the arguments presented above. Discourses on knowledge societies and organisations parallel to marketisation and management have reinforced demands for professional competences. Enterprising states and service organisations have emphasised the relations of autonomous professionals with clients and their demands as customers. Enterprising service organisations also entail their development into more fully fledged commercial organisations with enforced identity, management hierarchy and rationality. The management of autonomous professional work, by means of formal credentials before entrance into employment, is supplemented by recruitment with, and socialisation into, certain values and attitudes according to organisational cultures. Client control is partly exercised by the demands and evaluations of customers and their sovereignty to choose and exit from enterprising firms. Thus, professional competence tends to be less formally explicit and decontextualised, as in standardised credentials, and instead more personal, implicit, individual and connected with the contexts of positions, tasks

---

[35] M Considine, *Enterprising States: The Public Management of Welfare-to-Work* (Cambridge, Cambridge University Press, 2001).
[36] Webb, 'Work' (n 28).

and actual performance. This increased front line autonomy raises new requirements for self-regulated governmentality by professionalism.[37] In fact, marketing, contracting and auditing increase the demand for explicit accounting of professional competence. This quest for control by the work organisation's management will increase the demand for quality control and auditing, which by more or less bureaucratic means is trying to win back some control over the market-directed enterprise.[38] Thus, there is a dialectic between individual professional autonomy and collective organisational control, based upon two somewhat incompatible mechanisms—autonomy and discretion for the self-regulated professional–client relationship and individual implicit competence, versus possible exchange of professional employees and collective explicit knowledge, respectively. This is perhaps best illustrated by current dilemmas in general practice medicine where the wishes of patients to be seen, known and treated by one particular practitioner are incompatible with the efficient use of medical resources in General Practice Organisations. Legal practice is confronting similar dilemmas in large law firms seeking efficient use of their personnel.

II. ENTERPRISE AND PROFESSIONALISM: COMPLEMENTARITY

After the contradictions, it is important to consider the ways in which professionalism and enterprise are adapting and working together to produce new organisational forms. This section includes some of the strategies and tactics which are developing as professions adapt to emerging challenges and opportunities presented by cultures of enterprise. In addition, professionalism and enterprise might not always be polar opposites and mutually exclusive but could, instead, be mutually reinforcing.[39] Alternatively, we might deploy the notion of 'hybridity'[40] where different strands of professionalism and other organisational principles of enterprise coexist and co-penetrate each other, producing new hybrid arrangements. In particular, it seems that whatever management there is in professional organisations, it is more likely to have consensual rather than executive/directive connotations. Thus, Paul Adler et al[41] argue that the market, hierarchy and community are not necessarily mutually exclusive but can be mutually supportive. More market pressure often leads to more community-based practices such

---

[37] Fournier, 'The Appeal to "Professionalism"' (n 15).

[38] V Fournier and C Grey, 'Too Much, Too Little and Too Often: A Critique of Paul du Gay's Analysis of Enterprise' (1999) 6 *Organization* 107, 112.

[39] P Adler, S Kwon and C Hecksher, 'Professional Work: The Emergence of Collaborative Community' (2008) 19 *Organization Science* 359.

[40] JR Faulconbridge and D Muzio, 'Organizational Professionalism in Globalizing Law Firms' (2008) 22 *Work, Employment & Society* 7.

[41] Adler, Kwon and Hecksher, 'Professional Work' (n 39).

as in multidisciplinary teams and cooperative working which are consistent with occupational value and normative forms of professionalism.

The consolidation and complementarity of professionalism and enterprise would seem to arise also from the increased recognition that enterprise, organisation, management and managerialism are not only complex but also multilayered and multidimensional. Thus, management strategies are being used not only by organisations to control, and sometimes limit, the work of practitioners, but also by both practitioners and professional associations in the career development of particular practitioners and in order to improve the status and respect of a professional occupation and its standing.[42]

As a micro-level strategy, there is some evidence, particularly from health professionals such as nursing and midwifery[43] but also now from medical doctors[44] and teachers,[45] of individual practitioners acquiring qualifications in management (for example, the MBA) with the clear intention of furthering their careers. In the case of health professionals such as nurses and midwives this can also be interpreted as a collective mobility strategy as increasingly hospital management at middle and senior levels is perceived as a career opening for those with appropriate management credentials, experience and motivation.[46] It is important also to emphasise that for the individuals who move into management this is a move out of the profession's jurisdiction[47] and practice and into that of the organisation.

As a meso-level strategy, it is also interesting to note the work of Andreas Langer[48] in respect of social work in Germany. Masters level programmes for social workers in Germany are incorporating management training as a way of increasing the status, reputation and respect for social work as a

---

[42] See I Kirkpatrick, M Dent and P Kragh Jesperson, 'The Contested Terrain of Hospital Management: Professional Projects and Healthcare Reforms in Denmark' in D Muzio and I Kirkpatrick (eds), *Special Issue: Reconnecting Professional Occupations and Professional Organisations* (2011) 59 *Current Sociology* 489; M Noordegraaf, 'Remaking Professionals? How Associations and Professional Education Connect Professionalism and Organisation' in D Muzio and I Kirkpatrick (eds), *Special Issue: Reconnecting Professional Occupations and Professional Organisations* (2011) 59 *Current Sociology* 465.

[43] Bourgeault, Benoit and Davis-Floyd, *Reconceiving Midwifery* (n 12); T Carvalho, 'Redefining Professional Frontiers in Health: Negotiations in the Field' (Interim Meeting of ESA Research Network, Aarhus Denmark, June 2008).

[44] E Kuhlmann, 'Unsettling the Power–Knowledge Nexus in Professionalism: Multiple Dynamics in Healthcare' (Interim Meeting of ESA Research Network, Aarhus Denmark, June 2008).

[45] Gewirtz et al, *Changing Teacher Professionalism* (n 23).

[46] Kirkpatrick, Dent and Kragh Jesperson, 'The Contested Terrain of Hospital Management' (n 42).

[47] A Abbott, *The System of Professions: An Essay on the Division of Expert Labour* (Chicago, University of Chicago Press, 1988).

[48] A Langer, 'Academic Qualification Programmes for Professional Management: Managerial Expertise as One Facet of a New Professionalism' (Interim Meeting of ESA Research Network, Aarhus Denmark, June 2008).

professional occupation in the field of social services work. Following the Bologna process and standardisation of higher education levels in Europe, in Germany there is a substantial development of Masters programmes which qualify (in this case) social workers to apply for leadership positions in non-profit organisations and social services departments. These developments can be interpreted, therefore, as both a micro-level and meso-level strategy in respect of social work.

In addition, and as Daniel Muzio and Ian Kirkpatrick[49] explain, organisations can constitute sites for (and objects of) professional control and domination. The jurisdictional disputes and negotiations originally described by Andrew Abbott[50] are now being played out within enterprise organisations rather than in the wider arena of labour markets and education systems. The erosion of jurisdictions is exemplified by the capacity for contemporary law firms to form Alternative Business Structures (following the Legal Services Act 2007). At the same time, within organisations, occupations seek to process and control tasks and task divisions to suit their own occupational interests. The medical profession—particularly doctors employed by the state—continue to use their cultural authority and legitimacy to maintain dominance.[51] Peter Armstrong[52] describes competition between professionals in management (accountancy, engineering and personnel) as they seek to colonise key positions, roles and decision-making within large organisations. In these ways organisations can constitute arenas for inter-professional competition, professional conquest and enterprise and also intra-professional cooperation.

III. CONCLUSIONS

Professionalism has undergone profound changes and these have been seen as part of a state project to promote enterprise and an enterprise culture. In this context, Steven Brint has discussed an epochal shift from the rhetoric of trusteeship to the rhetoric of expertise.[53] The principles, strategies and methods of enterprise and organisation are deeply affecting most

---

[49] D Muzio and I Kirkpatrick, 'Introduction—Professions and Organisations—A Conceptual Framework' in D Muzio and I Kirkpatrick (eds), *Special Issue: Reconnecting Professional Occupations and Professional Organisations* (2011) 59 *Current Sociology* 389.

[50] Abbott, *The System of Professions* (n 47).

[51] D Coburn, 'Medical Dominance Then and Now: Critical Reflections' (2006) 15 *Health Sociology Review* 432; Freidson, *Professionalism* (n 7); G Larkin, *Occupational Monopoly and Modern Medicine* (London, Tavistock, 1983).

[52] P Armstrong, 'Changing Management Control Strategies: The Role of Competition between Accountancy and Other Organisational Professions' (1985) 10 *Accounting, Organizations and Society* 129.

[53] S Brint, *In an Age of Experts: The Changing Role of Professionals in Politics and Public Life* (Princeton, Princeton University Press, 1994).

professional occupations and expert groups, transforming their identities, structures and practices. Aspects of change certainly include the introduction of hierarchy, bureaucracy, output and performance measures and even the standardisation of work practices, all of which are more characteristic of organisational rather than professional forms of occupational control. When service sector professionals have proved enduringly difficult to manage and resistant to change, then an important part of the strategy has been to attempt to recreate professionals as managers, albeit with uneven success.[54] Thus, the discourse of enterprise becomes linked with discourses of professionalism, quality, customer service and care. Professionals are also tempted by the ideological components of empowerment, innovation, autonomy and discretion. Furthermore, attempts to measure and demonstrate professionalism actually increase the demand for the explicit auditing and accounting of professional competences. In this way, managerial demands for quality control and audit, target setting and performance review become reinterpreted as the promotion of professionalism. It is necessary to recognise, however, that output and performance measures also represent a 'discourse of competition'[55] or what Broadbent et al[56] term 'individualisation'. The danger is that social cohesion and institutional action are undermined while competition threatens both teamworking and collegial support. Thus, the quest for professionalism and accountability is highly competitive and individualistic, but it is also a bureaucratic means of regaining and exercising control over a market-directed enterprise staffed by professionals.

In public sector professions, control is increasingly achieved by means of normative values and self-regulated motivation. In professional services firms, a discourse of enterprise is fitted alongside the language of quality and customer care and the ideologies of empowerment, innovation, autonomy and discretion. In addition, this is also a discourse of individualisation and competition where individual performance is linked to the success or failure of the organisation. These all constitute powerful mechanisms of worker/employee control in which the occupational values of professionalism are used to promote enterprise and the efficient management of the organisation.

It is also important to recognise that some of the challenges to professionalism as an occupational value might also constitute challenges

---

[54] See Noordegraaf, 'Remaking Professionals' (n 42); F Mueller, C Carter and A Ross-Smith, 'Making Sense of Career in Big Four Accounting firm' in D Muzio and I Kirkpatrick (eds), *Special Issue: Reconnecting Professional Occupations and Professional Organisations* (2011) 59 *Current Sociology* 551.

[55] P Hoggett, 'New Modes of Control in the Public Services' (1996) 74 *Public Administration* 9, 15.

[56] J Broadbent, K Jacobs and R Laughlin, 'Comparing Schools in the UK and New Zealand' (1999) 10 *Management Accounting Research* 339.

to enterprise and a culture of enterprise. Some organisational techniques for controlling employees have affected the work of practitioners in professional organisations and limited the exercise of enterprise and development. One such handicap to both professionalism and enterprise is the imposition of targets in professionals' work such as in teaching and medicine,[57] as well as in para-professional occupations like the police.[58] The imposition of targets has had 'unintended' consequences on the prioritisation and ordering of work activities, and have brought with them a focus on target achievement to the detriment or neglect of other less measurable tasks and responsibilities. Also, increased regulation and form filling takes time which might arguably be better devoted to clients. The standardisation of work procedures, perhaps using software programs, is an important check on the underachieving practitioner, but can be a disincentive to both enterprise and to the creative, innovative and inspirational professional.

It is important to remember also that the way professionals regard their work and their working relationships is being changed too. The emphasis on internal as well as external markets, on enterprise and economic contracting, is transforming professionalism. In tendering, accounting and audit management, professionalism requires practitioners to codify their competence for contracts and evaluations.[59] 'Professional work is defined as a service product to be marketed, price-tagged and individually evaluated and remunerated; it is, in that sense, commodified'.[60] Professional service work organisations are converting into enterprises in terms of identity, hierarchy and rationality. Possible solutions to client problems and difficulties are defined by the organisation (rather than the ethical codes of the professional institution) and limited by financial constraints. The role of organisations as institutional entrepreneurs has also been identified, including the lobbying of professional institutions and the state to change professional regulation in their favour.[61]

---

[57] Gewirtz et al, *Changing Teacher Professionalism* (n 23); Dent, *Remodelling Hospitals* (n 25).

[58] V Boussard, *Sociologie de la gestion: les faiseurs de performance* (Paris, Belin, 2008).

[59] du Gay and Salaman, 'The Cult[ure] of the Customer' (n 14); Freidson, *Professionalism* (n 7); Lane, *New Public Management* (n 10).

[60] L Svensson and J Evetts (eds), *Conceptual and Comparative Studies of Continental and Anglo-American Professions* (Göteborg, Department of Sociology Göteborg University, 2003) 11.

[61] R Greenwood and R Suddaby, 'Institutional Entrepreneurship in Mature Fields: The Big 5 Accounting Firms' (2006) 49 *Academy of Management Journal* 27; N Malhotra, T Morris and CR Hinings, 'Variations in Organisation Form Among Professional Service Organisations' in R Greenwood, R Suddaby and M McDougald (eds), *Research in the Sociology of Organisations: Professional Firms* (Oxford, JAI Press, 2006) 171; R Suddaby, DJ Cooper and R Greenwood, 'Transnational Regulation of Professional Services: Governance Dynamics of Field Level Organisational Change' (2007) 32 *Accountancy, Organizations and Society* 333; R Suddaby and T Viale, 'Professionals and Field-Level Change: Institutional Work and the Professional Project' in D Muzio and I Kirkpatrick (eds), *Special Issue: Reconnecting Professional Occupations and Professional Organisations* (2011) 59 *Current Sociology* 423;

The commodification of professional service work entails changes in professional work relations. When practitioners become organisational employees then the traditional relationship of employer–professional trust is changed to one necessitating supervision, assessment and audit. Relationships between professionals and clients are also being converted into customer relations through the establishment of quasi-markets, customer satisfaction surveys and evaluations as well as quality measures and payment by results. The production, publication and diffusion of quality and target measurements are critical indicators for changing welfare services into a market.[62] The service itself is increasingly focused, modelled on equivalents provided by other producers, shaped by the interests of consumers and increasingly standardised. The increasing focus on marketing and selling expert solutions[63] connects professionals more to their work organisation than to their professional institutions and associations. Clients are converted into customers and professional work competencies become primarily related to, defined and assessed by the work organisation. The culture of enterprise is similarly discouraged by the control and predominance of the organisation.

In summary, the logics and culture of professionalism and enterprise are, at the same time, both similar and yet different, complementary and contrasting. However, some forms of regulation, bureaucracy and organisational practices and procedures might be constraining for both the normative values of professionalism as well as for the culture of enterprise. If professionalism and enterprise are to be reconciled then the organisational constraints on both need to be recognised.

J Flood, 'The Re-Landscaping of the Legal Profession: Large Law firms and Professional Re-Regulation' in D Muzio and I Kirkpatrick (eds), *Special Issue: Reconnecting Professional Occupations and Professional Organisations* (2011) 59 *Current Sociology* 507.

[62] Considine, *Enterprising States* (n 35).
[63] Brint, *In an Age of Experts* (n 53).

3

Financialisation by Proxy: The Case of Large City Law Firms

JAMES R FAULCONBRIDGE AND DANIEL MUZIO*

Lawyers have a primary duty to the courts and a secondary duty to their clients. These duties—including the attendant responsibilities such as client confidentiality and the rules relating to legal professional privilege—are paramount.[1]

THIS QUOTE, TAKEN from the publicity material of a corporate law firm, seems innocuous enough on the surface. Indeed, it reflects the principles of the professions that are enshrined in their codes of conduct.[2] However, as becomes clear when we return to it later in the chapter, such long-standing principles are increasingly exposed to new pressures associated with the financialisation of legal practice. Indeed, as illustrated by our analysis of large law firms, the penetration of financial logics into the management of professional firms is an important and so far relatively undocumented trend which may have some unexpected yet significant implications for professionals as well as consumers.

Outside the professions, the inflection of economic practice by the rubrics of financialisation is now a well-documented trend.[3] Uniting all these studies is a concern with the way the involvement of firms in capital markets and the rise of shareholder value logics have influenced strategy, first in the

---

* Parts of this chapter constitute a revision of a paper which was first published as: JR Faulconbridge and D Muzio, 'The Financialization of Large Law Firms: Situated Discourses and Practices of Reorganization' (2009) 9 *Journal of Economic Geography* 641, and appear here by kind permission of Oxford University Press.

[1] Slater & Gordon Lawyers (2007) Prospectus. Slater & Gordon Limited, p 9.

[2] Solicitors Regulation Authority, 'Code of Conduct 2011' (Solicitors Regulation Authority, 2014), available at: www.sra.org.uk/solicitors/handbook/code/content.page.

[3] See HJ Feng et al, 'A New Business Model? The Capital Market and the New Economy' (2001) 30 *Economy and Society* 467; J Froud et al, *Financialization and Strategy: Narrative and Numbers* (Abingdon, Routledge, 2006) for theoretical explanations; and PM O'Neill, 'Financial Narratives of the Modern Corporation' (2001) 1 *Journal of Economic Geography* 181; J Froud et al, 'Cars After Financialisation: A Case Study in Financial Under-Performance, Constraints and Consequences' (2002) 6 *Competition and Change* 13; A Pike, '"Shareholder Value" versus the Regions: The Closure of the Vaux Brewery in Sunderland' (2006) 6 *Journal of Economic Geography* 201, for empirical case studies.

United States and latterly in the United Kingdom and increasingly in other parts of Europe and Australia.[4] It has since become increasingly obvious that the logics of financialisation pervade economic life and that we are witnessing the 'capitalisation of everything'.[5]

In this chapter we interpret the structural transformation of the legal profession in England and Wales over the last 20 years through the concept of financialisation and propose this as an alternative to complement existing analyses which draw on the related concepts of de-professionalisation,[6] commercialisation[7] and managerialisation.[8] We show how privately held organisations, not listed on stock markets, have become enchanted by the logics of financialisation, mirroring the behaviours of market-listed, shareholder value-driven firms. In particular, we consider how the idea of 'financialisation by proxy' can be used to explain how increasingly performance-led and metric-driven models of corporate governance are redefining the management of law firms leading to the wide-ranging reconfiguration of traditional structures, values and practices.

As well as the introduction of the idea of financialisation by proxy, the contribution of this chapter is to show how the example of law firms is not only interesting insofar as it extends the analysis of financialisation to privately owned organisations, but also because it explores these processes within a professional context, a context traditionally assumed to be separate from the world of business, commerce and entrepreneurship.[9] In doing this, we highlight the peculiar proxy metrics and mechanisms through which these logics are being stretched, in another example of the 'capitalisation of everything',[10] into new and unexpected domains. This colonisation is inevitably a process fraught with tensions as the intended and unintended consequences of financialisation collide with the fundamental principles and long-standing practices of professional occupations. Thus,

---

[4] GL Clark, D Mansfield and A Tickell, 'Global Finance and the German Model: German Corporations, Market Incentives, and the Management of Employer-Sponsored Pension Institutions' (2002) 27 *Transactions of the Institute of British Geographers* NS 91; W Lazonick and M O'Sullivan, 'Maximizing Shareholder Value: A New Ideology for Corporate Governance' (2000) 29 *Economy and Society* 13; O'Neill, 'Financial Narratives' (n 3).

[5] A Leyshon and N Thrift, 'The Capitalization of Almost Everything: The Future of Finance and Capitalism' (2007) 24 *Theory, Culture & Society* 97.

[6] BH Burris, *Technocracy at Work* (New York, State University of New York Press, 1993); M Oppenheimer, 'Proletarianisation of the Professional' in P Halmos (ed), *Professionalisation and Social Change* (Keele, Keele University Press, 1973); MR Haug, 'De-Professionalisation: An Alternate Hypothesis for the Future' in P Halmos (ed) *Professionalisation and Social Change* (Keele, Keele University Press, 1973) 195.

[7] G Hanlon, 'Professionalism as Enterprise: Service Class Politics and the Redefinition of Professionalism' (1998) 32 *Sociology* 43.

[8] DJ Cooper et al, 'Sedimentation and Transformation in Organizational Change: The Case of Canadian Law Firms' (1996) 17 *Organization Studies* 623.

[9] MS Larson, *The Rise of Professionalism: A Sociological Analysis* (Berkeley, University of California Press, 1977).

[10] Leyshon and Thrift, 'The Capitalization of Almost Everything' (n 5).

we consider the wider societal implications arising from the financialisation of supposedly public safeguard services.[11] In particular we suggest that this drive towards fitter, leaner and meaner organisations and towards financial excellence might actually only benefit 'elite' professionals who are able to extract significant surplus from expanding subordinate groups in an increasingly elongated and reformulated division of labour. This is something that is likely to threaten the public interest, professional autonomy as well as long-standing professional institutions. Moreover, as documented by events following the recent economic crisis, it may also be financially unsustainable.[12]

The chapter unfolds over six sections. First, we present a brief overview of the literature on financialisation. We then present our methods before proceeding to analyse the restructuring of large law firms through the concept of financialisation. In particular we connect significant changes in the structure and practices of large law firms over the last 20 years or so to attempts to improve their financial performance, measured through the key metric of profits per equity partner (PEP). We argue how, as law firms increasingly manage with an eye to their position in the relevant league tables, PEP acquires a performative value as it redefines long-standing professional institutions such as promotion and career patterns as well as the very concept of the professional partnership itself (through developments such as lateral hires, de-equitisations and salaried partnerships). We then identify a number of vectors which have facilitated the spread of financialised logics and practices within the legal profession, and discuss some of the implications of these changes for professionals, their clients and the wider public. Finally, returning to these issues with the benefit of hindsight, we add a coda whereby we review some of the trends, arguments and predictions described in the original research (conducted in 2007–08) in light of developments in the post-financial crisis period (2008–13).

I. THEORIES OF FINANCIALISATION

Theories of financialisation are now well rehearsed and it serves little purpose to subject them to another comprehensive review.[13] Instead, we focus on the four main components of existing arguments: trends, agents,

[11] J Broadbent, M Dietrich and J Roberts, *The End of Professionalism? The Restructuring of Professional Work* (London, Routledge, 1997).

[12] S Ackroyd and D Muzio, 'The Reconstructed Professional Firm: Explaining Change in English Legal Practices' (2007) 28 *Organization Studies* 729; D Muzio and S Ackroyd, 'On the Consequences of Defensive Professionalism: The Transformation of the Legal Labour Process' (2005) 32 *Journal of Law and Society* 615.

[13] See M Pryke and P du Gay, 'Take an Issue: Cultural Economy and Finance' (2007) 36 *Economy and Society* 339; Froud et al, *Financialization and Strategy* (n 3) for reviews.

outcomes and critiques of financialisation and use these to understand recent changes in large corporate law firms in England.

The 'trend' of financialisation is not a particularly new one. As Feng et al[14] describe, it has existed since the 1990s but has received most attention since the dot.com bust of the early 2000s and the subsequent revaluation of high-tech firms using 'actual' rather than 'potential' performance metrics. A central component of such evaluations is, of course, the logic of shareholder value and measures such as Economic Value Added (EVA), Market Value Added (MVA), Shareholder Value Added (SVA), Total Shareholder Return (TSR) and Cash Flow Return on Investment (CFROI). As Julie Froud et al[15] point out, whilst such shareholder value logic is as much a discourse as a stable, agreed upon model of economic practice, it has come to dominate contemporary assessments of the success of firms. Crudely put, successful firms should deliver value by paying high dividends to shareholders and increasing their market value so as to offer substantial yields on investment.

The 'agents' promoting this phenomenon are diverse. Froud et al[16] describe how consultancies, such as Boston Consulting Group and Stern Stewart, propagated logics initially formulated by management gurus such as Rappaport and Stewart. This reminds us then of what Nigel Thrift[17] describes as the circuit of soft capitalism in which management gurus, the media and business schools advance economic practices claimed to optimise performance in the 'new' knowledge economy.[18] In addition, pension fund managers who are now some of the most active investors also vigorously promote the logics of shareholder value, through direct interventions at shareholder meetings.[19]

The 'outcomes' of this are, according to William Lazonick and Mary O'Sullivan,[20] a series of important structural changes, including a shift away from a 'retain and reinvest' allocative regime where growing the firm through the recycling of profits is the main priority, to a 'downsize and distribute' regime where cuts in the labour force and divestures shrink the size of the firm but allow more profit to be distributed to shareholders.

---

[14] Feng et al, 'A New Business Model' (n 3).

[15] Froud et al, *Financialization and Strategy* (n 3).

[16] ibid.

[17] N Thrift, 'The Rise of Soft Capitalism' (1997) 1 *Cultural Values* 29.

[18] See GL Clark, N Thrift and A Tickell, 'Performing Finance: The Industry, the Media, and its Image' (2004) 11 *Review of International Political Economy* 289; and C Greenfield and P Williams, 'Financialization, Finance Rationality and the Role of Media in Australia' (2007) 29 *Media Culture & Society* 415—on the role of the media in producing and disseminating the discourses of financialised practice.

[19] S Ackroyd, *The Organization of Business: Applying Organizational Theory to Contemporary Change* (Oxford, Oxford University Press, 2002); GL Clark, *Pension Fund Capitalism* (Oxford, Oxford University Press, 2000).

[20] Lazonick and O'Sullivan, 'Maximizing Shareholder Value' (n 4).

Lazonick and O'Sullivan argue that this has a number of effects. First, contrary to expectations, there are layoffs during periods of boom. Second, differentials between chief executive and worker remuneration are increasingly stretched. Third, and as a result of the previous two tendencies, returns to shareholders in the form of dividends and share buy-backs are significantly inflated.

Most would accept that there has been a discernible trend in this direction, but a number of 'critiques' of financialised logics and analyses of their effects have emerged that force us to look carefully at the wider implications. Perhaps most significantly it has been suggested that academics need to be more critical of the rhetorics of financialisation. As Froud et al[21] have argued, financialised logics and the discourses underlying them are varied, mutable and fluid, being enacted differently by both the consultants and firms that promote and employ them. They therefore question assumptions that a linear logic exists between corporate restructuring, increased 'shareholder value' and efficiency and effectiveness improvements, with existing evidence being equivocal at best. Instead, these authors promote a cultural economy perspective that recognises the power and legitimising effect of financialised discourses over the delivery of tangible results. Indeed, as they demonstrate from the example of the car industry, it is far from clear that financialised practices lead to more successful companies as weaker players can often deliver better shareholder value on paper, despite their shaky market position.

Our point of departure is to draw on these literatures and argue that they can be useful in analysing current trends in the organisation of large law firms in England. As already noted, existing studies of financialisation focus on capital market listed corporations in which the chief executive's primary role is to satisfy institutional investors and realise their demands for shareholder value. Law firms, with one Australian exception that we refer to below, are not market listed as of yet but seem to be increasingly displaying archetypal financialised logics. We attempt to explain this trend using insights from the literature described above so as to reveal some of the unexpected, troubling and potentially unsustainable consequences of recent financially focused practices.

II. METHODOLOGY

Our analysis is constructed using a triangulation of data from various sources. Quantitative material charting the composition and performance of large English law firms was taken from The Legal Business 100 survey

---

[21] Froud et al, 'Cars After Financialisation' (n 3); Froud et al, *Financialization and Strategy* (n 3).

between 1993, when records began, and 2008, when this research was conducted. This longitudinal analysis allows us to extrapolate historical trends in the financial performance and organisational structure of English law firms whilst also providing insights into the changing management practices that are associated with financialisation. We focus our analysis on the 10 largest firms, primarily because of the emphasis that these firms have placed on financialised management techniques in recent years. The trends identified are, nonetheless, relevant to the wider sample of firms analysed in the aforementioned survey, and are also relevant more broadly to large law firms worldwide, and in particular to US-based practices. However, here we focus on the largest firms in England to help tease out the geographically specific way in which these 'became financialised' in the late 1990s and early 2000s.

We also completed an extensive survey of articles in legal publications in 2007 aimed at practitioners in the United Kingdom (*The Lawyer*, *Legal Business* and *Legal Week*). This provided further detail of the changing financial performance and strategies of firms as well as insight into media reactions to these changes. Finally, we undertook 20 interviews during late 2006 and early 2007 in large corporate law firms in England. Interviewees were drawn from firms representing different segments of The Legal Business 100 survey, ranging from the largest, multi-office international firms through to nationwide firms and single office practices. Interviews lasted between 40 and 70 minutes, were recorded, transcribed and then coded. All interviewees were questioned about the strategy of the firm they worked for, recent changes to the organisation of the firm, working conditions and practices within the firm, managerial structures and styles and the impact of financial metrics (such as PEP) on their long-term strategies and day to day operations. Analysis of the interviews is used to help corroborate and explain the trends identified in the quantitative data collected.

III. FINANCIALISED LAW FIRMS?

Perhaps what makes the suggestion that law firms' behaviour is increasingly inflected by financialised logics so significant is the radical break such a change would imply from traditional notions of a professional firm. Law, as one of the few state sponsored professions, has, like accountancy, a fiduciary duty and, historically at least, is supposed to represent a public safeguard service.[22] As part of this duty, lawyers, as trustees of valued forms of skill and expertise,[23] are supposed to put the interests of their clients and of

---

[22] Broadbent, Dietrich and Roberts, *The End of Professionalism?* (n 11).
[23] S Brint, *In an Age of Experts: The Changing Role of Professionals in Politics and Public Life* (Princeton, Princeton University Press, 1994).

the public before their own interests. In this sense law firms have not been traditionally seen as organisations in which commercial logics prevailed. Of course, as Gerard Hanlon describes, such idealistic visions of what lawyers and law firms are and do, if they were ever accurate, have certainly been diluted by the rise of mega law firms with their business orientated, commercial outlook.[24] Indeed, today large corporate law firms are professional 'business' services firms, increasingly designed to lubricate the activities of global capitalism rather than to provide commercially disinterested public safeguard services.[25]

What these studies of the rise of the legal business service firms do not directly predict, however, is an outright obsession with financialised performance metrics and the unprecedented impact that these are having on the reorganisation of the legal profession. This is not to suggest that lawyers have not always been keen to make money.[26] However, in recent years there seems to have been a refocusing around financial performance underscored by new discourses and metrics of profitability that inevitably promotes different types of values, practices and structures.[27] This, we argue, is symptomatic of the 1990s and 2000s and coincides with not only the growing size of corporate law firms, but also with the rise of the shareholder society and the 'capitalisation of everything'.

A. The Performance Era and New Metrics of Success

The 1990s and especially the 2000s heralded a new period for law firms characterised by a new discourse: 'profits per equity partner' (PEP). Whilst not as familiar as its big brother (ie, shareholder) value and the associated metrics of EVA, MVA, SVA and CFROI, PEP has come to replace turnover as *the* measure of the success of a law firm. *The Lawyer*, one of the most influential legal publications in England, trumpeted the announcement that it would produce a 'Top of the PEPs' table in 2007 to provide 'the definitive inside track on the performance of the UK's biggest law firms'.[28] For firms the race was very much on to reach the top of this table as partners recognised the embarrassment associated with low levels

---

[24] G Hanlon, 'Institutional Forms and Organizational Structures: Homology, Trust and Reputational Capital in Professional Service Firms' (2004) 11 *Organization* 187.

[25] See also Cooper et al, 'Sedimentation and Transformation' (n 8) on the rise of 'Managerial Professional Business'.

[26] G Hanlon, *Lawyers, the State and the Market: Professionalism Revisited* (Basingstoke, Macmillan, 1999); D Sugarman, 'Bourgeois Collectivism, Professional Power and the Boundaries of the State. The Private and Public Life of the Law Society, 1825 to 1914' (1996) 3 *International Journal of the Legal Profession* 81.

[27] L Empson, *Managing the Modern Law Firm* (Oxford, Oxford University Press, 2007).

[28] The Lawyer, 'Who is Top of the PEPs?' *The Lawyer* (London, 11 June 2007), available at: www.thelawyer.com/who-is-top-of-the-peps/126383.article.

of PEP in a hyper-competitive marketplace. As the managing partner of Freshfields Bruckhaus Deringer commented about their past performance after restructuring delivered a massive rise in PEP, 'we did not have the financial performance that is necessary or appropriate for a firm of the calibre of ours'.[29] Similarly the managing partner of Eversheds commented after the announcement that they had broken the £500,000 PEP barrier, 'profitability has been one of our key targets over the past year, and with PEP breaking the £500,000 barrier, we have proven our ability to deliver on our promises'.[30]

Of course, the result of the new obsession is a devastating critique of firms failing to increase PEP. These firms are seen as poorly managed organisations in need of refurbishment. So when the firm Shoosmiths reported a 27 per cent increase in turnover but only a 3 per cent rise in PEP, these results were described as 'mixed' and blame was placed on 'a period of sustained expansion and a major recruitment drive across seven UK offices [that] have taken their toll on the firm's profitability'.[31] It would seem, then, that in the new epoch of financialisation, long-term investments associated with growth, which are typical of a 'retain and reinvest' regime,[32] are not necessarily seen as wholly positive. Indeed, such has been the focus of managing partners on the new PEP metric that, over the period under consideration, PEP in our sample of the top 10 law firms in England has risen by 157 per cent. As indicated by Table 1, this outstrips other financial indicators.[33] In the eyes of *The Lawyer*, this growth is a reflection of a series of unprecedented and controversial interventions on the organisational structure and division of labour in law firms, including the increasing recourse to 'brutal cost-cutting'[34] and the redefinition of the very notion of partnership. This is something which strikes a remarkable resemblance with the 'downsize and distribute' regime, which according to Lazonick and O'Sullivan,[35] is characteristic of processes of financialisation.

[29] The Lawyer, 'Download an Englishman, an Irishman and an American' Podcast, *The Lawyer* (23 February 2007), available at: www.thelawyer.com/19-february-2007/1162.issue.

[30] J Parker, 'Eversheds Confirms PEP to Break £500K' *The Lawyer* (London, 17 May 2007), available at: www.thelawyer.com/eversheds-confirms-pep-to-break-500k/125873.article.

[31] M Byrne, 'Shoosmiths Results Reveal Mixed Fortunes' *The Lawyer* (London, 4 June 2007), available at: www.thelawyer.com/shoosmiths-results-reveal-mixed-fortunes/126334. article.

[32] Lazonick and O'Sullivan, 'Maximizing Shareholder Value' (n 4).

[33] The Lawyer, 'The Global 100' *The Lawyer* (London, 2003); The Lawyer, 'The Global 100' *The Lawyer* (London, 2006).

[34] The Lawyer, 'Who is Top of the PEPs?' (n 28).

[35] Lazonick and O'Sullivan, 'Maximizing Shareholder Value' (n 4).

Table 1: Large English Law Firms: Key Financial and Labour Trends

Period	Revenues (% change)*	PEP* (% change)	Equity partners (% change)	Salaried partners (% change)	Associates (% change)	Leverage** ratios
2003–2008	26.9	53	–0.92	34.2	6.96	6.9 (2008)
1998–2003	9.6	24.2	72.9	N/A	96.7	6.7 (2003)
1993–1998	2.5	35.4	18.4	N/A	49.7	5.1 (1998)
1993–2008	42.5	157.2	103	N/A	215	3.9 (1993)

Source: Legal Business (2008) *The Legal Business 100, 1993–2008*. London, Legal Business.
* Data adjusted to 2008 prices based on Consumer Price Index
** Ratio of all salaried solicitors to equity partners
N/A = No data available due to small number of individuals in this category

B. Restructuring the Law Firm

We can begin our explanation of the restructuring associated with PEP fetishes in the 1990s when the first significant period of change was noted.[36] This was in many ways a period of unprecedented change as the structure of firms, which had been relatively static throughout the twentieth century, began to evolve. Indeed, as Stephen Ackroyd and Daniel Muzio report, throughout the 1990s a rapidly growing number of solicitors entered salaried employment as part of the first attempts by partners in law firms to drive up profitability and deflect the impact of a more hostile business environment by leveraging the performance and contribution of a rapidly expanding cohort of subordinates (non-partners) who did not share profits.[37] This stage is, however, the thin end of the wedge. As indicated by Figure 1, even more significant changes have occurred since 2000 with, by the year 2006, the associate to partner ratio in the legal profession climbing to around 1.8:1, an almost complete reversal of the ratio in the mid-1980s (1:2), as firms attempted to adopt what might be described as a leaner, more profitable model.

---

[36] Ackroyd and Muzio, 'The Reconstructed Professional Firm' (n 12); Hanlon, *Lawyers* (n 26).
[37] Ackroyd and Muzio, ibid.

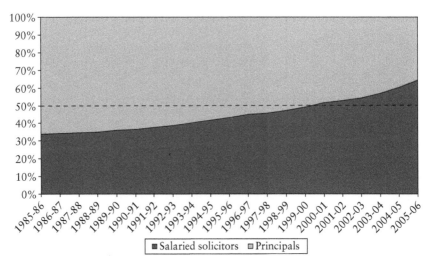

Figure 1: Ratio of Associates to Principals* in the Legal Profession in England and Wales—1985/85–2005/06
Source: Ratios calculated from the Solicitor Indemnity Fund (SIF) and the Law Society's Regis Database, as published annually in *Trends in the Legal Profession: Annual Statistical Report*, by the Law Society Strategic Research Unit (www.lawsociety.org. uk/policy-campaigns/research-trends/annual-statistical-reports/)
* Principals includes both equity partners and sole practitioners

This monumental transformation of the law from a predominantly self-employed to a predominantly employed occupation is underscored by a series of additional and drastic interventions in the profession's labour process and career structure. In particular, these interventions include the toughening and lengthening of promotion times and criteria. These have been extensively discussed elsewhere;[38] yet we want to focus on one particularly recent and important development: the case of the salaried partnership.

The salaried partnership is a significant innovation which stretches the meaning of partnership. The 'traditional' legal partnership was made up of equity partners only—individuals who owned a share of their firm, and therefore took a share of the profit it generated. Hence, profit per partner measures in the past were effectively the same as PEP measures. Increasingly, though, we are seeing salaried partners, whose remuneration is not linked to profits (besides the effect of bonus schemes), operating

---

[38] Ackroyd and Muzio, 'The Reconstructed Professional Firm' (n 12); S Bolton and D Muzio, 'Can't Live with 'Em; Can't Live Without 'Em: Gendered Segmentation in the Legal Profession' (2007) 41 *Sociology* 47; Muzio and Ackroyd, 'On the Consequences of Defensive Professionalism' (n 12).

as a new tier in organisational hierarchies. Indeed, not only are salaried partners found in most firms now but their numbers are growing significantly. As suggested by Table 1, salaried partners are, in our sample, the fastest, indeed the only, growing section of the professional labour force. Thus, salaried partnership, from an anomaly found only in a minority of firms, has been recast as a formal step in an increasingly elongated professional career structure. This introduction of new steps in the career ladder together with the broadening of existing ones has implied the elongation of hierarchies and the stretching of career spans. Writing in the 1980s, Richard Abel estimated an average wait of 5.7 years before becoming a full equity partner;[39] today, once an increasingly common stint as a salaried partner is factored into the equation, this has almost doubled to 10 years.[40]

The above changes to partnership and labour force structures, more generally, responds to a financialised logic. A salaried solicitor can generate substantially more fees than her labour costs (this surplus can oscillate between 2.5 and 4.8 times wage costs according to Abel).[41] Thus, increasing the number of salaried staff relative to profit sharing partners leads to an increasing volume of surplus which can be used to maintain and expand equity partner income levels. Indeed, according to Hanlon,[42] large firms have operationalised this logic by considering for partnership only those solicitors who generate three times more income than their remuneration costs. The rule of the game is simple: increase the number of people who bake the cake whilst stabilising or reducing the number of people who can share the cake.[43] Larger helpings will inevitably follow. Salaried partnership contributes to this strategy by increasing leverage whilst providing at the same time an expectation management tool.

The financial logic associated with these developments emerges clearly in Table 2. As it shows, the majority of PEP is now actually produced through the appropriation of surplus generated by subordinate workers, including this new category of 'lesser' partners. In this context, the manipulation of staffing ratios becomes an effective route for increasing profitability and a standard aspect of law firm management.

Most radically, recent interventions have also sought the reduction of equity partner headcount in a period of boom for legal services. Indeed,

---

[39] RL Abel, *The Legal Profession in England and Wales* (Oxford, Basil Blackwell Books, 1988) 205.
[40] M Brivot, H Lam and Y Gendron, 'Digitalization and Promotion: An Empirical Study in a Large Law Firm' (2014) 25(4) *British Journal of Management* 805.
[41] Abel, *The Legal Profession in England and Wales* (n 39) 206.
[42] Hanlon, *Lawyers* (n 26).
[43] DH Maister, *Managing the Professional Service Firm* (New York, Free Press, 1993).

Table 2: Leverage in Action—An Illustration

	Partners	Senior fee earner	Junior fee earner
Hourly rate (HR) £	220	190	140
Notional hours pa (HH)	1,300	1,300*	1,300*
Notional income pa (NI) (HR x HH) £	286,000	247,000	182,000
Remuneration (R) £	450,000	90,000	50,000
Income/remuneration ratio (NI/R)	0.63	2.74	3.64

Data provided by Muzio (2004)

as indicated by Table 1, between 2003 and 2008 the number of equity partners employed in the top 10 firms in the United Kingdom contracted by almost 1 per cent despite revenues growth of 27 per cent. Although a proportion of this reduction will be accounted for by natural wastage, these trends corroborate growing anecdotal evidence of de-equitisation (redundancy of equity partners). According to some[44] this strikes at the heart of the very nature of the legal profession, as, in a dramatic break with the past, it signifies how partners, the owners of the firms, are also increasingly viewed as cost to be efficiently and ruthlessly managed. 'Chopping out the dead wood' or 'weeding the garden', to use common expressions, is a useful instrument in today's increasingly bloated, heterogeneous and geographically dispersed partnerships, where informal control may be somewhat less effective.[45] Yet, the gradual reduction in equity partners may be more than a simple short-term managerial intervention targeted at seriously under-performing employees.[46] Instead, the reduction seems to also be bound up with the quest of sustaining and expanding profitability. Thus, the updated strategy may be to actually reduce rather than simply stabilise those who share the cake, whilst of course continuing to expand those who participate to revenue generation.

The recent changes discussed here suggest that developments in the profession's labour process which originally emerged in the 1990s as defensive moves[47] were carried through and indeed intensified in what for law firms

---

[44] J Flood, 'Lawyers as Sanctifiers: The Role of Elite Law Firms in International Business Transactions' (2007) 14 *Indiana Journal of Global Legal Studies* 35.

[45] Freshfields Bruckhaus Derringer won an employment tribunal where a former partner claimed he was unjustifiably de-equitised because it was deemed that the firm had taken proportionate steps in pursuit of a legitimate (profit enhancing) goal: M Byrne, 'Revealed: Mid-Market Firms Say "Yes" to Floatation' *The Lawyer* (London, 25 June 2007), available at: www.thelawyer.com/revealed-mid-market-firms-say-yes-to-floatation/126748.article.

[46] Empson, *Managing the Modern Law Firm* (n 27).

[47] Muzio and Ackroyd, 'On the Consequences of Defensive Professionalism' (n 12).

was a period (between 2002 and 2007) of unprecedented growth and profitability. This parallels trends identified by Lazonick and O'Sullivan[48] in the corporate sector and in particular the shift towards a 'downsize and distribute allocative regime', whereby even financially successful firms continuously reorganise their activities and turn to their labour process as an avenue for sustained profitability and shareholder return. Thus, the growing attention for financialised metrics and practices and the unprecedented impact that these are having on the structure of the legal profession is certainly tied to the self-interested agency of those who stand to benefit from these changes: equity partners. Yet, there are other significant vectors of change beyond self-interest. It is to these other vectors of financialisation that we now turn our attention.

IV. VECTORS OF FINANCIALISATION

A. Political–Economic Realignments

The legal 'Big Bang' that took place in 1990 opened the English legal market to overseas law firms for the first time.[49] Previously many US firms had entered London to provide advice on US law to transnational corporations. After 1990, however, these firms increasingly began to provide English law advice and compete with the 'magic circle' firms Clifford Chance, Linklaters, Freshfields, Allen & Overy and Slaughter and May. This created new competition and, most significantly for our argument here, positioned English incumbents against competitors with significantly higher levels of profits. This had two effects.

First, it created reputational problems for English firms. Law firms live and die on their reputations and, in a financialised world where profitability is the only accepted measure of success and the quality of the firm, being less profitable than your US counterpart causes reputational problems. Second, and more pragmatically, the more profitable US firms were able to pay solicitors significantly more money and, therefore, poach star players from English firms. As one senior partner commented about this dilemma:

> I think it's fair to say that they [reports of PEP] must have some impact. For example potential recruits may regard them as significant. Perhaps some clients make a judgment on the quality of a law firm by how well it seems to be doing in those terms. So you cannot completely ignore the league tables ... What we do have is a sense of a need for comparability purposes to know that we are not

---

[48] Lazonick and O'Sullivan, 'Maximizing Shareholder Value' (n 4).
[49] B Cullen-Mandikos and A MacPherson, 'US Foreign Direct Investment in the London Legal Market: An Empirical Analysis' (2002) 54 *The Professional Geographer* 491.

lagging behind on competitors, that we're not making our partners or our staff work harder for less benefit ... And so if you were not financially success[ful] you would have to find some other means of retaining or attaining staff and that could be more difficult.[50]

It could then be argued that US law firms themselves were vectors of financialisation. And undoubtedly this is true to some extent as English firms copied their rivals who had begun to leverage higher numbers of solicitors to partners, used up-or-out promotion mechanisms,[51] deployed dual-tier partnership arrangements and crucially enjoyed better profitability levels at an earlier stage. But convergence around 'best' (in this case intended as 'most profitable') practice is not the only relevant trend at play.

In the post-2000 era we must also turn our attention to the enabling role of the regulatory 'Big Bang' connected with the UK's Legal Services Act 2007. This Act, through the introduction of Alternative Business Structures, paves the way for the potential overhaul of the traditional governance, regulation and structure of legal practice. A key provision, here, is the acceptance of outside (meaning non-lawyer) ownership of law firms. In this context, most radically, law firms may be able to attract external investors as shareholders and 'go all the way' with a full stock exchange flotation. Indeed, at the time this research was conducted, it was anticipated that up to 50 per cent of the firms in *The Lawyer's* UK 100 survey might seek outside investors and even stock exchange listing.[52]

Whilst the full implications of the Act are still emergent and perhaps slower than originally expected,[53] its provisions seem likely to support the financialised logics and practices here described. Indeed, part of the logic of the new financial metrics such as PEP is to provide an acceptable basis for the valuation of law firms so as to facilitate investment decisions.[54] Partners may therefore be keen to maximise the value of their partnership equity by enhancing PEP and ultimately the supposed value of the firm to outside investors. In this respect it is interesting that, at the time this research was conducted, we were beginning to see in the specialist legal press proxy (multi-billion pound) stock market valuation for the UK's leading law firms.[55]

---

[50] Senior partner, Top 10 firm.

[51] M Galanter and T Palay, *Tournament of Lawyers: The Transformation of the Large Law Firm*, 1st edn (Chicago, University of Chicago Press, 1991).

[52] Byrne, 'Revealed' (n 45).

[53] S Chadderton, 'Legal Services Board Concedes "No Big Bang" in Five Years Since LSA' *The Lawyer* (London, 4 April 2012), available at: www.thelawyer.com/analysis/the-lawyer-management/abs-news-and-analysis/legal-services-board-concedes-no-big-bang-in-five-years-since-lsa/1012083.article.

[54] S Mayson, 'Building Sustainable Capital: A Capital Idea' in L Empson (ed), *Managing the Modern Law Firm* (Oxford, Oxford University Press, 2007) 141.

[55] See, eg, G Ringshaw, 'Focus: Making a Bundle' *The Sunday Times* (London, 8 July 2007).

Legislation, therefore, seems to have acted as a powerful vector in facilitating the shift from financialisation by proxy to 'real' financialisation. In addition, the very centrality of law firms as intermediaries in the newly emergent 'economy of permanent restructuring'[56] has also exaggerated the willingness of law firms to change their structure. Large corporate law firms now service clients that are constantly merging, de-merging, reorganising and refinancing their operations. They produce the legal structures that facilitate 'downsizing and re-distribution'[57] processes in their clients and inevitably these logics have caught the attention of managing partners themselves.[58] This is, then, an important component of this process of financialisation by proxy. Law firms have become so embroiled in the logics and practices of financialised management on behalf of their clients that they have begun to absorb and recreate these in a process of institutional isomorphism.[59] In addition, other actors have also been important in driving change.

B. Cultural Economy and Law Firm Management

As described in the opening sections of the chapter, various agents of financialisation have an important role in reproducing the discourses that influence corporate actors. In particular, management gurus and consultancies have in recent years increasingly turned their attention to advising law firms. Perhaps the most important guru for law firms is David Maister. His books which include *Managing the Professional Service Firm*[60] and *First Among Equals: How to Manage a Group of Professionals*[61] are bestsellers, having sold over 2.5 million copies on Amazon alone. In them Maister offers various prescriptions for managing everything from partner motivation to overseas office networks. Significantly, profitability is a key issue in all of these texts. In *Managing the Professional Service Firm* a whole chapter is dedicated to this issue early on in the book. Here readers are reminded that:

> In a partnership, the ultimate measure of profitability is (or should be) profit per partner, which is driven by three main factors, margin, productivity, and leverage

---

[56] Froud et al, *Financialization and Strategy* (n 3).
[57] Lazonick and O'Sullivan, 'Maximizing Shareholder Value' (n 4).
[58] As even the most senior partners in London's law firms are paid significantly less than many of the bank clients they work for, this trend is likely to have further driven the desire of partners to optimise their own profits so to affirm their elite status.
[59] See Cooper et al, 'Sedimentation and Transformation' (n 8).
[60] Maister, *Managing the Professional Service Firm* (n 43).
[61] PJ Mckenna and D Maister, *First Among Equals: How to Manage a Group of Professionals* (London, Simon & Schuster, 2002).

... 'profit per partner' should be viewed as the professional firm equivalent of 'return on equity'.[62]

Leaders of law firms have listened to such advice and used it as a cue for the adoption of the types of structural changes occurring in market-listed firms as a response to financial pressures.

The media also deserves careful consideration because of the central role some publications have played in championing financial logics. This has taken place both in the financial press (for example, *The Financial Times* (FT)) and professional publications such as *The Lawyer*. The FT issues annual 'innovative lawyers' awards, one category in 2007 being 'Management'; the winner was Eversheds for its partner profit-sharing scheme. The categories of award have now changed;[63] in 2014, instead of referencing profitability, evidence was required of how law firms are, 'responding to the economic challenges of slow growth in Europe, changing client expectations, new competition and the increasing internationalisation of legal services'.[64] The influence of such publications (because of the way they historically analysed, ranked and publicised the PEP performance of firms) should also not be underestimated. Mirroring the findings of Gordon Clark, Nigel Thrift and Adam Tickell,[65] and Greenfield and Williams,[66] it seems that the way the media portrays certain types of action has helped sway the behaviour of managing partners in law firms. Winning an award from the FT or being top of the PEPs in tables produced by *The Lawyer* and others is seen as important proxy for quality and performance and as such a concern for management. As one interviewee commented:

> Whether we're first, second or third has a cosmetic benefit sometimes but frankly we want to be towards, well we want to be at the top end of these tables. If we're at the top end of the tables we're happy.[67]

V. PROBLEMATISING FINANCIALISATION IN THE LAW FIRM

It seems then, that various factors have produced the significant changes in the structuring of law firms over recent years. Of course, as Lazonick

---

[62] Maister, *Managing the Professional Service Firm* (n 43) 31.

[63] Financial Times, 'FT Innovative Lawyers Ranking and Awards, Europe 2014' *The Financial Times* (London, 10 February 2014), available at: www.ft.com/cms/s/2/2380bf14-9248-11e3-9e43-00144feab7de.html#axzz368mNQ0Ni.

[64] ibid.

[65] Clark, Thrift and Tickell, 'Performing Finance' (n 18).

[66] Greenfield and Williams, 'Financialization' (n 18).

[67] Senior Partner, Top 10 firm.

and O'Sullivan and Froud et al[68] amongst others show, the adoption of financialised practices is not without consequences for the core workforce of firms, for clients, for society at large and somewhat paradoxically, for the long-term performance of the firms in question. These issues form the focus of the discussion below. As we show, the changes law firms have initiated have both intended and unintended consequences worth further examination.

A. Professional Lives: Towards the Law Factory?

As reported, recent changes have involved the elongation and formalisation of professional hierarchies and the emergence of two-tier partnerships with associate lawyers being asked to wait longer before they are offered partnership.[69] The 'tournament of lawyers'[70] is also becoming increasingly contested as promotion is decoupled from seniority and technical competence[71] and subjected to the requirements of the business case (will the lawyer generate profits) and ultimately to the necessities of retaining and improving satisfactory financial ratios.

Perhaps one of the most justifiable logics connected with the proliferation of salaried partners is, then, its role in managing career expectations and combating attrition by offering associates who otherwise would not be promoted the title and status of being a partner. However, paradoxically, despite the intention to provide an expectation management tool, frustration is often caused by the fact that on many occasions the profit generating threshold for admittance to any form of partnership places substantial— some might say unreasonable—demands on lawyers. At the same time, the temptation to use more salaried partners to expand the firm's revenue base without decreasing individual partner takings becomes irresistible, further reproducing the problem as there is actually an incentive not to promote people beyond salaried partnership level. As one interviewee described his experience of this process:

> I've got a lot of friends at [firm x] and they have really squeezed partnership and it's difficult to get partnership at [firm x] now because they want to, you've probably read it in the *Lawyer* if you read that, they want to get to four hundred thousand pounds per equity partner. The only way they are going to do that is

---

[68] Lazonick and O'Sullivan, 'Maximizing Shareholder Value' (n 4); Froud et al, 'Cars After Financialisation' (n 3).

[69] See also WD Henderson, 'An Empirical Study of Single-Tier versus Two-Tier Partnerships in the Am Law 200' (2006) 84 *North Carolina Law Review* 1691.

[70] Galanter and Palay, *Tournament of Lawyers* (n 51).

[71] Hanlon, *Lawyers* (n 26).

reduce the partners. [Lawyer x] is a guy who has come across here from [firm y], he only joined us a month ago as partner, fantastic bloke, very able, corporate lawyer and he was told by his immediate boss [at firm x] that 'we want you to be a partner because you are capable but if we squeeze the numbers to make the PEP target you won't make it for a few years'.[72]

For those stuck in the middle, the new profit focus has potentially significant consequences. Whilst the 'elites' of law firms, the equity partners, reap handsome rewards from rising PEP, non-equity partners and especially the rafts of leveraged associates face new challenges as they fulfil the role of cogs (profit generators) in increasingly large law machines. Consequently, as the income gap separating junior solicitors and partners from their profit-sharing equity partner seniors widens,[73] and as promotion tracks become more competitive and tortuous, workloads increase, work–life balance deteriorates and promotion tournaments become more fractious. Sixteen hour days and six or seven day working weeks are now not uncommon as lawyers strive for promotion and are leveraged to deliver rises in PEP. These tensions of course reap a personal as well as a professional toll. In particular, the combination of extended partnership tracks and growing stress levels are said to be the cause of the now significant attrition rates experienced by large English firms,[74] despite unprecedented financial success. Indeed, many firms are now asking whether it is possible to extract profits from an already stretched group of workers:

> You get to a certain level—say the £500,000 partner profits point—and then squeezing more out of the machine becomes increasingly difficult; particularly if you are not going for the big de-equitisation push. You cannot ask associates to do much more than they are doing.[75]

B. Public Interest

All this may seem of little concern beyond the confines of the law firms' walls. But, in theory at least, professionals such as lawyers 'heal our bodies,

---

[72] *Lawyer*, Top 25 large English law firm.

[73] Eg, in the large English 'magic circle' firms (Clifford Chance, Freshfields Bruckhaus Derringer, Linklaters and Allen & Overy, the ratio of starting salaries to 'top of equity' pay is approximately, on average, 1:17 or £65,000 to £1,105,000. Even starker is the ratio between those at the bottom of the partnership ladder in 2006 and those at the top which was, on average, 1:4.8. In 2001, the ratio of top of equity to bottom of equity was 1:2.4 (based on data in *The Lawyer* (2003; 2006). Many also expect the changes associated with the Legal Services Act 2007 to be replicated elsewhere meaning discussions of financialisation may have relevance outside the English context of this chapter.

[74] Attrition rates are now at around 23%. For a historical review of these attrition rates, see the annual law firms survey published by PWC: PWC, '2013 Annual Law Firms' Survey' (PWC, 2013), available at: www.pwc.co.uk/business-services/law-firms/home.jhtml.

[75] Quoted in *Legal Week*: C Edmond, 'Associate Fears Grow as Firms Stretch Leverage' *Legal Week* (19 July 2007), available at: www.legalweek.com/legal-week/news/1176830/associate-fears-grow-firms-stretch-leverage.

measure our profits and save our souls'.[76] Professional projects[77] have historically justified their claims, privileges and rewards on the basis of rhetorics of altruism and public service. This is what Steven Brint[78] refers to as the social trusteeship ideal of professionalism whereby the professions have consistently highlighted their role as depositories of socially relevant forms of knowledge, thus giving them the ability to solve problems of great public and personal importance.

In today's post-Enron context, many would be rightly sceptical of suggestions that professionals and corporate lawyers in particular provide publicly spirited services. Nevertheless, despite the new realities of commercialisation, corporate lawyers do still maintain important statutory roles and have deontological responsibilities, which inevitably clash with the unfettered pursuit of economic return. As officers of the court lawyers have a duty to serve justice and uphold the law, whilst the nature of their fiduciary relationship with clients implies that they have to prioritise the client's best interests (subject to not stepping outside the law), sometimes at the expense of their own profit maximisation. For example, if a client has to be advised not to pursue a particular deal or form of restructuring for legal reasons the law firm will potentially lose income. New financialised models which emphasise profitability and success in the PEP league tables raise questions about the ability of lawyers to maintain this 'disinterested' position and their fiduciary duties.

Indeed, in May 2007 when the Australian firm Slater & Gordon floated on the Australian stock exchange the profession entered a new era where profit making has to have a formal place in management decisions. This is where the chapter's opening quote, taken from Slater & Gordon's initial public offering brochure, becomes significant:

> Lawyers have a primary duty to the courts and a secondary duty to their clients. These duties—including the attendant responsibilities such as client confidentiality and the rules relating to legal professional privilege—are paramount given the nature of the Company's business as an incorporated Legal Practice. There could be circumstances in which the lawyers of Slater & Gordon are required to act in accordance with these duties and contrary to other corporate responsibilities and against the interests of Shareholders and the short-term profitability of the Company.[79]

The quote captures the inherent tensions between the profession's duties and the new preoccupations connected with financialisation, flotation and

---

[76] A Abbott, *The System of Professions: An Essay on the Division of Expert Labour* (Chicago, University of Chicago Press, 1988).

[77] Larson, *The Rise of Professionalism* (n 9).

[78] Brint, *In an Age of Experts* (n 23).

[79] Slater & Gordon, 'Prospectus' (Slater & Gordon, 2007) 84, available at: www.slatergordon.com.au/docs/prospectus/Prospectus.pdf.

the expectations of outside investors.[80] Can lawyers maintain this balance effectively? Are overworked associates and partners capable of fulfilling their duties and of managing conflicting demands to the best of their ability? Furthermore, does the consumer and indeed society benefit from such changes in emphasis and practice even when these are justified in the terms of client focus and value added?

In many ways such questions take us back to the work of Adolf Berle and Gardiner Means who studied the dangers of separating ownership and control in firms because of the moral hazard it creates.[81] Similarly the work of Michel Aglietta and Antoine Rebérioux[82] on the problems of CEO share options as a mechanism for ensuring the performance of firms also seems relevant here. In short, this work suggests that financialised performance metrics might create a conflict of interest with partners and those managing law firms potentially prioritising their own and the firms gain—ie, profitability—in lieu of fiduciary duty and at the cost of the client's best interests. Staffing transactions with cheaper forms of less qualified professional labour, such as legal executives and trainees, leveraging the work of junior professionals, using computerised case management systems to reduce the number of solicitors needed, and having solicitors simply signing off paperwork associated with a case rather than actively work on it are all examples of the outcomes of profit-driven strategising. As the factory system replaces craft production, costs are reduced but clients may be potentially deprived of the benefits associated with bespoke, professionally led advice.

Whilst we are hesitant to make too many claims and predictions, clearly such issues should be considered in future debates. Indeed, an intensification of financially driven restructuring is possible in the English context over the forthcoming years as firms seek to improve PEP still further in preparation for flotation on stock exchanges or the attraction of external investors. As Stephen Mayson[83] argues, those firms with high PEP are likely to be more attractive to investors and so PEP rates and league tables are likely to become even more important in the post-Legal Services Act epoch.[84] However, our interviewees did argue that few large firms were likely to rush to find external investors because of concerns about the reputational

---

[80] Although it should be noted that only two other firms have followed suit and floated: IHL Group and Quindell. More flotations may be seen as more ABSs come on line in England and Wales.

[81] A Berle and G Means, *The Modern Corporation and Private Property*, 2nd edn (New Jersey, Transaction Publishers, 1999).

[82] M Aglietta and A Rebérioux, *Corporate Governance Adrift: A Critique of Shareholder Value* (Cheltenham, Edward Elgar, 2005).

[83] Mayson, 'Building Sustainable Capital' (n 54).

[84] Many also expect the changes associated with the Legal Services Act 2007 to be replicated elsewhere meaning discussions of financialisation may have relevance outside the English context of this chapter.

dangers associated with the demise of partnership governance.[85] Indeed, reassuringly some were even beginning to ask questions about the dangers of the PEP 'game'. For instance, in 2007, the editor of *Legal Week* suggested that the financialised model of the law firm was already contested.[86]

VI. CONCLUSION AND CODA

In this chapter we have sought to do two things. First, to explore the way the logics of financialisation have penetrated large English law firms in recent years. We have described this as a process of 'financialisation by proxy' because of the way ideals and discourses have moved into the world of legal services from the world of the stock market through newly created metrics and mechanisms (PEP league tables). In doing this we have examined both the nature of the changes associated with this process and the agents involved in spreading financialised logics and practices within law firms. Second, we have begun to unpack some of the most striking consequences of this process of change and how this connects with other key trends identified in the literature, such as internal stratification, commercialisation and managerialisation. It is well known that financialised management has implications for workers[87] and consumers[88] and here we have begun to examine these debates from the perspective of law firms.

We originally conducted this research in 2008 at a point where the legal profession had enjoyed a prolonged and intense period of economic expansion but was facing the global financial crisis. Returning to this work has given us the opportunity to review our original arguments and observations in light of recent developments in the post-financial crisis period. Interestingly, data in the UK Legal Business 100 for 2009–13 showed a reversal of many of the trends registered in the previous 15 years and discussed in our original publication.[89] What is most noteworthy here is not so much the decline in financial indicators such as PEP (–32 per cent) or Revenues per Lawyer (–10 per cent), something which is to be expected in the context of an economic slowdown, but the more structural trends such as the decrease in leverage ratios which by 2013 had dropped to five salaried professionals per equity partner from a ratio of 6.9:1 in 2008. The

---

[85] See also L Empson and C Chapman, 'Partnership Versus Corporation: Implications of Alternative Governance for Managerial Authority and Organizational Priorities in Professional Service Firms' (2006) 24 *Research in the Sociology of Organizations* 145.

[86] See: Editor's Comment, 'End of the Road for PEP' *Legal Week* (19 July 2007), available at: www.legalweek.com/legal-week/analysis/1176781/editor-comment-end-road-pep.

[87] Lazonick and O'Sullivan, 'Maximizing Shareholder Value' (n 4).

[88] Froud et al, *Financialization and Strategy* (n 3).

[89] Legal Business, 'Legal Business 100' (Legal Business, 2013), available at: www.legalbusiness.co.uk/index.php/component/taxonomy/Legal%20Business%20100.

fact that this figure is closer to the 1993 value of 3.9:1 than to the ratio only five years earlier, speaks to the intense process of restructuring and de-leveraging that the profession has embarked upon in the post-crisis period. Of course, deleveraging points to some significant changes in underlying headcount trends, with most growth, occurring, for the first time in 20 years, at partner rather than associate level.

What does this means for our original thesis on the financialisation of the legal profession? Most simply it may suggest that financialisation is a conjunctural rather than an epochal trend, as it relies on and contributes to the broader economic cycle. This is best illustrated by the example of leveraging, which acts as a source of profitability whilst salaried workers can generate a sufficiently large surplus relative to their cost of labour. This is fine in periods of economic growth but in recession leverage can rapidly turn from a source of profitability to a liability, as firms have to maintain large fixed costs without generating the necessary volumes of fees. Law firm staff have to be paid their salaries regardless of the firm's profitability, whereas the partners can have their income greatly reduced in line with the profitability of the firm. Thus, most basically, the trend towards leveraging described in our original paper depended on an expanding legal services market and was reversed as soon as this condition disappeared. This of course echoes the general criticisms of the suitability of PEP as a performance metric, which began to surface, as described in the previous section, even during the expansion in the 2000s. Second, it is also worth considering whether leveraging requires a certain type of labour-intensive transactional work which may be more amenable to delegation to cheaper and less experienced forms of labour, such as the due diligence work associated with Mergers and Acquisitions activity or the intense document checking associated with capital markets operations. As soon as this work disappeared following the crisis, not only did profitability decline but leveraged business models became less viable.

These developments are not, per se, incompatible with financialisation, as the structural adjustments described above may be motivated by attempts to protect financial performance in a changing economic context. Thus, whilst during periods of growth financial performance could be best served through leveraging, during a slowdown this was best achieved through its opposite. As such, it may be possible that firms have used the justification of the crisis to radically change the size and shape of their partnership to protect profitability, better position themselves for future growth[90] or even

---

[90] M Taylor, 'Clifford Chance to Cut Partners in Firmwide Reshaping' *The Lawyer* (London, 4 February 2009), available at: www.thelawyer.com/clifford-chance-to-cut-partners-in-firmwide-reshaping/136594.article; K Ganz, 'Clifford Chance to Make 80 London Lawyers Redundant' *The Lawyer* (London, 8 January 2009), available at: www.thelawyer.com/clifford-chance-to-make-80-london-lawyers-redundant/136200.article; B Moshinsky,

make the firm more attractive for a sale.[91] This of course would still imply that, whilst the structure and behaviour of firms is indeed changing, financialised strategies and practices continue to drive their management and to exercise a significant influence on the structure of the profession. One thing that appears clear, though, from the prominence of criticisms in the media, the development of alternative metrics such as 'earnings per partner' and the declining frequency of media citations, is that the hegemony of PEP as a performance indicator is increasingly contested.[92]

'Linklaters to Axe Up to 70 Partners in Massive Shake Up' *The Lawyer* (London, 23 January 2009), available at: www.thelawyer.com/exclusive-linklaters-to-axe-up-to-70-partners-in-massive-shake-up/136424.article; M Taylor, 'Linklaters: 270 London Jobs to Go' *The Lawyer* (London, 29 January 2009), available at: www.thelawyer.com/linklaters-270-london-jobs-to-go/136509.article; M Byrne, 'Costs in Translation' *The Lawyer* (London, 5 July 2010), available at: www.thelawyer.com/costs-in-translation/1004932.article.

[91] C Griffiths, 'Focus: Equity Partnership and EPP: Slash and Earn' *The Lawyer* (London, 13 September 2010), available at: www.thelawyer.com/focus-equity-partnership-and-epp-slash-and-earn/1005478.article.

[92] See, eg, C Griffiths 'Dentons, The American Lawyer Row, and Why PEP is Not "Meaningless"' *The Lawyer* (London, 13 June 2014), available at: www.thelawyer.com/analysis/behind-the-law/dentons-the-american-lawyer-row-and-why-pep-is-not-meaningless/3021911.article.

4

Delivering Family Justice: New Ways of Working for Lawyers in Divorce and Separation

MAVIS MACLEAN

T HIS CHAPTER DRAWS on work in progress in Oxford on the delivery of family justice in late modern society and argues that we may be moving away from a lawyer-centred child-focused family justice system towards a more diverse, less regulated world of greater consumer choice with a new emphasis on private ordering. The drivers for change include both austerity and the recent deregulation of legal services. The changes are dynamic and exciting, but the concerns arising are how far family justice in its emerging form will be able to meet the needs of the vulnerable. A diverse but fragmented market in professional intervention for those facing the challenges of family change through divorce or separation is a long way from the welfare state ethic of access to justice as part of citizenship. We are seeing increasing inequalities between those, on the one hand, whose choices are not constrained by limited resources, and those, on the other, who are not able to purchase information, advice and support. These inequalities will impact on two groups of third parties: children and the public purse, if the clusters of problems associated with family change remain unresolved.[1]

I. HOW IMPORTANT ARE FAMILY LAWYERS FOR COUPLES, AND PARTICULARLY PARENTS WHO END THEIR RELATIONSHIPS?

When we began empirical work on family law in Oxford 20 years ago, our concern was the differential impact of the legal process on men and

---

[1] G Cookson, 'Analysing the Economic Justification for the Reforms to Social Welfare and Family Law Legal Aid' (2013) 35 *Journal of Social Welfare and Family Law* 21.

women going through divorce. We found in our survey of 718 divorced adults screened out from a general population survey, that legal advice was used by almost all the women with children[2] and the key outcome was the movement of resources from non-resident fathers to mothers with the care of dependent children. As the divorce rate rose to a peak in the early 1990s,[3] and the demand for legal aid rose with it, government began to question the value of legal intervention and to warm to the idea of what was first called conciliation and later mediation, ie, an alternative form of dispute resolution. As the Law Commission in 1990 set out the need to move away from any reference to matrimonial offence to divorce on request if a marriage had irretrievably broken down,[4] the government moved mediation centre stage in a consultation document, 'Looking to the Future: Mediation and the Ground for Divorce', followed, in 1995, by a White Paper of the same name.[5] A summary of the proposed legislation by the Lord Chancellor's Department in 1996 entitled 'Marriage and the Family Law Act 1996' described the policy options as a choice between litigation, or arm's length negotiation by solicitors and mediation, the latter being the preferred choice.

The contrast between the claims made for the emerging mediation service and the disparagement of the work of lawyers was so marked, that we felt compelled to take a closer look at the lawyers,[6] while our colleague Robert Dingwall began to study the new profession of mediation.[7] Our study of family solicitors comprised a survey of cases, combined with observation at first hand of the daily work of a number of family practitioners dealing with clients of varying economic status and a range of divorce-related matters. We found solicitors to be offering not only legal information and advice, but also active support on the cluster of problems facing men and women experiencing family breakdown. The first task was always to ensure a roof over the heads of any children involved and then to find a way to pay for it. A vulnerable client on legal aid might be helped in the course of working out financial arrangements with related problems in employment, or debt management. We observed solicitors setting up meetings with local authority housing departments to agree a plan for rent arrears, giving out

---

[2] J Eekelaar and M Maclean, *Maintenance after Divorce* (Oxford, Clarendon Press, 1986) 92.

[3] In the 1993 OPCS General Household Survey 165,000 divorces were recorded: Office of Population Censuses and Surveys, 'General Household Survey 1994' (Table 2.24, OPCS, 1994).

[4] Law Commission, *Ground for Divorce* (Law Com No 192, 1990).

[5] Lord Chancellor's Department, *Looking to the Future—Mediation and the Ground for Divorce* (Cm 2424, 1993); Lord Chancellor's Department, *Looking to the Future—Mediation and the Ground for Divorce: The Government's Proposals* (Cm 2799, 1995).

[6] See J Eekelaar, M Maclean and S Beinart, *Family Lawyers: The Divorce Work of Solicitors* (Oxford, Hart Publishing, 2000).

[7] R Dingwall, 'Divorce Mediation: Should We Change Our Mind?' (2010) 32 *Journal of Social Welfare and Family Law* 107.

home phone numbers to anxious parties in domestic violence cases and even visiting a local hospital to take instructions from a client who was unwell. These solicitors were offering help with problems, managing these when they could not be solved and supporting clients when they could not be managed. The focus was far wider than simply dispute resolution. Where there were disputes, the lawyers were negotiating with their clients to try to reach a position which would be within the range of what a court would accept if the matter, despite the solicitor's best efforts to reach agreement, were to come to court. And if both lawyers were able to do this, then settlement was likely to follow either in the form of an informal arrangement, or if certainty was required in the case of a property division or arrangements for children, then a consent order would be sought from the court to establish enforceability. The lawyers were dealing with third parties on behalf of clients, identifying potential as well as actual difficulties, and aiming to avoid future conflict when circumstances changed on remarriage or the arrival of new children. The Solicitors Family Law Association (SFLA, the forerunner to Resolution) had by this time established a code of practice for its 5000 members which in paragraph 1.1 required members to:

> Advise, negotiate and conduct proceedings in a manner calculated to encourage and assist the parties to achieve a constructive settlement of their differences as quickly as may be reasonable whilst recognising that parties may need time to come to terms with their new situation.[8]

In our study of divorcing parents,[9] 19 per cent of our sample of 249 formerly married parents—screened out from a general population sample[10]—had taken no professional advice; 74 per cent had seen a lawyer, 79 per cent of whom were legally aided; 53 per cent had seen 'only' a lawyer; 20 per cent a lawyer and another professional; 1 per cent had seen both a mediator and a lawyer; and others had seen Relate counsellors and spiritual advisers.[11]

From what we observed it seemed that there was little consumer-led demand for substituting an alternative form of professional intervention in divorce, though a small number of the divorcing population were seeking, in addition to the advice of lawyers, the help of others, mainly marriage counsellors and spiritual advisers. At this time the mediators largely came from a counselling background and were working in the not-for-profit sector, focusing on helping in a less formalistic way with disputes over arrangements for children. They were thought by the early researchers to be rather reluctant to extend their work to money issues.[12]

---

[8] Solicitors Family Law Association, 'Code of Practice', para 1.1, Resolution 2014.
[9] M Maclean and J Eekelaar, *The Parental Obligation* (Oxford, Hart Publishing, 1997).
[10] ibid, 155.
[11] ibid, 133.
[12] See J Walker, P McCarthy and N Timms, *Mediation: The Making and Remaking of Cooperative Relationships—An Evaluation of the Effectiveness of Comprehensive Mediation* (Newcastle, Relate Centre for Family Studies, 1994).

II. POLICY PRESSURE ON FAMILY LAWYERS

Government appeared to work on the assumption that lawyers, far from restraining the adversarial inclinations of their clients (as we and others had observed), were instrumental in increasing conflict, and with legal aid payment for service by the hour were, as suppliers, creating demand for their services. Mediators on the other hand, specialising in dispute resolution and coming from the voluntary sector, were thought to offer a new cost-effective and constructive alternative to the work of courts and lawyers, the latter represented again in policy statements as focused only on litigation and adjudication. In his speech to the UK Family Law Conference on 25 June 1999, Lord Irvine said:

> The agreements reached in mediation have a rational basis; they are the result of constructive negotiation between those concerned ... People are able to see that scoring points and settling wrongs, real or imagined, will not be helpful in future ... Parties are more likely to adhere to agreements they have made themselves rather than orders imposed from outside.

For the latter statement there was no evidence. And the former appeared to us to be based on a misperception of what lawyers do. We suggest it is inaccurate to present mediation and litigation as the only alternative strategies. Such a dichotomy ignores the negotiation work of lawyers and courts that function in a culture of settlement so strong that lawyers have even been criticised by Gwyn Davis for failing to represent the interests of their clients with sufficient vigour.[13] Even now, only 7 per cent of applications to court in divorce-related matters result in a contested final hearing.[14]

The response of the lawyers at this stage was to stay in touch with and embrace the skills of mediation, some training and practising as mediators. This might be interpreted as defending their place in the family justice system, but equally, as openness to new ways of supporting clients. Lawyers and mediators now work together in the SFLA/Resolution, which embraces all those working in family law with a commitment to dealing with disputes in a constructive way, encouraging agreement and supporting the umbrella organisation for the emerging mediation profession, the Family Mediation Council. But differences between lawyer mediators and non-lawyer mediators (often referred to as the not-for-profit sector) remain the subject of discussion.

Although the attempt of the Family Law Act 1996 to move to divorce on request supported by the provision of information and a period of reflec-

---

[13] G Davis, *Partisans and Mediators* (Oxford, Clarendon Press, 1998).
[14] See further E Hitchings, J Miles and H Woodward, *Assembling the Jigsaw Puzzle: Understanding Financial Settlement on Divorce* (Bristol, University of Bristol, 2013).

tion and consideration was not implemented in full, the role of mediation was further promoted through changes to legal aid which required those seeking financial support to attend a meeting at which they would be told about the benefits of mediation.[15] In a subsequent evaluation for the Legal Services Commission[16] it was found that only one in three or four of these meetings led to full mediation, and that, although parties were generally positive, the process was not apparently leading to high rates of settlement. It was Dingwall's view that:

> [G]overnment support for mediation reflects professional enthusiasm with little regard to the very low client base ... this has come about because the story of mediation with its association with reasonableness and compromise—is appealing and secondly because the government has accepted the mediators' argument that spiralling legal costs can be cut through by diverting cases to mediation.[17]

While the pressures on government spending had led to the gradual tightening of control over legal aid expenditure through contracting and auditing, the current economic crisis under the Coalition government has led to acute pressure on the legal aid budget. This resulted in the Legal Aid, Sentencing and Punishment of Offenders Act 2012 (LASPO) which effectively removed private family work from the scope of the legal aid scheme. There are exceptions for cases where safety is a concern, or where circumstances are exceptional.[18] But public funding is available for financially eligible applicants to access mediation, and a little help from lawyers.[19] And under the provisions of the Children and Families Act 2014, what is currently an expectation will, once the Act is implemented, become a requirement that all applicants to the Family Courts in private law matters must first attend a Mediation Information and Assessment Meeting to encourage their participation in mediation rather than seeing lawyers as the first port of call.

III. THE RESPONSE OF THE LAWYERS

How is the legal profession's role in providing family justice changing in response to these pressures? While cuts in legal aid provision seriously threaten the ability of family solicitors and the family Bar to help low-income clients, other changes have made the profession more free to develop and adapt the way they work. The Clementi Report to the Lord Chancellor,

---

[15] Family Law Act 1996, s 29.

[16] G Bevan and G Davis, *Monitoring Publicly Funded Mediation: Report to the Legal Services Commission* (London, LSC, 2000).

[17] Dingwall, 'Divorce Mediation' (n 7) 107.

[18] At the time of writing, February 2014, only eight exceptional cases where human rights issues arise had been helped.

[19] If the client is eligible, under LASPO a small fee is available to instruct a lawyer to draft a consent order.

followed by the Legal Services Act 2007, instituted firmer regulation of professional conduct, but at the same time opened the way to advertising legal and related services and to new forms of business structure where lawyers work with other professionals. A restructuring of legal services thus began. In 2013, on examining 40 websites set up by Resolution members we found an increasingly businesslike approach to marketing, with new specialist services being added to the traditional legal menu, including: advocacy, forensic accountancy, tax management, in-house ADR services—such as mediation, collaborative law and collaborative light (where lawyers from both sides meet with clients and negotiate face to face but promise to withdraw from the case if it cannot settle and court proceedings are expected)—and a new interest in early neutral evaluation and arbitration. Individual lawyers are working with new partners in new business settings, such as financial services. Attention is being paid to cutting costs in some cases by not having a formal office, meeting clients at home or in a serviced office while communicating by phone and email. 'Unbundling' or doing specific tasks rather than taking on a case in its entirety is increasing, and fixed-price packages of work are being offered including, for example, managing a non-conflicted divorce. Care is taken to make sure that itemised elements of work are carried out by the most cost-effective member of staff, moving away from the all round personal care tradition of solicitors' practice. Firms appear to be offering fewer training contracts and placing greater reliance on legal executives. Increasing numbers of law graduates unable to get training contracts are however turning to this as an alternative career path, taking CILEX (Chartered Institute of Legal Executives)[20] examinations and working as Chartered Legal Executives. As legal executives they are developing specialist knowledge and skills and can offer considerable expertise at lower cost. Groups of sole practitioners are forming networks or 'pods' to be able to cover all aspects of family practice, and also to spread the risk of offering fixed-price packages. A number of firms are specifically offering non-adversarial family law and even 'holistic' family law with life coaching sessions available. Software improvements have made it possible to work independently with minimal administrative backup.

All family lawyers are under financial pressure, from those working with low-income clients who are losing income following the cuts in legal aid through to those dealing with higher-income clients where the recession has impacted on the rate of divorce and the ability to cope with the financial implications at a time of economic uncertainty. New ways of arranging payment have developed. 'Pay as you go' schemes and scale rates linking

---

[20] Recognised as an approved regulator in March 2014.

charges to client income have developed for poorer clients.[21] At the upper income levels there are offers of help with financing payment, and the development of client loans secured on the outcome of a settlement but accessed by the lawyer who is able to draw down on a monthly basis (though there are concerns that any such plan involving the proceeds of a loan to underwrite the legal expenses might be construed as champertous). Requests for unbundling do not arise only for financial reasons, but also come from clients who are better informed, familiar with the internet and wish to keep control of their affairs by doing as much of the work for themselves as they can. They also include, for example, the work arising from a mediation memorandum of understanding where a consent order is to be drafted.

Law firms seem to be taking a more proactive approach to marketing, developing high visibility on local and national media, making effective use of social media, analysing carefully how clients approach the office whether by personal recommendation or use of the internet. We have even been told of payments to existing clients in recognition of their help in recommending friends and colleagues to use the firm. There are apparently no rules against this, though it seems to sit uncomfortably with the traditional ethics of the profession. Initial free consultations are offered partly as a pro bono activity but also as a 'taster' for the product. Fixed fees help to reduce the uncertainty about costs which were problematic for potential clients. Alternatively an initial client meeting can be used to estimate the final costs of a case. The new fee structures make brutally clear the cost advantages of avoiding conflict. IT and finance services are being outsourced more often, which does not always reduce costs but advertising does appear to increase turnover and increase visibility. Despite some gloomy evidence from the Law Society of the impact of LASPO and threats from substitutes to legal practice leading to consolidation and change,[22] there is also therefore clear evidence of an energetic response to the economic and policy pressures by legal firms.

IV. NEW FORMS OF 'LEGAL' SERVICES: ALTERNATIVE BUSINESS STRUCTURES AND ONLINE SERVICES

So far we have been looking at the ways in which lawyers are attempting to deal with the pressures of cuts in public funding and the wider impact of the recession, in the context of government policies which tend to see lawyers

---

[21] See, eg, the Simpson Millar website: www.simpsonmillar.co.uk—a large firm with offices in 10 major cities. In 2013 it was offering an early estimate of total legal cost and charges of £75 an hour plus VAT to those who would formerly have been eligible for legal aid pre LASPO.

[22] See, The Law Society, 'Legal Services Industry Part 1: An Overview' (Law Society, 2012) 245.

as the problem and ADR as the solution.[23] But there are also new forms of service emerging. Solicitors are working in settings other than legal firms. The new business structures include tax specialists and accountants constituting a financial services firm with family law as a subsidiary service. And a high street business best known for its grocery stores, The Co-operative Society, has set up the Co-operative Legal Services as one of the first Alternative Business Structures. The service offers an informative website, fixed-price non-contested divorce—originally £450 including VAT—and a package including mediation set up with the not-for-profit service, National Family Mediation, at a cost of £750 to cover both child-related and financial issues.[24] The service began in London but plans to expand nationally.

Taking a step further, perhaps the most innovative services are those being offered on the web. Here, information, advice and help, together with advertising of more traditional existing services, comprise a rapidly changing world not yet sufficiently researched or regulated. We have looked briefly at the professional client care services provided by lawyers and have referred to the challenge from ADR. But with the online services we are seeing a range of provisions from general information, often free, through more tailored information at some cost, to advice, support and service provisions with a striking element of self-help. Instead of the traditional pattern of walking into the high street lawyer's office with the legal aid logo in the window and being helped with a range of problems associated with divorce or separation, the online user now surfs the net to find what is needed. It is not always clear who is offering the service which, unlike the work of solicitors which is covered by the Solicitors Regulatory Authority (SRA), is largely unregulated. Having made the small survey which we describe below, we found that these services range widely from helpful information well prepared by not-for-profit organisations, with accurate description of the current law and what people generally do (Frequently Asked Questions and answers), through government websites offering the necessary forms, and solicitors advertising their services, through to more aggressively commercial websites offering a range of material not all of which is accurate, helpful or free, but may cause problems for those who part with money and receive little benefit and may even increase their difficulties.

Our small survey of online information and advice on divorce was carried out in 2013 by 'googling' the following search terms:

— DIY divorce
— Divorce advice
— Divorce petition forms

---

[23] A Boon, 'Professionalism under the Legal Services Act 2007' (2010) 17 *International Journal of the Legal Profession* 195.

[24] No VAT is payable if the service is delivered by a not-for-profit agency.

— Divorce papers
— Online divorce.

We used these terms at monthly intervals in May and June 2013, using different internet addresses, and examined the first Google page to come up. The process yielded 41 entries in May. Excluding two press stories of celebrity divorces we were left with 39 sites, 11 of which came up more than once, leaving 28 contactable sites of which one was not yet up and running. On reading the information presented and following up with phone calls for clarification where necessary and a number given, we grouped the Google entries into six categories:

1. Solicitors (9) advertising their services, plus Co-operative Legal Services (total 10).
2. Independent advice (4) including the Citizens Advice, Netmums and Mumsnet, and the independent Money Advice Service.
3. Government websites (2).
4. Non-legal practitioners (3) including two counsellors and a mediator.
5. Commercial services (3) Money Supermarket, Lawpack and WH Smith.
6. New specialist providers of online divorce services (6).

Solicitors firms dominated the entries, advertising services which included fixed-price packages. But the two most visible organisations which came up in response to every search term used were Quickie Divorce, a new online specialist provider, and the government websites, one of which provided easy access to the divorce petition forms, while the other was expressed in specialist terminology and less helpful to the layman. What do the new specialist online services offer? Is the internet releasing a plethora of easily accessible and sometimes free sources of advice, easily accessible to those going through divorce? Might they be able to fill the gaps in provision left by LASPO?

There are concerns: for example, it may not be easy for the potential consumer to make an informed choice. Divorce On Line appears with the tag 'official' and an 0330 phone number saying 'get started today!' but sits next to an advert from the not-for-profit organisation, Wikivorce, saying 'Online Divorce … you sure? Why risk it? Our solicitor divorce costs less than a divorce on line'. It is not always clear whether a site is offering the advice of a 'lawyer', ie, anyone with a law degree, or a paralegal, or a qualified solicitor, with professional qualifications whose work is regulated by the SRA. When we asked in follow-up phone calls whether the providers were lawyers, we received a range of answers from the confusing 'Yes, er, I mean no' to 'we are lawyers but not working as lawyers', to the clearer 'we are legal executives, we can handle non-contested matters' and intriguingly 'a firm of solicitors does our legal work for us'. On closer examination, what looked like a new specialist provider could turn out to be a traditional legal firm, for example: Divorce Rights, Law Shop, Alternative Family Law, sounded 'new' but Divorce Rights, on close examination of the website and a follow-up phone call could be clearly identified as an internet-based service operated and managed nationwide by a network of solicitors firms providing legal services. And on the other hand, Divorce Aid: Solicitors sounded like a firm of solicitors, but on close examination of the website turned out to be a service which helps the client to find a firm of solicitors. It is not always easy to draw a clear line between the new online specialists and solicitors working in new ways.

To take one example, Quickie Divorce claim to have been used by 15,000 people in 2012, which amounts to 18 per cent of all divorces in England and Wales for that period. The website states, 'Your divorce petition can be initiated now for just £37. Or you can have all the divorce forms you'll need to send to the court completed for you for just £67'. Court fees are not mentioned. An 0800 free telephone advice line is offered where, 'Our teams of experts can give guidance on all matters relating to divorce process, and also help you choose which service is right for you'. There is no offer of legal advice, only advice on process and choice of service. But this is a technical distinction unlikely to be clear at first sight to a layman. There is also a 'personal plus' service which includes 'all the benefits of our Personal Service plus a Clean Break Agreement and Lifetime Will (worth a total of £195) for just £135'. This clean break agreement is said to be a consent order. Reassurance is provided as to professional oversight of the service: 'Enjoy the security of knowing that a panel solicitor is overseeing your case from start to finish and that all the necessary forms will be completed for you from issuing the petition until your Decree Absolute is in your hand'. The response to a phone call was quick, friendly but brief, and insistent that they could only deal with cases where there was no dispute. When asked about whether they were solicitors it was clearly stated that they were not, but that they would send out clean break order forms to an external solicitor to check. So it seems that Quickie Divorce offer a no frills document management service for non-contentious divorce without in-house lawyers. It could well be suitable and helpful to those seeking a quick affordable divorce where there are no issues, but is unlikely to help those where issues arise in the course of proceedings.

A more complex service is offered by the not-for-profit service, Wikivorce, who claim to have helped an even larger number of people last year—50,000—over half the divorcing population. The website offers clear and accurate information on how to proceed, gives advice on avoiding conflict with exemplary staged information and guidance on how to help yourself and offers clearly defined packages of divorce services at £179 for the divorce only, £139 for financial settlement and £279 for both managed by a solicitor. They help with access to mediation, divorce support groups, and provide a Divorce Calculator which works out an estimate for a fair financial settlement for ancillary relief proceedings in England and Wales based on individual data. The advertised 0800 number was not answered on our call, but a friendly and informative gentleman called back within 15 minutes in response to a missed call to answer our queries about lawyer involvement. It was explained that a large legal firm helped them pro bono, and that no Wikivorce matter is dealt with other than by a lawyer, though at different grades. For example, divorce forms would be filled in by a paralegal or FILEX. Registering for the Divorce Calculator was quick and easy. This asks for information on husband's and wife's income, then their household needs in three categories: essential, childcare costs and lifestyle costs, and finally, a statement of assets and liabilities. The calculator also explains how a court would approach any calculation, with the first portion of income allocated on prioritised needs and any surplus allocated on lifestyle, contribution made and compensation for detriment. Any user would need to collect together the necessary information, and have a basic level of computer literacy, but the programme is commendably clear and competent. The website also offers a price comparison table giving the fixed-price details and website link for solicitor managed divorce in 30 legal firms. For example, Nelsons, a firm specialising in legal aid, was said to charge £229 (May 2013) and Brethertons £600. The highest price quoted was Woolley and Co at £870 and the lowest, unsurprisingly was Wikivorce, at £179. Altogether an interesting contribution to divorce services, though hard to classify as a legal service.

The last online special service to come up in response to our search terms was Divorce Online, which offered a range of services: from £45 for all the forms and a guide to filling them in and sample letters to send to the court; £189 for a managed divorce; £229 with a clean break; through to £385 for solicitor managed divorce. The website helpfully offered a link to the Bar Council's guide for litigants in person, and the Bar Pro Bono Unit. It was difficult to ascertain from the website the level of qualified solicitor involvement, but an 0330 phone number and a postal address were provided. The phone was answered quickly, as Online Legal Services, and there was a willingness to answer questions. When I asked whether this was in fact a firm of lawyers the answer was 'no, we are paralegals, qualified to take two people who are willing, through the divorce process. We deal with amicable divorce'. The message is clear: disputes cost money.

If the internet surfer is looking for free, rather than low cost, advice the options are more limited. A number of the options we found in an earlier limited search were not advice and were not free. For example, Expert Answers asks what the answer to your question is worth to you and says that the higher the sum you are willing to pay the quicker you will receive an answer—possibly refreshingly honest and may well be what happens in other settings! Truelegaladvice at legal-advice-centre.co.uk, gave good summaries of the legal position but no advice. LawWorks clinics supported by the Law Society offer a free half hour interview plus basic advice, to 90 minutes and a draft letter from qualified lawyers but warned of a possible eight-week wait for an appointment (as at September 2013).

Perhaps the last word on specialist online legal services should go to Rocket Lawyer, which aims to deliver legal services via a 'freemium' model using an interactive online interview process to create straightforward legal documents, and offering to create divorce settlement agreements for those without disputes but intriguingly using American terminology. The aim is to be accessible and affordable, extending the range of consumer choice— described by the *Law Society Gazette* as disruptive but not destructive.[25]

V. OBSERVATIONS

Times are changing. Instead of easy access to legal aid for the majority of divorcing parents, we have a rather beleaguered legal profession making serious efforts to become more affordable and accessible by offering a wide range of services from the traditional hourly paid 'full legal', to fixed-price packages, 'unbundling' and lawyer-led private ordering in the form of arbitration, collaborative law, lawyer mediators and lawyer managed or supported online services. Other professionals are involved in the enterprise—from accountants to life coaches, and non-lawyer mediators sometimes working in joint ventures with therapists or counsellors. Business models range from firms with offices in every large city (and abroad) with full administrative backup, to sole practitioners in virtual offices and volunteers and paralegals servicing websites. It is a whole new world of innovative and exciting ways of supporting men and women, particularly parents, through divorce and separation. But is this range of services making it easier to find help with the range of problems associated with family change, and in particular the need to resolve conflict and find fair and enforceable ways of dividing property and making arrangements for the care of children? Or is the withdrawal of public funding seriously affecting those with fewer resources, including limitations due to literacy or health or language? Is the gap left by LASPO being filled, or is this task being left to the less than wholly successful 'Sorting out Separation' (SOS) government web app, launched rather hurriedly by DWP late last year, which hopes to guide those contacting it to the help they feel that they need? The site has been much improved but did not inspire early confidence by referring to the divorce law of the United Kingdom (since corrected), when of course Scotland has a rather different system.

---

[25] J Goodman, 'Rocket Lawyer: Disruptive Not Destructive' *Law Society Gazette* (London, 17 December, 2012), available at: www.acq5.com/rocket-lawyer-disruptive-not-destructive.

What direction might we expect legal services to take over the coming decade? Sadly, little hope remains of a return to more generous government support, though it is possible that more attention may be paid to low-cost advice systems based on the web. There is clearly potential for further development here, but for many of the most vulnerable adults affected it is hard to see how online services can ever be sufficient without some form of person-to-person backup.

The debate of the 1990s about the relative roles for mediators and lawyers is changing its shape, as lawyers train as mediators and display their appreciation of the part mediation has to play in dispute resolution. Mediation has become one of a number of alternative ways of dealing with disputes, rather than the only way as hoped by government, whether we take the 'A' in ADR to mean alternative to the courts, or to stand for appropriate or assisted. There is still a lack of clarity among the public about the exact nature of mediation. We are familiar with the distinction between lawyers and non-lawyer mediators, but we now have lawyer mediators setting up mediation services within their legal practice, which may offer many other additional services, or offering mediation sessions at other legal practices. We have non-lawyer mediators working alone or in combined services offering therapy or counselling related to divorce and separation but also other family issues, such as parenting classes, or child therapy, or working in lawyers' offices as part of a large range of services or as the sole addition to traditional legal practice. The variations are far too great for us to go on considering mediation and legal work as in opposition. Lawyers have long valued the techniques for dispute resolution developed in mediation, while mediators value and need the financial expertise of the legal professions and the need for precise drafting of consent orders in order to secure an enforceable agreement. This may be necessary not only for the peace of mind of the parties, but technically essential if they wish to alter a mortgage agreement or change the legal title to a property.

The next step is to develop a more sophisticated and detailed understanding of what exactly the various forms of service can offer, what they cost, who is offering them and which are helpful for which kinds of situations. And above all to identify ways in which the different forms of intervention can develop ways of working together to make sure that gaps are filled and costs controlled.

Our current research in Oxford has now reached the stage of observing the work of different practitioners and can begin to offer some tentative comment on some of the differences in practice. On the basis of early observations, we suggest the following possible ways of differentiating the work done in mediation from the work of lawyer-led negotiation not intended to result in litigation (though it may involve applying to court for a consent order):

— In mediation the participants are usually together in one room with the practitioner. They bring to the meeting the matters on which they disagree, and define the aim of the meeting. The practitioner is able to talk to them both during the meeting, but not outside it by phone or in person. Emails are normally shared. This makes for a faster exchange of views which can lead to faster resolution of an issue but sometimes to faster divergence where there is no time for reflection as there may be with solicitors managing an exchange of views. A mediator cannot have direct dealings with a third party, such as a mortgage adviser or bank, and the information available in financial mediation is presented by the parties and is not verified by the practitioner. Mediators vary in their willingness to make suggestions to participants, for example about the timing or location of contact, or the disposal of the matrimonial home. Mediators are required to advise participants to seek legal advice when considering making a binding agreement usually in the form of a consent order which will need to be drafted by a lawyer though some mediators prepare drafts. A recent judgment from the President of the Family Division,[26] supporting the making of an arbitral award into a consent order by a fast-track process, also commented on the possibility of this practice developing for decisions reached by other ADR routes including mediation. The mediator is free to withdraw from the mediation if the participants appear to be moving towards a manifestly inappropriate resolution. In working on child-related issues, the mediator is required to remind the parties to consider the needs of the children but is not required to seek their welfare in any agreement as the paramount consideration as would be the case in a legal setting under the Children Act (England and Wales) 1989. Mediation sessions may be spread out over some months, either due to availability or to the need to take things gradually to mitigate hostility.

— Solicitors traditionally have a closer, more supportive relationship with their individual client, though this may be changing with unbundling. They also have a working relationship with the solicitor for the other party which may affect progress towards a resolution of any dispute. The lawyer, however, has a wider brief for offering advice on potential problems as well as resolving specific existing disputes. Part of the task is to foresee and advise the client about possible future problems arising (for example, on re-partnering or the birth of new children), and to make sure any arrangement minimises future difficulties. This is easily interpreted as 'stirring up trouble', but may well achieve the opposite. The solicitor is available (at a cost) to the client by phone at any time, and can be asked to do specific tasks. A local solicitor is likely to have information on local housing costs and school catchment areas, which

---

[26] *S v S* [2014] EWHC 7 (Fam).

will be brought in when making suggestions. A key difference is the possibility of achieving discovery and verifying information, and acting directly with third parties such as banks and mortgage firms. There is usually no need for further work except in the unlikely event of a contested court hearing.

Costs are a key element in consumer choice of service, and at present it may be difficult to work out what these might be for the various combinations of items of service required. Mediation charges commonly range from £90 to £250 per hour (plus VAT) for each participant. Three to five sessions of 90 minutes are a common pattern sometimes with a charge for 20 minutes' administration for writing up notes for each session. The total cost might range from £1000 to £2000 for each participant. For a publicly-funded participant, the limit is £756 per client for all issues sole mediation,[27] plus £100 for drafting a memorandum of understanding. In addition, there is likely to be some further expenditure on legal advice and help in drafting a consent order, plus court fees for the divorce procedure. Solicitor mediators commonly charge at the same hourly rate whether mediating or acting as a lawyer, but there may of course be fixed-price packages available for defined procedures including non-conflictual divorce. Full legal service in a highly conflicted complex case can carry extremely high costs. For an extreme example we might look to the case of *Radmacher v Granatino*[28] before the Supreme Court. *The Telegraph*[29] reported legal costs of £2 million, though it may have been twice this sum. The cost of collaborative law is high, and carries the risk of having to start work with a new legal adviser if settlement is not achieved. Arbitration fees are privately negotiated. Counselling may run alongside use of mediation or legal services.

The calculations for the layman are daunting. The cost of using mediation for specific issues needs to include the cost of some legal intervention to secure enforceability in finance and to deal directly with the third parties involved in any credit arrangement. The intervention of a lawyer at a difficult point in financial mediation might circumvent the need for lengthy debate of an option which is technically not feasible. On the other hand, going straight to a lawyer may result in high costs if conflict is not well managed, or a speedy resolution of the matter by a solicitor who practices non-adversarial family law where the other side is similarly advised, possibly using mediation for a specific issue. The calculations are difficult. To say that mediation is quicker and cheaper may or may not be the case; it could be argued that going straight to court as a self-representing litigant

---

[27] Civil Legal Aid Remuneration Regulations 2013, SI 2013/422.
[28] *Radmacher (formerly Granatino) v Granatino* (Rev 4) [2010] UKSC 42.
[29] R Mendick, 'Heiress Katrin Radmacher and the £100 Million Prenuptial Agreement' *The Telegraph* (London, 17 October 2010), available at: www.telegraph.co.uk/women/sex/divorce/8068458/Heiress-Katrin-Radmacher-and-the-100m-prenuptial-disagreement.html.

might sometimes be the cheapest option. It is not one which government would like to see taken up.

It is perhaps more helpful to look at what the various forms of intervention can do best, and where they might work better. In a non-conflicted case it may be tempting to buy a fixed-price package from a lawyer or online service, advertised as suitable for a non-conflicted case, but it is important to recognise that conflict may appear or disappear over the course of a separation/divorce. It may be important to choose a package, like those offered by Co-operative Legal Services, where transition from a simple to a more complex package is built into the system.

So, to summarise, what interventions are currently out there for the consumer of divorce services and what do they offer? Mediation offers a sometimes painful and not always conclusive face to face trust building exercise, leading towards a resolution of the issues as identified by the parties. For enforceability, further work is required from lawyers. Regulation of the service is still rather unclear. Full legal services offer a costly but supportive service including examination of current and potential issues, work with third parties and usually a negotiated outcome which will carry enforceability. The work is regulated. Unbundling increases client control and helps to limit costs, as do fixed-price packages, but these packages need to be chosen with care. Online services from lawyers and non-lawyers carry low costs, but the client as a one-time purchaser under stress and without expert information is vulnerable to exploitation or inadequate service. Services purchased online are not yet subject to effective regulation.

And what do we know of the choices consumers are actually making and the costs those choices incur? Based on a survey of 866 adults involved in divorce over the last five years, YouGov published a report in 2013 on the costs of divorce.[30] They found that of the 25 per cent of people who had arranged their own divorce without individual legal help, fewer than a third had used websites, mainly to find free information and advice. Over half the sample had used a solicitor. Of the divorces in their sample, 20 per cent had cost less than £1k, 44 per cent less than £2k and only a quarter over £5k, but this sample included a number of pre-LASPO cases. The pace of change is now so fast that we might expect an updated survey to find greater use of the online services, or perhaps smaller numbers of divorces costing less than £1k.

As Julia Evetts shows in chapter two of this volume, the divide between professions, enterprise and the market is not as clear-cut as we might expect. In family law, full client care from a professional, at a market price, is no longer available except to the rich. A free market with incomplete reg-

---

[30] Helpfully summarised in Comment, 'DIY Divorce Report' (2013) 43 (August) *Family Law*.

ulation is developing in other forms of service. Mediation, while it has not, as government had hoped, fully substituted for legal services, is becoming more and more important in a different way as a valued part of the package of professional support services for divorcing and separating couples and their children. It sits well, as do the changes in legal services and the emergence of online services, with the move towards giving more responsibility to the consumer in law, as in medicine and education. However, with greater autonomy and choice in an unregulated world come the undeniable risks for vulnerable parties who lack the purchasing power, essential skills or resilience to navigate their way through the legal complexities and emotional pressures of family breakdown.

5

Judicial Diversity and the 'New' Judge

ROSEMARY HUNTER

THERE IS NO doubt that judicial practices and subjectivities have undergone a major transformation since the 1990s. In *The New Judiciary* published in 1999, Kate Malleson pointed to the growth in size of the judiciary and the expansion of its policymaking role, especially through judicial review and more recently the Human Rights Act, as the major sources of change.[1] In this chapter I want to focus on three different sources of change. Two are more generalised—neo-liberalism and bio-politics. The third is more specific but also more of a newcomer—the equality and diversity agenda within the judiciary. The chapter attempts to trace the impact of these developments and the relationships between them, in order to arrive at some conclusions about the desirable attributes of the 'new' judge. But as cultural and socio-legal studies repeatedly remind us, the new does not inexorably drive out the old; rather, different subjectivities and temporalities continue to coexist, in varying relations of tension, accommodation and hierarchy. Thus, it is also necessary to pay attention to the extent to which the 'old' judge maintains his position in the judicial constellation.

I. NEO-LIBERALISM

The first set of developments might broadly be grouped under the heading of neo-liberalism. The neo-liberal concern to minimise the state and make the most efficient use of scarce public resources, and the notion that efficiency is best achieved through the use of management techniques derived

---

[1] K Malleson, *The New Judiciary: The Effects of Expansion and Activism* (Aldershot, Ashgate, 1999) 1.

from the private sector,[2] has resulted in a dramatic departure from the traditional conception in the adversarial system of the judge as passive arbiter.

First, the judge must now be a case manager.[3] It is no longer acceptable to leave it to the parties to determine their own timetable for litigation. Rather, the judge must take control, move the matter forward, set timetables for case preparation and the filing of material, ensure that the parties have complied with these directions and sanction them if they have not. The parties are, in turn, enjoined to cooperate with each other in relation to disclosure and the identification of issues in dispute, in order to optimise their use of judicial and court time. This was one of the central elements of the Woolf reforms to civil justice,[4] but it applies in criminal cases as well.[5] In her research on the influence of neo-liberalism in the Magistrates' Courts in East Kent, Lucy Welsh has identified, among other things, the way in which case management and case management forms have restructured summary criminal proceedings.[6] Judicial case management is facilitated by individual docket systems.[7] A judge is more likely to maintain control over a timetable and to sanction failures of compliance if they have responsibility for handling the case from beginning to end. This, in turn, effects a subtle transformation in the relationship between the judge and the parties. The judge is no longer a distanced and interchangeable decision-maker. The identity of who sits under the wig and gown thus becomes more important. He or she is expected to enter into a potentially long-term relationship with the parties and to develop a personal familiarity with the details of their case. Indeed, evidence suggests that litigants value such a relationship and prefer judicial continuity, finding it stressful and disorienting to appear

---

[2] See, eg, D Harvey, *A Brief History of Neoliberalism* (Oxford, Oxford University Press, 2005) 65; M Power, *The Audit Society: Rituals of Verification* (Oxford, Oxford University Press, 1997) 43; M Powell, *Modernising the Welfare State: The Blair Legacy* (Bristol, Policy Press, 2008) 7, 8.

[3] See, eg, Civil Procedure Rules, Rule 1.4 and Part 3; Criminal Procedure Rules, Part 3; Family Procedure Rules, Rule 1.4 and Part 4.

[4] Malleson, *The New Judiciary* (n 1) 165.

[5] See, eg, Home Office, Department for Constitutional Affairs and Attorney General's Office, 'Delivering Simple, Speedy Summary Justice' (Home Office, DCA and AG, 2006); H Riddle, 'The Stop Delaying Justice! Initiative' *Law Society Gazette* (London, 19 January 2012), available at: www.lawgazette.co.uk/63857.article; Ministry of Justice, *Swift and Sure Justice: The Government's Plans for Reform of the Criminal Justice System* (Cm 8388, 2012).

[6] L Welsh, 'Magistrates, Managerialism and Marginalisation: Neoliberalism and Access to Justice in East Kent', PhD in progress, Law School, University of Kent. See also L Welsh, 'Are Magistrates' Courts Really a "Law Free Zone"? Participant Observation and Specialist Use of Language' (2013) 13 *Papers from the British Society of Criminology Conference* 3.

[7] For detailed discussions of an individual docket system, see Australian Law Reform Commission, *Review of the Federal Civil Justice System* (ALRC DP 62, 1999) paras 10.44–10.71; C Sage and T Wright with C Morris, 'Case Management Reform: A Study of the Federal Court's Individual Docket System' (Law and Justice Foundation of New South Wales, 2002), available at: www.lawfoundation.net.au/ljf/site/templates/reports/$file/CaseManagementReform.pdf. In the United Kingdom see, eg, Jackson LJ, 'Review of Civil Litigation Costs: Final Report' (The Stationery Office, 2010) 278–79, 327, 391–93, 431; Ryder J, 'Judicial Proposals for the Modernisation of Family Justice' (Judiciary of England and Wales 2012) 6, 7.

before a different judge each time they attend court.[8] Individual dockets may, however, clash with other elements of efficiency. For example, in England and Wales there is a heavy reliance on part-time, fee-paid judges, both to supplement the full-time, salaried judiciary and to enable the system to 'try out' potential full-time judges for suitability before taking the risk of a salaried appointment with tenure for life. It is impossible to achieve judicial continuity with part-time judges who may sit for only 15 days per year. Nevertheless, individual dockets are often held up as the ideal in discussions of judicial administration.[9]

Another element of efficiency is to avoid the use of judicial and court time altogether by the promotion of settlement in civil cases and guilty pleas in criminal cases. Although in criminal cases judges do not usually play an active role in achieving a guilty plea (though they may, if requested, give a sentence indication),[10] in civil cases they are certainly expected to be active in encouraging the parties to reach their own agreement rather than proceeding to adjudication,[11] which may include referring the parties for mediation and/or creating and reinforcing a 'culture of settlement' in the court. This was another central element of the Woolf reforms to civil justice,[12] and is also a notable feature of the family justice system, as a recent book by Mavis Maclean and John Eekelaar amply attests.[13] In their observations of 37 private family law matters, the single largest amount of time was spent by judges 'facilitating an agreed outcome' (38 per cent of the total time spent on these matters), followed by 'managing preparations for hearing' (22 per cent). Adjudication, by contrast, took up only 11 per cent of the time of the judges observed.[14]

Neo-liberal performance management techniques borrowed from the private sector classically include the use of Key Performance Indicators (KPIs) to measure the achievement of desired performance standards. New Labour's devotion to KPIs, and the kinds of perverse incentives they can create—both to manipulate the statistics and to ignore areas of activity not

---

[8] Eg, House of Commons Justice Committee, *Operation of the Family Courts* (Sixth Report, House of Commons Justice Committee, 2011) paras 210–11; Family Justice Review, 'Final Report' (MOJ, DfE, Welsh Government, 2011) 86; J Macfarlane, 'The National Self-Represented Litigants Project: Identifying and Meeting the Needs of Self-Represented Litigants—Final Report' (Ontario, University of Windsor, Faculty of Law, 2013) 99.

[9] See Welsh, PhD in progress (n 6).

[10] *R v Goodyear (Karl)* [2005] EWCA 888; Attorney General's Office, 'Attorney General's Guidelines on the Acceptance of Pleas and the Prosecutor's Role in the Sentencing Exercise' (rev, AGO, 2009).

[11] Civil Procedure Rules, Practice Direction: Pre-Action Conduct; Family Procedure Rules, Part 3, Practice Direction 3A, now reinforced by the Children and Families Act 2014, s 10.

[12] Lord Woolf, 'Access to Justice: Final Report to the Lord Chancellor on the Civil Justice System in England and Wales' (Her Majesty's Stationery Office, 1996) ch 10.

[13] J Eekelaar and M Maclean, *Family Justice: The Work of Family Judges in Uncertain Times* (Oxford, Hart Publishing, 2013).

[14] ibid, 82.

subject or susceptible to measurement—are now well known, for example, in relation to the police[15] and the NHS.[16] This has not prevented the development and application of KPIs for the justice system, although the extent to which they are aimed at producing justice is questionable. Indeed, the main enemy seems to be delay, since time is numerically measurable while the quality of decision-making is not.

To give just one example, the recent Family Justice Review, chaired by economist and businessman, David Norgrove,[17] recommended that proceedings in which a local authority is applying to take a child into care should be completed in a maximum of six months.[18] This is a laudable aim—of course questions about children's care and welfare should be determined as quickly as possible, especially when they are at risk of suffering significant harm. But as a KPI, this standard is problematic. First, the 'average' duration of care proceedings at the time of the report was 48 weeks in Family Proceedings Courts and 61 weeks in County Courts,[19] so bringing this down to a 'maximum' of 26 weeks was an extremely challenging demand. Much work has been done in the interim and the 'average' duration is now somewhat closer to 26 weeks, but that is still nothing like a 26-week 'maximum'.[20]

The reduction so far has been achieved via the adoption of two main strategies. The first has been to ensure that applications are better prepared before proceedings are issued.[21] This, in turn, means that it may take longer for proceedings to be issued in the first place. Thus, from the perspective of the child concerned, the time taken may not be much less, but for the purpose of the KPI, time only starts running once the court application is made. Second, a significant amount of time in Family Court proceedings is spent in the preparation of expert reports from psychologists, psychiatrists

[15] See, eg, BBC News, 'Police Forces Facing Dozens of New Performance Targets' (19 September 2013), available at: www.bbc.co.uk/news/uk-24148129; BBC News, 'Police Fix Crime Statistics to Meet Targets, MPs Told' (19 November 2013), available at: www.bbc.co.uk/news/uk-25002927.

[16] See, eg, The King's Fund, 'Have Targets Improved NHS Performance?' (The King's Fund, 2010), available at: www.kingsfund.org.uk/projects/general-election-2010/key-election-questions/performance-targets.

[17] See: www.gov.uk/government/people/david-norgrove.

[18] Family Justice Review, 'Final Report' (n 8) 31, 103–07. This time limit has now been enshrined in legislation by the Children and Families Act 2014, s 14 (amending s 32(1)(a) of the Children Act 1989).

[19] Family Justice Review, 'Final Report' (n 8) 91.

[20] The average duration of care and supervision proceedings had fallen to an average of 42.2 weeks by the time of the Family Justice Board, 'Family Justice Board Annual Report 2012–13' (MOJ, 2013) 3, and to under 35 weeks by the last quarter of 2013. Still, only 60% of 'standard track' cases nationally commenced after 1 April 2012 were completed within 26 weeks, with considerable local variations (statistical reports to Kent Family Justice Board, January 2014).

[21] J Munby, 'View from the President's Chambers: The Process of Reform' (2013) 43 *Family Law* 548, 551; J Munby, 'View from the President's Chambers: The Process of Reform: The Revised PLO and the Local Authority' (2013) 43 *Family Law* 680; J Munby, 'View from the President's Chambers: The Process of Reform: An Update' (2013) 43 *Family Law* 974.

or other child welfare professionals. This is at least partly due to the fact that there is only a limited number of experts available to undertake forensic work—especially at legal aid rates—so their services are much in demand.[22] In addition, thorough assessments of the family and the child's relationships with various family members take time.[23] The solution has been to minimise the use of expert reports. Judicial case management in care cases now involves 'cracking down' on expert reports and only permitting expert involvement when it absolutely cannot be avoided.[24] Of course this reduces delay and to that extent is in the interests of the child. But whether a child's welfare is better served simply by accelerating proceedings or by full and expert assessment of their needs and how they can best be met is an unaddressed question. An alternative approach which would make the 26-week target much more achievable would be a large injection of resources into the Court Service, local authorities and legal aid, but that is clearly not on the agenda.

With KPIs come performance improvement groups. These are groups of judges and other key players in each local area which meet to review performance against KPIs, to analyse the reasons for failure to meet KPIs and to devise measures for improving performance.[25] Many judicial hours are now spent on a regular basis poring over Court Service statistics and developing strategies to achieve better numbers. As well as their performance against KPIs, local groups are shown their performance against other areas, and against their performance in previous quarters. Woe betide the area which finds itself in the bottom quartile, or whose figures go backwards rather than showing continuous improvement.

In sum, the neo-liberal judge is one who spends a significant amount of their time managing cases and promoting settlement rather than making decisions. They may have a more personal relationship with litigants than would previously have been the case. They work within a KPI-driven regime and are expected to contribute to the labour of performance improvement. Legal knowledge and traditional judicial performance are de-emphasised in favour of a more bureaucratised approach, part administrator and part

---

[22] Family Justice Review, 'Final Report' (n 8) 121–22, 125. See also C Sturge and P Bhari, 'Experts: Maintaining and Expanding the Pool' (2005) 35 *Family Law* 156; G Ives et al, 'Is there an Expert in the House? The Future for Expert Witnesses' (2013) 43 *Family Law* 1041.

[23] Especially residential assessments, the value of which was questioned by the Family Justice Review, 'Final Report' (n 8) 120; Family Justice Review, 'Interim Report' (MOJ, DfE, Welsh Assembly Government, 2011) 110.

[24] See Family Procedure Rules, Part 25, especially Rule 25.1 (amended January 2013); J Munby, 'View from the President's Chambers: Expert Evidence' (2013) 43 *Family Law* 816; and now the Children and Families Act 2014, s 13.

[25] In family law, the national Performance Improvement Sub-Group is a sub-group of the Family Justice Board; and each local Family Justice Board has its own local Performance Improvement Group comprising judges, Cafcass managers, local practitioners, local authority legal officers and relevant HMCTS managers.

service worker. This might appear to be a more feminised job description than one requiring traditionally masculine judicial authority.

II. BIO-POLITICS

Michel Foucault identified the rise of the human sciences through the nineteenth and twentieth centuries as instituting a new form of power, one based on knowledge of and expertise in human behaviour, in contrast to the older form of coercive juridical power.[26] Under the regime of bio-power, human behaviour is regulated through discourses of normalisation, and through the inducement of self-discipline via the internalisation of behavioural norms. In her 1989 book *Feminism and the Power of Law*, however, Carol Smart took issue with the notion that bio-power would simply displace juridical power, and instead observed various ways in which juridical power and bio-power entered into alliances, with bio-power gaining added force through mechanisms of legal coercion, and juridical power gaining added legitimacy by drawing on and incorporating knowledge derived from the 'psy' disciplines.[27]

It is no coincidence that *Feminism and the Power of Law* appeared in the same year as the Children Act 1989. The Act's centralisation of child welfare has done much to turn family law into a thoroughly bio-politicised field. Child welfare knowledge is not the province of judges or the law but of social workers, psychologists and psychiatrists.[28] As a result, in order to fulfil the statutory mandate to give paramount consideration to the welfare of the child,[29] family judges have been drawn into a relationship with bio-political experts: Cafcass[30] officers, social workers, child and family psychologists, child and adolescent psychiatrists and paediatricians.[31] The

---

[26] See M Foucault, *The Birth of Biopolitics: Lectures at the Collège de France, 1978–79* (London, Picador, 2008); M Foucault, *The Order of Things: An Archaeology of the Human Sciences* (London, Routledge, 1970) esp ch 10; M Foucault, *Power/Knowledge: Selected Interviews and Other Writings 1972–1977* (New York, Pantheon Books, 1980).

[27] C Smart, *Feminism and the Power of Law* (London, Routledge, 1989) 8–9, 14–20, ch 5, 162–63.

[28] See, eg, J Masson, 'The Role of the Judge in Children's Cases' (1988) 7 *Civil Justice Quarterly* 141; A Diduck and F Kaganas, *Family Law, Gender and the State*, 3rd edn (Oxford, Hart Publishing, 2012) 392.

[29] Children Act 1989, s 1.

[30] Children and Family Court Advisory and Support Service—the Family Court child welfare service. Cafcass officers are social workers who fulfil a range of functions focused around advising the court on children's welfare.

[31] This relationship is forged by a variety of mechanisms in both private and public law. In private law these include: the undertaking of safeguarding checks by Cafcass prior to the first hearing in every case brought under s 8 of the Children Act 1989; the involvement of a Cafcass officer at the first hearing of every such case; the preparation by Cafcass officers of welfare reports under s 7 of the Act; the appointment of a guardian in cases in which the child is made a party to proceedings; and provision for expert reports under Part 16 of the Family Procedure Rules. In public law these include: the preparation of cases and reports in care or supervision order and adoption proceedings by local authority social workers, independent social workers and 'psy' professionals, as discussed above.

Cafcass officer, children's guardian and experts are sources of objective 'truth' about the child's welfare based on disciplinary knowledge, whereas the claims made about the child's welfare by the child's parents are inherently self-interested and uninformed, and hence less reliable. It follows that the recommendations of Cafcass, the guardian and/or any expert are more likely to be adopted by the court than the contentions of either parent; or if Cafcass, the guardian or expert supports a parent's position, that parent is most likely to succeed. This is recognised, for example, by the practice of the former Legal Services Commission of withdrawing legal aid from a party prior to final hearing when the expert's report went against them, on the basis that they no longer had a reasonable prospect of success.[32] As discussed earlier, however, one problem with experts is that they disrupt the courts' regime of speed and efficiency, and so judges are now enjoined to do without them. Eekelaar and Maclean also suggest on the basis of their recent observations in Family Courts that overworked social workers and Cafcass officers, subject to their own regimes of speed and efficiency, are now more interested in getting cases off their books than in focusing on the child's welfare. As a consequence, the judicial role now extends to monitoring and regulating these professionals and holding them to account.[33]

But even in the absence of welfare professionals, debates about child welfare in family law deploy behavioural science research evidence in support of contending positions.[34] What do we 'know' about the effects on children of limited contact with one parent, or of dividing their time between both parents, or of the effects of staying contact for babies? Fathers' rights advocates find support in attachment theory.[35] Women's organisations

---

[32] See, eg, L Trinder et al, 'Litigants in Person in Private Family Law Cases' (MOJ, forthcoming).

[33] Eekelaar and Maclean, *Family Justice* (n 13) 1–8, 109, 111, 117.

[34] Eg, GT Harold and M Murch, 'Inter-Parental Conflict and Children's Adaptation to Separation and Divorce: Theory, Research and Implications for Family Law, Practice and Policy' (2005) 17 *Child and Family Law Quarterly* 185; S Gilmore, 'Contact/Shared Residence and Child Well-Being: Research Evidence and its Implications for Legal Decision-Making' (2006) 20 *International Journal of Law, Policy and the Family* 344; S Gilmore, 'The Assumption that Contact is Beneficial: Challenging the "Secure Foundation"' (2008) 38 *Family Law* 1226; A Barnett, 'The Welfare of the Child Revisited: In Whose Best Interests? Part I' (2009) 39 *Family* Law 50; A Barnett, 'The Welfare of the Child Revisited: In Whose Best Interests? Part II' (2009) 39 *Family Law* 135; L Trinder, 'Shared Residence: A Review of Recent Research Evidence' (2010) 22 *Child and Family Law Quarterly* 475; S Harris-Short, 'Resisting the March Towards 50/50 Shared Residence: Rights, Welfare and Equality in Post-Separation Families' (2010) 32 *Journal of Social Welfare and Family Law* 257; B Fehlberg et al, 'Caring for Children After Parental Separation: Would Legislation for Shared Parenting Time Help Children?' (London, Nuffield Foundation, 2011).

[35] See, eg, 'Bonding—The Attachment Theory—Fathers' Rights' on YouTube: www.youtube.com/watch?v=SMTIlXavtqU, and various other websites; citing JB Kelly and ME Lamb, 'Using Child Development Research to Make Appropriate Custody and Access Decisions for Young Children' (2000) 38 *Family Court Review* 297. See also J Masson, J Hunt and L Trinder, 'Shared Parenting: The Law, the Evidence, and Guidance from Families Need Fathers' (2009) 39 *Family Law* 831.

invoke research on the damaging effects of domestic violence on children.[36] Neither are family judges passive recipients and transmitters of child welfare knowledge. Rather, as Smart prefigured, they authorise 'a legal version' of child welfare knowledge which does not necessarily reflect its disciplinary origins.[37] In their book *How the Law Thinks About Children*, Michael King and Christine Piper argue that child welfare knowledge, as adopted and relayed by family judges, is a simplified, reductionist version of the original, which loses many nuances and inconvenient details.[38] Recent legislative efforts to specify presumptions about children's welfare bear out this point even more starkly.[39] In Australia, in the wake of one such effort, research is now underway to determine how child welfare knowledge can be functionally incorporated into judicial decision-making so as to enable the courts to reach more 'correct' or 'appropriate' decisions.[40]

But it is not only family law which has been touched by the tentacles of bio-power. The advent of problem-solving courts in a number of countries has involved a shift from adjudication—and specifically the determination of guilt or innocence in summary criminal proceedings—to a more bio-political focus on the causes of offending. Problem-solving courts aim to stop the revolving door of offending, conviction, imprisonment, release and reoffending by addressing the underlying problem that brings a person repeatedly back to court in the first place, such as substance abuse or violence, and often other related problems as well.[41] Specialist courts such as drug courts and domestic violence courts take a multidisciplinary approach and apply insights about human behaviour, motivations and behavioural change as much as the law.[42] The aim is to reduce recidivism not by means of harsher sentences but by social interventions to break the cycle of offending.

[36] Eg, C Sturge and D Glaser, 'Contact and Domestic Violence: The Experts' Court Report' (2000) 30 *Family Law* 615; M Coy et al, 'Picking Up the Pieces: Domestic Violence and Child Contact' (Rights of Women, 2012) 10–12.

[37] Smart, *Feminism and the Power of Law* (n 27).

[38] M King and C Piper, *How the Law Thinks About Children*, 2nd edn (Aldershot, Ashgate, 1995).

[39] Especially in Australia: Family Law Amendment (Shared Parental Responsibility) Act 2006 (Cth), partially reversed by the Family Law Legislation Amendment (Family Violence and Other Measures) Act 2011 (Cth). In the United Kingdom, see now the Children Act 1989, s 1(2A) and (2B), inserted by the Children and Families Act 2014, s 11.

[40] See H Rhoades, 'Legislating to Promote Children's Welfare and the Quest for Certainty' (2012) 24 *Child and Family Law Quarterly* 158; H Rhoades, G Sheehan and J Dewar, 'Developing a Consistent Message about Children's Care Needs Across the Family Law System' (2013) 27 *Australian Journal of Family Law* 191.

[41] M King et al, *Non-Adversarial Justice* (Annandale, Federation Press, 2009) 18. See also, eg, G Berman and J Feinblatt, 'Problem-Solving Courts: A Brief Primer' (2001) 23 *Law & Policy* 125; JL Nolan, *Reinventing Justice: The American Drug Court Movement* (Princeton, Princeton University Press, 2003); JL Nolan, *Legal Accents, Legal Borrowing: The International Problem-Solving Court Movement* (Princeton, Princeton University Press, 2011); S Whitehead, 'Innovation to Meet Local Needs' (2013) 69 *Magistrate* 6.

[42] King et al, *Non-Adversarial Justice* (n 41) 17, 139–40. See also, eg, G Thomson and C Edwards, 'Problem-Solving Courts: Two Case Studies' (2013) 69 *Magistrate* 10.

Offenders who plead guilty are diverted for treatment or intervention programmes, with the judge acting as coach in encouraging and assisting them
to reform their lives rather than simply being an arbiter handing down
punishment.[43]

A step further on is therapeutic jurisprudence, which again brings principles and practices from behavioural sciences into the courtroom.[44] The
aim of therapeutic jurisprudence is to minimise the law's negative effects
and maximise its positive effects on the well-being of, usually offenders,
but sometimes also victims, including their psychological and emotional
well-being.[45] There is a clear synergy between problem-oriented courts
and therapeutic jurisprudence.[46] For example, in drug courts, the judge is
required to maintain contact with the offender while they are subject to
pre-sentence programmes, and possibly also post-sentence, in order to support their behavioural reform. This is personal contact, direct engagement
with the offender, unmediated by counsel, involving the forging of affective
links.[47] A therapeutic judge may also apply these principles in the general
courtroom, being actively concerned with the people coming before them
rather than maintaining an authoritative distance. In the words of King
et al, 'Though therapeutic judging is not social work it does require a
greater commitment of emotional energy than does traditional judging'.[48]
The notion of judging as emotional labour has been explored by Sharyn
Roach Anleu and Kathy Mack in their study of Australian magistrates.[49]

King et al summarise the implications of these various bio-political developments for the person of the judge;[50] to take on board these developments,
they say, the judge needs to have an 'expanded legal mind', one which is
more open and interdisciplinary, as well as having greater interpersonal
skills. They have to be prepared to take 'an expanded view of the nature of
the legal problem and its effect on those involved' and to 'demonstrate an
ethic of care towards those coming before the courts'. They must encourage
participation, engage in problem-solving and apply interpersonal skills and

---

[43] King et al, *Non-Adversarial Justice* (n 41) 139–40, 213; Thomson and Edwards,
'Problem-Solving Courts' (n 42).

[44] King et al, *Non-Adversarial Justice* (n 41) 17.

[45] ibid, 22. See also DB Wexler, *Therapeutic Jurisprudence: The Law as a Therapeutic
Agent* (Durham, Carolina Academic Press, 1990).

[46] See, eg, P Bentley and N Bakht, 'Problem Solving Courts as Agents of Change' (2004) 15
Commonwealth Judicial Journal 7.

[47] ibid, 16.

[48] ibid.

[49] S Roach Anleu and K Mack, 'Magistrates' Everyday Work and Emotional Labour'
(2005) 32 *Journal of Law and Society* 590. The term 'emotional labour' was coined by Arlie
Hochschild in A Hochschild, *The Managed Heart: Commercialization of Human Feeling*
(Oakland, University of California Press, 1983).

[50] King et al, *Non-Adversarial Justice* (n 41) 212.

therapeutic techniques rather than exercising coercion and control.[51] Once again, as with the neo-liberal judge, this appears to be a more feminised job description than the traditional form of masculine judicial authority. It is notable, however, that problem-solving courts, therapeutic jurisprudence and routine family justice operate at the lower levels of the judicial hierarchy—in Magistrates Courts and County Courts—and that the more senior judiciary appear thus far substantially untouched by the bio-political turn.[52]

III. THE EQUALITY AND DIVERSITY AGENDA

After decades of feminist campaigns for equality and representation, and in a context in which higher courts make decisions with increasingly wide-reaching consequences, it has become clear that a judiciary composed almost entirely of middle-aged to elderly, white, middle to upper-class men is no longer politically acceptable.[53] Compared with other countries, the United Kingdom came to this realisation remarkably late.[54] The question then became how to achieve a more diverse judiciary. A variety of answers to this question have been provided internationally.[55] The answer adopted in England and Wales has been a managerial one—a bureaucratised appointment process has been substituted for the previously personalised

[51] For a study on the effect on judges of working in courts applying principles of therapeutic jurisprudence, see P Fulton Hora and DJ Chase, 'Judicial Satisfaction when Judging in a Therapeutic Way' (2003/04) 7 *Contemporary Issues in Law* 8. For an argument that problem-solving judges require 'a high level of emotional intelligence' in order to juggle their judicial (impartial, independent) and problem-solving (engaged, empathetic) roles, see J Duffy, 'Problem-Solving Courts, Therapeutic Jurisprudence and the Constitution: If Two is Company, Is Three a Crowd?' (2011) 35 *Melbourne University Law Review* 394.

[52] It is arguable that bio-politics have entered the Family Division of the High Court by virtue of the nature of the work undertaken by that Division, but it is also notable that this is the Division with the highest proportion of women judges.

[53] For an international overview of the entry, advancement and current representation of women in the judiciary, see U Schultz and G Shaw, 'Introduction: Gender and Judging: Overview and Synthesis' in U Schultz and G Shaw (eds), *Gender and Judging* (Oxford, Hart Publishing, 2013) 7. In England and Wales, the latest courts diversity statistics showed that women made up 11% of Lord Justices of Appeal, 17% of High Court judges, 19% of Circuit Judges and 27% of District Judges (County Courts): see: www.judiciary.gov.uk/publications/diversity-statistics-and-general-overview-2013. Not included in these statistics is the fact that only one of the 12 Justices of the Supreme Court (8%) is a woman.

[54] The Lord Chief Justice, Lord Taylor, acknowledged in 1992 that there was an 'obvious' gender imbalance in the judiciary—but confidently asserted that a 'substantial number of appointments' would be made in the next five years to redress this: 'The Judiciary in the Nineties' (Richard Dimbleby Lecture, 1992). Discussion of the issue did not really begin in earnest until the mid to late 1990s: see E Rackley, *Women, Judging and the Judiciary: From Difference to Diversity* (Abingdon, Routledge, 2013) 32–33, 71–72.

[55] See SJ Kenney, *Gender and Justice: Why Women in the Judiciary Really Matter* (Abingdon, Routledge, 2013); Schultz and Shaw, *Gender and Judging* (n 53).

one, centred on a transparent application process and appointment on merit.[56]

There are obvious limitations to this model. While it provides greater equality of opportunity in the appointment process, it does not guarantee greater diversity as a result. The statutory duty of the Judicial Appointments Commission (JAC) is to select candidates 'solely on merit',[57] hence much turns on what is taken to constitute 'merit'. The statutory structure tends to suggest that merit and diversity are quite separate things. For example, the JAC must 'have regard to the need to encourage diversity in the range of persons available for selection',[58] but there is no requirement to have regard to any need to encourage diversity in the range of persons actually selected. The recently enacted Crime and Courts Act 2013 'clarifies' that it is not incompatible with appointment 'solely on merit', where two candidates are of equal merit, to prefer one of them over the other for the purpose of increasing diversity,[59] but this again suggests that the candidates' merit is to be determined in the first place without any reference to the value of increasing diversity.[60]

In terms of the conduct of the appointment process, the JAC has put considerable effort into diversifying the recruitment pool, by means of outreach to under-represented groups, research on aspirations and attitudes towards judicial office and efforts to dispel 'myths' that judicial appointment is 'not for the likes of me'.[61] As with neo-liberal responsibilisation and therapeutic jurisprudence, the emphasis is on changing the behaviour of the individual—'don't be shy, apply!'—rather than addressing systemic structural and cultural barriers to the achievement of equality and diversity.[62] Certainly at entry level, however, the JAC has done much to ensure that the applicant pool is more reflective of the broad profile of those within the profession who meet the minimum statutory qualifications required for appointment.[63]

---

[56] See Judicial Appointments Committee, 'Selection Process' (JAC, 2014), available at: jac.judiciary.gov.uk/selection-process/selection-process.htm.

[57] Constitutional Reform Act 2005, s 63(2).

[58] Constitutional Reform Act 2005, s 64(1). This provision is expressly made subject to the requirement of selection 'solely on merit': s 64(2).

[59] Crime and Courts Act 2013, Sch 13, Pt 2, amending, inter alia, s 63 of the Constitutional Reform Act 2005.

[60] This inference is borne out by the approach the JAC intends to take to the implementation of the equal merit provision, announced in April 2014: Judicial Appointments Commission, 'Equal Merit Provision: JAC Policy' (JAC, 2014), available at: jac.judiciary.gov.uk/about-jac/2767.htm.

[61] See Accent, 'Barriers to Application to Judicial Appointment: Report' (JAC, 2013); Judicial Appointments Commission, 'Information for Prospective Applicants' (JAC, 2014), available at: jac.judiciary.gov.uk/static/documents/JAC_Mythbusting_paper_Oct_2012_Final.pdf.

[62] See, eg, Rackley, *Women, Judging and the Judiciary* (n 54) 91.

[63] See Judicial Appointments Commission, 'Judicial Selection and Recommendations for Appointment Statistics, April 2013 to September 2013' (JAC, 2013) 23–24, Tables A1 and A2—Applications compared with pre-Judicial Appointments Commission; Judicial Appointments Commission, 'Equality Objectives Performance Report 2013–2014' (JAC, 2014), available at: jac.judiciary.gov.uk/about-jac/351.htm.

After entry level, though, the recruitment pool becomes progressively narrower. In addition to the statutory criteria, the Lord Chancellor imposes 'non-statutory criteria' which require experience at a lower level before moving to the next step in the hierarchy. So before being eligible for a salaried appointment, applicants must have served at least two years in a fee-paid role,[64] and before moving to a higher rank, applicants must have gained experience as a judge of a lower rank. So only Deputy District Judges or Recorders may become District Judges, only Recorders or District Judges may become Circuit or Crown Court judges. Only Recorders or Circuit, Crown Court or Deputy High Court judges may become High Court judges. Only High Court judges may become Court of Appeal judges, and only Court of Appeal judges may become Supreme Court judges (Lord Sumption being the exception that conclusively proved the rule). This means that as one moves up the judicial hierarchy, the eligible pool becomes less and less diverse, and the time it will take until the more diverse recent entrants become eligible for higher appointment gets longer and longer.

In relation to the question of merit, the JAC has developed a list of six qualities and abilities required of all judges, comprising 'intellectual capacity', 'personal qualities', 'an ability to understand and deal fairly', 'authority and communication skills', 'efficiency' and 'leadership and management skills'.[65] The 'efficiency' and 'leadership and management skills' criteria are in line with the requirements of neo-liberal judging. 'Intellectual capacity' is as one would expect. 'An ability to understand and deal fairly' requires 'an awareness of the diversity of the communities which the courts and tribunals serve and an understanding of differing needs'. Clearly this does not require one actually to be from a non-traditional background. 'Personal qualities' and 'authority and communication skills' are a mix of the old and the new. More traditional (masculine) judicial attributes include 'sound judgement', 'decisiveness', 'objectivity', 'ability to inspire respect and confidence' and 'ability to maintain authority when challenged'. Newer qualities include 'ability and willingness to learn and develop professionally' and

---

[64] Eg, the Information Pack for a currently available post as a Salaried Judge of the First Tier Tribunal states: 'The Lord Chancellor expects that candidates for salaried posts will have sufficient directly relevant previous judicial experience', a requirement which will be waived 'only in wholly exceptional cases'. 'Directly relevant experience' is defined as meaning 'sitting as a judge in a salaried or fee-paid capacity, for fee-paid judges this should be a period of at least two years or 30 sitting days since appointment': Judicial Appointments Commission, 'Information Pack' (JAC, 2014), available at: jac.judiciary.gov.uk/static/documents/00854_-_ Information_Pack.pdf.

[65] Judicial Appointments Commission, 'Qualities and Abilities' (JAC, 2014), available at: jac.judiciary.gov.uk/application-process/qualities-and-abilities.htm. It is interesting to compare these with the Judicial Studies Board's 'Framework of Judicial Abilities and Qualities' for the High Court and Circuit and District Benches (Judicial Studies Board, 2008), available at: www.judiciary.gov.uk/wp-content/uploads/JCO/Documents/Training/framework_AandQ_081008.pdf, which overlaps to some extent, but is otherwise much more 'old school'.

'ability to explain the procedure and any decisions reached clearly and succinctly to all those involved'. The relative weight to be given to these various attributes is left entirely open.

Finally, while the old system of 'secret soundings' has gone,[66] it is replaced by a statutory requirement for the JAC to consult with 'a person ... who has held the office for which the selection is to be made or who has other relevant experience'.[67] In the case of High Court appointments, the Lord Chief Justice is also 'likely' to be consulted.[68] So while no longer secret, there are still 'soundings', which rely on the applicant being known to and considered 'sound' by the relevant statutory consultee/s.

Thus, while the new appointment process is certainly transparent, its terms are a hybrid (very likely a compromise) between engendering the 'new' judge and maintaining the old. It is hardly surprising, then, that the JAC's results have also been mixed, with increasing diversity at the lower levels but a much slower pace of change as one ascends the judicial hierarchy.[69]

Following appointment comes judicial training. In earlier times, the only training judges were thought to need in common law systems was having had long experience as a successful barrister. But if judges are now more numerous and more diverse, and if they are now expected to perform tasks such as case management, one cannot necessarily rely on them all having had the right kind of experience.[70] In Malleson's words, 'the judiciary changed from a club to a profession, hence the advent of judicial training'.[71] Newly appointed part-time judges are now required to attend a residential induction course,[72] with further induction seminars before they can become 'ticketed' for specialist jurisdictions. Continuing education is also mandatory for salaried Crown Court, Circuit and District Judges.[73] The courses

---

[66] For an account of this system, including critical views, see House of Commons Constitutional Affairs Committee, 'Judicial Appointments and a Supreme Court' (First Report, House of Commons Constitutional Affairs Committee 2004) 44–46. See also G Drewry, 'Judicial Appointments' [1998] *Public Law* 1.

[67] Constitutional Reform Act 2005, s 88(3).

[68] Judicial Appointments Commission, 'Statutory Consultation' (JAC, 2014), available at: jac.judiciary.gov.uk/selection-process/selection-process.htm#Statutory_Consultation.

[69] See Judicial Appointments Commission, 'Updated Analysis of the Trends in the Diversity of Applications and Recommendations Made by the JAC' (JAC, 2014), available at: jac.judiciary.gov.uk/static/documents/Updated_trends_2013_9.pdf. For a graphic representation of the pace of change at different levels of the judiciary, see K Malleson, 'The Presence of Women in the British Judiciary' (The Judge is a Woman Conference, Université Libre de Bruxelles, November 2013), available at: www.law.qmul.ac.uk/eji/docs/121825.pdf.

[70] Malleson, *The New Judiciary* (n 1) 162.

[71] ibid, 163.

[72] See Courts and Tribunals Judiciary, 'Training' (Judiciary, 2014), available at www.judiciary.gov.uk/about-the-judiciary/training-support/judicial-college/training.

[73] See Judicial College, 'Prospectus April 2014–March 2015 Courts Judiciary' (Judicial College, 2014) 10; Judicial College, 'Strategy of the Judicial College 2011–2014' (Judicial College, 2014) paras 17–18, available at: www.judiciary.gov.uk/about-the-judiciary/training-support/judicial-college/strategy-2011-14. See also P Darbyshire, *Sitting in Judgment: The Working Lives of Judges* (Oxford, Hart Publishing, 2011) 104; Malleson, *The New Judiciary* (n 1) 167.

offered by the Judicial College are mainly subject specific (criminal law, civil law, family law, administrative law) but there is one course titled 'the business of judging', and modules within subject-matter seminars are dedicated to case management. Continuing education is, however, only optional for High Court judges,[74] and is not mentioned for Court of Appeal or Supreme Court judges.[75] Notably, judicial training in England and Wales is run by the judiciary—the aim being for more experienced judges to pass on their accumulated wisdom to new entrants—in order to avoid any perceived threat to judicial independence.[76]

Even more potentially threatening to judicial independence is judicial performance evaluation. This has long been a feature of civilian systems and has also been widely introduced in the United States, but remains controversial in England and Wales and other common law jurisdictions.[77] A recent Onati workshop on evaluating judicial performance (May 2013) discussed issues such as what aspects of judicial performance should be evaluated; who should evaluate judicial performance—other judges, lawyers, litigants?; measurement issues in judicial performance evaluation and potential gender bias in evaluation measures; and the relationship between judicial performance and court performance evaluation.[78]

The relationship between judicial performance evaluation and the equality and diversity agenda, however, was made clear by the Advisory Panel on Judicial Diversity, chaired by Baroness Neuberger, in 2010. One of the Panel's recommendations was that 'an appraisal system owned and run by the judiciary should be implemented to cover all levels within the judiciary'.[79] The stated rationale for this was that:

> Judicially led appraisal is key to enabling talented judges from diverse backgrounds to progress in their careers more effectively. Appraisal needs to address

[74] Judicial College, 'Prospectus' (n 73).

[75] According to Malleson, this is because the higher levels of the judiciary are still club-like (ie, small and homogeneous), plus there is less need for consistency of approach at those levels: Malleson, *The New Judiciary* (n 1) 165.

[76] Darbyshire, *Sitting in Judgment* (n 73) 104.

[77] On the United States, see National Centre for State Courts and links provided therein: National Center for State Courts, 'Judicial Performance Evaluation: Resource Guide' (NCSC, 2014), available at: www.ncsc.org/Topics/Judicial-Officers/Judicial-Performance-Evaluation/Resource-Guide.aspx. For comparison between the United States and other jurisdictions, see S Colbran, 'A Comparative Analysis of Judicial Performance Evaluation Programmes' (2006) 4 *Journal of Commonwealth Law and Legal Education* 35.

[78] The workshop programme is available at: Onati International Institute for the Sociology of Law, 'Workshop Calendar 2013' (IISJ, 2013) www.iisj.net/iisj/de/workshop-calendar-2013.asp?cod=7014&nombre=7014&prt=1&sesion=1347.

[79] Advisory Panel on Judicial Diversity, 'The Report of the Advisory Panel on Judicial Diversity 2010' (MOJ, 2010) Recommendation 46, available at: www.equality-ne.co.uk/downloads/759_advisory-panel-judicial-diversity-2010.pdf.

diversity specifically so that those with unusual career paths can access the development and opportunities and advice they need to progress.[80]

Two issues may be drawn out here. One is an implicit acknowledgement that diversifying the pool and the profile of appointees at entry level is not sufficient to satisfy the demand for a more diverse judiciary at all levels. Those entrants also need to be able to progress upwards within the judiciary. Following from this is a concern that diverse entrants may not simply 'trickle up' in accordance with their proportions among entry level appointments. In other words, as in the legal profession more generally, there is a risk that judges from non-traditional backgrounds may find themselves anchored to the 'sticky floor' at the bottom of the judicial hierarchy and fail to progress at the same rate as their peers who more resemble the traditional incumbents of judicial office. Once again, the remedial model employed is one of addressing individual deficits. Judges from diverse backgrounds are to be properly acculturated, assimilated, inculcated with appropriate norms of behaviour and steered in the right direction so they are able to overcome their unpropitious origins and made capable of progression. The criteria for progression will not change, but those from diverse backgrounds can be helped to meet them by means of appropriate advice and development opportunities. An interesting question here is what is meant by an 'unusual career path'. Given the rigidity with which career paths and qualified pools are defined, one can only assume that this refers to solicitors or academics who have not followed the 'usual' route to judicial office via the Bar.

The implementation of the Advisory Panel's recommendation has been slow. According to the latest annual report of the Judicial Diversity Taskforce, an appraisal process for Recorders has been designed and agreed, and was piloted from September 2013—three and a half years after the recommendation was made. Following the pilot, the Judicial Office was to 'evaluate the outcomes' and 'identify the next steps'.[81] Recorders have presumably been chosen for piloting because, as indicated earlier, they have an identifiable career path—they are on track either to the Crown/Circuit Court or the senior judiciary. So it is really necessary to ensure they are suitable. Although not mentioned by the Judicial Diversity Taskforce, there is also an appraisal system for Deputy District judges, with the results used in the selection process if a Deputy District judge applies for appointment as a full-time District judge.[82] There is much less recognition of a career path and therefore presumably much less necessity for appraisal in the case of District judges and Crown/Circuit Court judges. Also currently being piloted is a process for 'review and providing feedback' to High Court

---

[80] ibid, 148.
[81] Judicial Diversity Taskforce, 'Improving Judicial Diversity: Progress Towards Delivery of the "Report of the Advisory Panel on Judicial Diversity 2010"' (MOJ, 2011) 35.
[82] I am grateful to Sonia Harris-Short for providing me with this information.

judges in the Chancery Division.[83] Again, this is a group with a clear career path, but because of their seniority and in line with their lack of need for training, this is notably not an appraisal system.

The final element of the equality and diversity agenda to be noted relates to the diversity of court users and the need to ensure equality before the law. This is connected to the judicial attribute concerning 'an ability to understand and deal fairly'. The fact that court users are diverse and require equal treatment is another relatively belated discovery. The 'Equal Treatment Benchbook', a guide to assist judges in being socially aware, sensitive to differences and fair to everyone, was first promulgated in the late 1990s and has subsequently been substantially revised and expanded (most recently in 2013) into a comprehensive tome. Even the summary document, 'Fairness in Courts and Tribunals',[84] runs to 76 pages. Topics covered include age discrimination; children and young people; disability; domestic violence; gender; gender reassignment; interpreters, intermediaries and signing; language and terminology; race; religion and belief; sexual orientation; social exclusion and poverty; unrepresented parties; and vulnerable adults. The fact that judges are expected to absorb and give effect to all this information is a far cry from the distanced impersonality of the past. Again, there are hints of therapeutic jurisprudence, an ethic of care and personal engagement with litigants.

In particular, increasing numbers of litigants in person have put significant pressure on the notion of the judge as passive arbiter[85] and require judges to interact directly with litigants without the mediating presence of counsel. Recommendations from various sources have suggested that substantial changes to judicial practice are required where litigants in person are involved.[86] For example, Richard Moorhead suggests that in order to achieve both procedural and substantive justice for litigants in person, different elements of judge-craft need to be deployed: not a rigid adherence to impartiality and objectivity but communication and empathy. Communication needs to work in both directions 'allowing greater freedom in the manner and content of communication that litigants could engage in' and 'communicating the principles on which disputes should be decided early, simply and clearly'.[87] Empathy includes 'engag[ing] directly with the litigant's social world and their perceptions of the dispute' and

---

[83] Judicial Diversity Taskforce, 'Improving Judicial Diversity' (n 81) 35.

[84] Courts and Tribunals Judiciary, 'Fairness in Courts and Tribunals' (Judiciary, 2012), available at: www.judiciary.gov.uk/publications/fairness-in-courts-and-tribunals.

[85] See, eg, R Moorhead, 'The Passive Arbiter: Litigants in Person and the Challenge to Neutrality' (2007) 16 *Social and Legal Studies* 405.

[86] Eg, Moorhead, ibid; Judicial Working Group on Litigants in Person, 'Report' (Judiciary of England and Wales, 2013) available at: www.judiciary.gov.uk/publications/judicial-working-group-lip-report/; Trinder et al, 'Litigants in Person' (n 32).

[87] Moorhead, 'The Passive Arbiter' (n 85) 417, 422.

striving to achieve a form of fairness that is influenced by what the parties view as fair.[88] Once again, these prescriptions sound like a more feminised approach to judging.

IV. CONCLUSION

In summary, the three drivers of change identified—neo-liberalism, bio-politics and the equality and diversity agenda—have permeated up the judicial hierarchy to different degrees, but in each case, their influence becomes more attenuated the higher one goes. Consequently, we find 'new' judges clustered towards the bottom of the judicial hierarchy, with 'old' judges remaining at the top.

In 1999, Malleson noted the degree of role differentiation between judges by rank, so that senior judges enjoyed an expanding constitutional role while the lower ranks performed a 'largely social service role' and part-time judges engaged primarily in dispute resolution.[89] In 2014, any difference between part-time judges and the lower ranks of salaried judges is not so clear—they are all engaged in dispute resolution, performing a social service role, interacting directly with parties, managing timetables, striving to meet KPIs and being trained and developed. I have argued that the requirements for judicial performance at this level dovetail neatly with the equality and diversity agenda, in that women can meet these requirements just as well as—if not better than—men. At the same time, the JAC's merit criteria are sufficiently flexible to allow greater emphasis to be placed on 'old' judicial qualities for more senior appointments, and this preservation of the 'old' judge at higher levels is facilitated by the progressively narrowing eligibility pool and requirements for statutory consultation. One is left with the uncomfortable conclusion that women are being appointed in greater numbers to the lower ranks of the judiciary because the nature of the judicial role at that level calls for more stereotypically feminine skills, while the definition of 'merit' at senior levels maintains its stereotypically masculine associations, with the result that women continue to be excluded from those positions. There appears to be ongoing difficulty in recognising women as having the kind of 'merit' necessary to fulfil the role of the 'old' judge. It follows that the profile of the senior judiciary may only undergo significant change if the nature of the job was to change substantially.

As noted above, Malleson identified the expanding constitutional role of the judiciary brought about by the growth in judicial review and the advent of the Human Rights Act as largely the preserve of senior judges. While judges at lower levels have been subject to the forces of bureaucracy,

[88] ibid, 417, 419.
[89] Malleson, *The New Judiciary* (n 1) 165.

managerialism and bio-power, senior judges have retained the ability to constrain the activities of the executive through the exercise of juridical power. One of the current government's ambitions is to wrest power from the judiciary by severely curtailing the scope for judicial review[90] and repealing the Human Rights Act.[91] If that occurs, the glass ceiling for the 'new' judge may be shattered in the process.

[90] See A Horne and J Dawson, 'Judicial Review: Government Reforms—Commons Library Standard Note' (17 February 2014), available at: www.parliament.uk/briefing-papers/sn06616/judicial-review-government-reforms.

[91] Conservative Party, 'Invitation to Join the Government of Britain: The Conservative Manifesto 2010' (Conservative Party, 2010) 79; A Travis, 'Conservatives Promise to Scrap Human Rights Act After Next Election' *The Guardian* (30 September 2013), available at: www.theguardian.com/law/2013/sep/30/conservitives-scrap-human-rights-act.

6

The LETRs (Still) in the Post: The Legal Education and Training Review and the Reform of Legal Services Education and Training—A Personal (Re)view[1]

JULIAN WEBB

T HE LEGAL EDUCATION and Training Review (LETR) has been the latest in a long line of formal reviews of legal education and training in England and Wales. Developed and funded by the three largest front line regulators,[2] its launch was announced at the 2010 Lord Upjohn Lecture by Legal Services Board (LSB) chair David Edmonds.[3] As the largest review of legal education and training since the 1971 Ormrod Report,[4] it was intended from the outset to be distinctive in approach. In fact it could be described as a 'first' in a number of respects. It was the first review to be constructed as a research-led, two-stage process. It was the first to extend its reach to the whole legal services sector. It was also the first to be defined in primarily regulatory terms, and to take place in the context of a set of statutorily defined objectives and responsibilities as regards legal education and training.[5]

---

[1] As the title points out, this is a personal reflection and evaluation of the LETR Report and subsequent developments. It does not set out to represent the collective views of the LETR research team (except insofar as those are published and acknowledged here), though the whole piece inevitably reflects ideas and influences shared during the two years we worked together. My particular thanks to Jane Ching for information, advice and reality checks while writing this chapter.

[2] The Bar Standards Board (BSB), ILEX Professional Standards (IPS) and the Solicitors Regulation Authority (SRA).

[3] D Edmonds, 'Training the Lawyers of the Future—A Regulator's View' (2011) 45 *The Law Teacher* 4.

[4] Committee on Legal Education, *Report of the Committee on Legal Education* (Cmnd 4595, 1971) (Ormrod Report).

[5] See ss 1 and 4 of the Legal Services Act 2007 which respectively set out a range of regulatory objectives for legal services regulators, and charge the LSB to assist in the maintenance

This chapter aims to set the LETR in its primary contexts, to briefly discuss the main conclusions and recommendations of the 2013 LETR Report[6] and identify progress that has been made on its implementation. The chapter concludes by evaluating the progress that has been made so far and reflecting on some of the future challenges the reform process faces.

I. THE BACKGROUND TO THE REVIEW

The LETR has not taken place in a vacuum. To be properly understood it needs to be read in the context of changes to the national and global legal services market, to systems of professional (including education and training) regulation and by a growing international debate about the nature and functions of legal education itself.[7]

A. The Global Legal Services Market

The transformation of the global legal services market has been an important *motif* in recent debates about both the future of the profession and the role of legal education and training, though the implications of such changes are far from certain. As a recent review of the research has noted:

> There seems to be little dispute over the fact that change is inevitable; or over the causes of the change; or even over the idea that something must be done to respond to the coming changes. While there's a fairly unprecedented consensus about the problem, the same cannot be said about a solution. It's possible that the lack of a clear path to follow may merely reflect reality: there may be no obvious solutions to offer in the face of what could be described as a mounting existential crisis for law firms.[8]

It is suggested that there are at least three major trends that are likely to influence the scale, scope and focus of legal education and training.[9]

---

and development of standards of education and training for (authorised) legal service providers.

[6] Legal Education and Training Review, 'Setting Standards: The Future of Legal Service Education and Training Regulation in England and Wales' (SRA, BSB and CILEX, 2013), available at: www.letr.org.uk.

[7] The context is discussed at length throughout the LETR Literature Review, and in the main Report, notably in ch 3, but *seriatim*. This chapter draws extensively on those data, and updates the original analysis where possible.

[8] Canadian Bar Association, 'The Future of the Legal Profession: Report on the State of the Research' (Legal Futures Initiative, 2013), available at: www.cbafutures.org/The-Reports/State-Of-Research.

[9] Except where otherwise indicated, this section draws chiefly on the data presented in the LETR Report, ch 3.

First, we are seeing the emergence of new ways to deliver legal services. Increased competition is present across the sector, allied with increased pressure from purchasers/consumers who are looking for faster and often cheaper services, and, particularly in the commercial sector, greater value added from their suppliers. This is requiring providers to innovate: more flexible and transparent billing practices; better knowledge management; outsourcing; more customised client solutions; and, conversely, routinising and automating transactions where possible. This risks creating new regulatory challenges, for example, in respect of assuring the quality of work, and achieving necessary levels of supervision across the legal workforce. It also impacts future demand for lawyers and raises questions about the skills the regulated workforce will require.

There has been a significant reduction in numbers of fee-earners during the recession, and a decline in numbers of training contracts and pupillages.[10] Despite signs of recovery, the training market in particular appears, so far, to have remained largely static. At the same time we are seeing in at least some firms a much greater use of outsourcing, substituting contract lawyers and paralegals for permanent admitted staff and (relatively expensive) trainees.[11] Although it is still relatively difficult to predict any overall trend, it is more likely than not that such changes are becoming a permanent feature of the market. This may help keep the demand for trainees relatively depressed, though some of this effect may be offset by businesses opening up and exploiting previously under-served markets.

In terms of knowledge and skills development, chapter 2 of the LETR Report identified a general need to enhance commercial and 'social' awareness, to develop writing skills and communication, legal research skills and digital literacy of those entering practice. The Report also highlighted the importance down the line of enhancing lawyers' competences in client relationship management, project and risk management, as well as the higher management skills needed to provide organisational leadership in a

---

[10] In 2011–12, 4869 training contracts were registered as compared with 5441 in 2010–11 and 6303 in 2006–07. There are signs that Legal Practice Course (LPC) applicant numbers are adjusting to market conditions; in 2013–14, the number of full-time LPC students fell by 8% from the previous year, leaving some 6500 approved places (technically) unfilled. The total number of LPC applications has fallen by about 37% since 2008: see Law Careers.Net, 'The Number of LPC Students Continues to Decline' (16 December 2013), available at: www.law-careers.net/Information/News/The-number-of-LPC-students-continues-to-decline-16122013. Applications to the Bar continue to be more resistant to market effects. Bar Professional Training Course applications fell only marginally, by 2.7%, in 2011–12, while enrolments actually increased by 23.1% to over 1800 students. Numbers of new pupillages have continued to decline steadily, from 527 in 2006–07, to 438 in 2011–12: 'Bar Council, Bar Barometer: Trends in the Profile of the Bar 2013' (Bar Council, 2014), available at: www.barstandards-board.org.uk/media/1584380/barometer_report_112pp_tuesday_3.pdf.

[11] In addition to the LETR data, see J Tsolakis, 'Building Tomorrow: A Perspective on the Legal Market' (Royal Bank of Scotland, 2014) 9, available at: www.rbs.com/content/dam/rbs/Documents/News/2014/03/perspective-on-the-legal-market.pdf.

rapidly changing world. Moreover, with a growing focus on sales, client relationship and knowledge/process management functions, it became apparent that the sector was starting to create new hybrid roles, for both admitted and paralegal/support staff which require some very different combinations of technical legal, IT and business skills.[12]

Second, the current interplay between marketised systems of legal services funding and legal education has had a significant impact on the ability of the legal system to deliver social justice. Not only are opportunities to work in legal aid and public or third sector legal services declining,[13] the disproportionate rewards of commercial legal practice, especially when combined with the spiralling cost of legal education, act as a disincentive to students to consider such work. To that extent the pull of commercial practice can be seen as actively distorting the market for training by producing a very substantial oversupply of potential lawyers to the commercial sector, while areas of social welfare law experience unmet need.[14] Moreover, further cuts to publicly funded/third-sector legal services are likely to impact the diversity of the (traditional) legal professions and further limit their contribution to social mobility.[15] There has already been considerable consolidation into larger entities, and it must be open to question whether further consolidation, diversification of activity and the search for alternative modes of organising[16] and funding legal services by themselves will fill a growing access to justice gap. Unless there is radical change it is likely that more consumers will either have to 'lump it', rely on self-help, or turn to more accessible 'unregulated' providers.[17] Despite moves in the United

---

[12] See also R Susskind, 'Provocations and Perspectives' LETR Briefing Paper 3/2012 (LETR, 2012), available at: www.letr.org.uk/briefing-and-discussion-papers/index.html; R Susskind, *Tomorrow's Lawyers: An Introduction to Your Future* (Oxford, Oxford University Press, 2013).

[13] N Byrom, 'The State of the Sector: The Impact of Cuts to Civil Legal Aid on Practitioners and Their Clients' (ilegal/University of Warwick, 2013), available at: www2.warwick.ac.uk/fac/soc/law/chrp/projects/legalaidcuts/153064_statesector_report-final.pdf.

[14] Cp GK Hadfield, 'The Price of Law: How the Market for Lawyers Distorts the Justice System' (2000) 98 *Michigan Law Review* 953.

[15] See, eg, A Cullingworth, G Samarsinghe and S Jamma, 'YLAL Social Mobility Report: One Step Forward, Two Steps Back' (2014) March *Legal Action* 7.

[16] Eg, the potential to reduce costs by 'unbundling' or 'rebundling' legal services. Thus, a growing number of family law practices, including Co-operative Legal Services use unbundling to offer a range of divorce packages involving different levels of professional management or support of the process. Liverpool law firm Morecrofts has similarly been reported as having created a range of unbundled services to assist clients in navigating the small claims jurisdiction: see N Rose, 'Are Small Claims Becoming a New Law Firm Battleground?' *Legal Futures* (14 April 2014), available at: www.legalfutures.co.uk/latest-news/are-small-claims-becoming-new-law-firm-battleground.

[17] Data produced for the Legal Services Board, highlighted in the LETR Report, para 3.122, already indicate that over half of consumer legal problems are addressed outwith traditional law practice. 'Unregulated' here is used specifically to mean entities not regulated under the LSA or equivalent to deliver legal services. This does not necessarily imply that services are provided at lower quality or lower cost than a 'regulated' service provider.

States and Canada to enhance access by licensing paralegals to operate as independent practitioners with limited practice rights, such options have not so far received significant consideration or support in the United Kingdom, outside the LETR Report.[18] Third, regulation itself is being used as a driver of change. This can particularly be observed in the liberalisation of ownership rules for legal businesses through the regulatory framework for 'alternative business structures' (ABSs) in England and Wales.

ABSs are a small but growing sector of the market. By the end of 2013 the Solicitors Regulation Authority (SRA), the largest licensing body for ABSs, had authorised a total of 241 such entities, with overall figures indicating that there are now over 300 ABSs operating in the market.[19] Delays to the introduction of the SRA's licensing regime, and the relatively lengthy approval process meant that the LETR research was able to say very little about the ABS phenomenon, and the extent to which ABSs will be the game changer that has been predicted is still quite hard to gauge. However, there is at least an argument that these regulatory reforms have played a role in accelerating competition and innovation, even where the innovators are not necessarily adopting the ABS structure to do it.[20] The likely entry by three of the 'big four' accountancy firms also suggests that the impact of ABSs is not going to be limited to the high street or mid-tier. Once again these various developments may have some impact on workforce development and training needs within the sector, though this is difficult to qualify or quantify at present.

In short, the not unreasonable assumption is that at least some aspects of legal education and training will have to respond to these changing dynamics as law schools prepare the next generation of legal professionals for the ways in which legal services are being organised and delivered now and in the future, not, as Richard Susskind put it, in the 1980s.[21] The problem is that, while these three drivers raise multiple questions about the future directions of legal practice, so far there have been very few answers, especially from within the profession itself.

---

[18] Legal Education and Training Review, 'Setting Standards' (n 6) paras 6.101–6.141, and Recommendations 22 and 23.

[19] D Bindman, 'ABSs Top 300 Mark with Latest Licencees Demonstrating Variety of New Legal Breed' *Legal Futures* (16 April 2014), available at: www.legalfutures.co.uk/latest-news/abs-top-300-mark-latest-licencees-demonstrating-variety-new-legal-breed.

[20] Riverview Law is an example of a new entrant which did not launch as an ABS; Riverview was almost certainly the first firm to build its business model and its entire brand around fixed-fee pricing; however, what was more significant from our perspective was the way in which it has eschewed the classic partnership management model, invested heavily in IT and in a strong, market-facing, client relationship development programme, and developed its skills base accordingly. The entry of new online service providers like Rocket Lawyer and Legal Zoom which provide DIY legal services at the front end, backed up by a referral network of solicitors willing to offer services at a heavily discounted rate has also not been contingent on ABS approval.

[21] Susskind, 'Provocations' (n 12).

B. The New Political and Moral Economy of Professional Regulation

The new political and moral economy of professional regulation also provided a significant but less obvious subtext to the work of the LETR research team. Since the 1980s, the confluence of consumerism, scholars critical of the legal professional 'project', and neo-liberal governments and international agencies suspicious of professional monopolies have placed the profession under intense ideological and economic scrutiny.[22] In the process the underlying norm of professional self-regulation has itself come into question as evidence has mounted that traditional systems of lawyer regulation suffer from flaws that are 'significant, systemic and structural'.[23]

In the wake of these challenges, modes of regulation and enforcement activity have begun to evolve in some quite profoundly different ways. Change—or at least the potential for change—thus far has been most apparent in a number of increasingly liberalised common law jurisdictions in Australia, the United Kingdom and the Republic of Ireland,[24] but growing pressure for reform is also being felt across Europe.[25] The Legal Services Act 2007 (LSA) has been very much at the sharp end of these developments.

The LSA regulatory framework is predicated on a model which assumes that a liberalised market, driven by competition and supported where necessary by regulation, is the best protector of both the public and consumer interest. This ideological change is carried through into practice via a number of mechanisms:

— The creation of regulatory objectives: the LSA is relatively unusual (in legal services settings) for specifying a range of regulatory objectives against which both the regulators and their regulation is to be judged.[26] The section 1 obligation to 'encourage an independent, strong, diverse and effective' legal profession in particular has been used to justify the

---

[22] See, eg, RL Abel, *English Lawyers between Market and State: The Politics of Professionalism* (Oxford, Oxford University Press, 2003); F Stephen, *Lawyers, Markets and Regulation* (Cheltenham, Edward Elgar Publishing, 2013) ch 5.

[23] D Rhode and A Woolley, 'Comparative Perspectives on Lawyer Regulation: An Agenda for Reform in the United States and Canada' (2012) 80 *Fordham Law Review* 2789.

[24] See, eg, S Mark and T Gordon, 'Innovations in Regulation—Responding to a Changing Legal Services Market' (2009) 22 *Georgetown Journal of Legal Ethics* 501; R Devlin and A Cheng, 'Re-Calibrating, Re-Visioning and Re-Thinking Self-Regulation in Canada' (2010) 17 *International Journal of the Legal Profession* 233; L Terry, S Mark and T Gordon, 'Adopting Regulatory Objectives for the Legal Profession' (2012) 80 *Fordham Law Review* 2685; J Webb, 'Regulating Lawyers in a Liberalized Legal Services Market: The Role of Education and Training' (2013) 24 *Stanford Law & Policy Review* 533.

[25] NJ Philipsen, 'Regulation and Competition in the Legal Profession: Developments in the EU and China' (2010) 6 *Journal of Competition Law and Economics* 203; Stephen, *Lawyers* (n 22) 73–82.

[26] On the nature and use of regulatory objectives in legal services regulation, see Terry, Mark and Gordon, 'Adopting Regulatory Objectives' (n 24).

regulators taking what Edmonds describes as a 'deep interest in the education and training of lawyers'.[27] Regulators are also required to ensure that 'all' the regulatory objectives are at least considered in, if not actively advanced by, their work on education and training.

— By creating a system of autonomous frontline regulators, overseen by a supervisory body with statutory authority (the LSB), the LSA reforms have sought to create both new (co-)regulatory spaces between the regulatory agencies, while also opening the market up to regulatory competition (ie, competition between regulators).[28] These changes should, to a greater degree than historically, insulate regulatory agencies from professional capture, and reduce the risks of regulatory monopoly, but they also add to the complexity and fragmentation of the regulatory environment.

— By encouraging frontline regulators to develop both entity and outcomes-focused regulation (OFR) in England and Wales, the LSB has sought to expand the available regulatory toolkit and increase regulatory flexibility and responsiveness to the legal services market.

The creation of this new regulatory complex has potentially significant implications for education and training.

First, it moves competence and competition centre stage. Andy Boon has observed that the LSA can be read as an attempt to use competition to reinvigorate and reconstruct law as a liberal profession in the public interest, or to undermine professionalism as a mechanism of occupational control.[29] In fact, it may be arguable that these are not alternatives, but part and parcel of a revised, stripped down, version of professionalism in which professional competence and responsibility is assured by a mixture of heightened competition and (limited) bureaucratic control. The emphasis on competence is critical here. Competence is both an end in itself and a means by which the regulators advance consumer and public interest objectives. Such an approach inevitably highlights the central 'regulatory' role for education and training.

Second, a greater emphasis on entity and OFR necessitates finding a proper balance between the regulatory requirements placed on entities and individuals, and raises questions, particularly in the context of continuing professional development (CPD) and workforce supervision, as to how much responsibility for quality assurance should be delegated by the regulator to those involved in delivering the education and/or training.

---

[27] Edmonds, 'Training the Lawyers of the Future' (n 3) 4, 6.
[28] See Stephen, *Lawyers* (n 22) 116–19.
[29] A Boon, 'Professionalism under the Legal Services Act 2007' (2010) 17 *International Journal of the Legal Profession* 195, 199.

Third, the move to OFR also raises whether there needs to be a substantial cultural change within the regulatory function, so that the regulatory role itself becomes more about educating, providing information and expert advice and promoting standards to the regulated community.[30] Boon has also argued that OFR introduces a system of 'situational ethics' which will require different education and training to a 'rules-based' system.[31]

C. International Trends in Legal Education and Training

The LETR has also taken place in the context of significant changes to the scale and demographics of legal education and a growing transnational debate about its nature and functions.

Despite marked structural variations between systems which reflect much of their local history, there are significant convergences and common problems. Much of this can be associated with the interplay of globalisation and the new (national) political economy of higher education. In the wake of the Washington Consensus, higher education policy internationally has become increasingly framed within the neo-liberal agenda of creating a global 'knowledge economy', a discourse that values higher education more as an economic than a cultural good, and which has led to higher education becoming treated as a private economic good, to be privatised, marketised, commoditised and deregulated or re-regulated in the name of efficiency.[32]

While higher education institutions often see themselves as the objects of globalisation they are also key agents in the process. We should not overlook the extent to which they have been active participants in the changes that have been introduced, for example, in the increased emphasis on productivity or 'performativity' as measured by research and teaching audit,[33] the growing stakeholder culture[34] and enhanced efforts to demonstrate student employability and links with the world of work.[35]

---

[30] See N Smedley, *Review of the Regulation of Corporate Legal Work* (London, Law Society, 2009) 22.

[31] Boon, 'Professionalism' (n 29) 293.

[32] See M Thornton, *Privatising the Public University: The Case of Law* (Abingdon, Routledge, 2012); N James, 'Power-Knowledge in Australian Legal Education: Corporatism's Reign' (2004) 40 *Sydney Law Review* 587. Note also how within the EU the 'Lisbon Process' has, since 2001, increasingly sought to tie EU higher education policy to a competitive agenda, geared to increasing the sector's 'export value', and challenging the 'market lead' that has been enjoyed by US and Australian universities over their continental European counterparts.

[33] Thornton, *Privatising the Public University* (n 32) 113, 187–88.

[34] See F Cownie (ed), *Stakeholders in the Law School* (Oxford, Hart Publishing, 2010).

[35] P Brown, A Hesketh and S Williams, 'Employability in a Knowledge-Driven Economy' (2003) 16 *Journal of Education and Work* 107; MP Moreau and C Leathwood, 'Graduates' Employment and the Discourse of Employability: A Critical Analysis' (2006) 19 *Journal of Education and Work* 305.

At a more systemic level, the globalisation of legal education can also be seen in large part as a cipher for massification, internationalisation and Americanisation. Massification—the rapid expansion of higher education— is a direct consequence of the equation, within the knowledge economy discourse, of global competitiveness with the development of a highly educated workforce. It is not a phenomenon unique to law, but law's popularity with potential students makes it a fertile ground for university expansion, and thus attractive to university senior managers. Massification has taken place across many systems and has often involved not just increased recruitment (usually for proportionately less resource), but substantial restructuring of the higher education sector and its infrastructure, as, for example, in the abolition of formal distinctions between traditional universities and higher technical institutions in Australia, Germany and the United Kingdom.

Internationalisation is commonly seen as one of the significant cultural benefits of a globalised higher education. In England and Wales, law is one of the largest recruiters of international students.[36] Law schools have been influenced by internationalisation, leading to a greater cultural diversity among staff and students, enhanced mobility and internationalisation and transnationalisation of the curriculum, though relatively few have actually used it to radically rethink their offering.[37] The professional law curriculum, on the other hand still tends to be viewed, predominantly, as jurisdiction specific. Where content is professionally prescribed, it is primarily domestic law. If internationalisation represents an opportunity for law schools, it can represent a challenge for professional 'relevance' and authority over both the curriculum and the institution.

Existing jurisdiction-based qualification pathways have also created challenges for regulation. They tend to restrict the route to qualification for international students rather than open it up.[38] Moreover, mobility requirements in the EU have increased rather than reduced the complexity of pathways (by adding registered European and foreign lawyers, Bar Transfer Test (BTT) and Qualified Lawyer Transfer Scheme (QLTS)

---

[36] In 2011–12 there were over 20,000 international students studying the subject at undergraduate and postgraduate level, representing 22% of the total law student population: UK Council for International Student Affairs, 'International Student Statistics: UK Higher Education' (UKCISA, 2014), available at: www.ukcisa.org.uk/Info-for-universities-colleges--schools/Policy-research--statistics/Research--statistics/International-students-in-UK-HE/#.

[37] But note the developments at McGill Law School in Montreal: H Dedek and A de Mestral, 'Born to Be Wild: The "Trans-Systemic" Programme at McGill and the De-Nationalization of Legal Education' (2009) 10 *German Law Journal* 889; J Bedard, 'Transsystemic Teaching of Law at McGill: "Radical Changes, Old and New Hats"' (2001) 27 *Queen's Law Journal* 237.

[38] See, eg, C Silver, 'Holding onto "Too Many Lawyers": Bringing International Graduate Students to the Front of the Class' (2013) 3 *Oñati Socio-Legal Series* 533, available at: papers.ssrn.com/sol3/papers.cfm?abstract_id=2298682; J Flood, 'Legal Education in the Global Context: Challenges from Globalization, Technology and Changes in Government Regulation' (LSB, 2011), available at: papers.ssrn.com/sol3/papers.cfm?abstract_id=1906687.

graduates, and equivalent transferees into the smaller professions). These developments need to be factored in to our understanding of a modern education and training system. The regulatory framework created in Europe by the Establishment and Mutual Recognition/Professional Qualification Directives[39] has required licensing authorities to look far more closely at the scope, nature and comparability of training regimes. Changes to the Professional Qualification Directive, permitting mobility in cases where a migrant can claim partial access to a reserved activity,[40] may force the system (albeit on a case-by-case rather than sectoral basis) closer to a form of activity-based regulation, perhaps policed by restricted practising certificates.

Americanisation has also grown apace.[41] The American model of graduate 'professional school' legal education has spread over the last decade and has already taken hold in Canada, Australia and Japan. It is also gaining influence in China and other parts of east Asia. The United States and the United Kingdom have traditionally dominated the market for international law students. The New York Bar and American LLMs have in recent years become more available and more popular with international students, arguably challenging the English market in postgraduate and professional legal education, and raising some concerns that English law and law firms might lose visibility and standing thereby.[42]

D. Shaping the Debate

While the debate in each jurisdiction has reflected its own mix of global phenomena and local conditions,[43] increased numbers, growing international competition in both the legal services and legal education markets, and concerns about the capacity of legal education systems to provide

---

[39] See N Rogers, R Scannell and J Walsh, *Free Movement of Persons in the Enlarged European Union* (London, Sweet & Maxwell, 2012) 227, for a survey of the legislative developments in this area up to 2012.

[40] The amending Directive 2013/55/EU entered into force in February 2014, giving Member States a two-year implementation period. See by way of background, J Lonbay, 'Activity Based Regulation—EU Perspectives on Partial Access to Reserved Activities' (*Julian Lonbay's EU Legal Blog*, 9 March 2012), available at: www.julianlonbay.wordpress.com/2012/03/09/activity-based-regulation-eu-perspectives-on-partial-access-to-reserved-activities.

[41] See Flood, 'Legal Education in the Global Context' (n 38); S Chesterman, 'The Evolution of Legal Education: Internationalization, Transnationalization, Globalization' (2009) 10 *German Law Journal* 877; see also RA Brand and D Wes Rist (eds), *The Export of Legal Education: Its Promise and Impact in Transition Countries* (Farnham, Ashgate, 2009).

[42] See, eg, Legal Education and Training Review, 'Setting Standards' (n 6) para 2.114; cp C Silver, 'The Variable Value of US Legal Education in the Global Legal Services Market' (2011) 24 *Georgetown Journal of Legal Ethics* 1.

[43] Cp, eg, contributions to the recent Special Issue of the *International Journal of the Legal Profession*: 'Too Many Lawyers' (2012) 19 *International Journal of the Legal Profession*.

relevant and effective preparation for practice are common themes across jurisdictions and have, to varying degrees, driven a plethora of reviews since the early 2000s.

The underlying transformation caused by the massification and marketisation of legal education can be seen as a significant causal factor, fuelling the debate around the complex interplay between law student and lawyer numbers, the costs of legal education, employability and access to the profession. Thus, for example, in Canada, the 2009 review of the Common Law degree[44] was largely triggered by quality and parity concerns as the profession faced both a growing influx of Canadians seeking admission with overseas law degrees, and proposals to create the first new Canadian law schools for 25 years. In England and Wales, concerns over costs and student numbers have been a significant driver of criticisms of the existing vocational training for solicitors and barristers. In particular, they were a key subtext in the Wood Reviews of the (then) Bar Vocational Course and pupillage between 2008 and 2010.[45] The inability of those reviews to come up with a magic bullet solution has meant that the problem has continued to fester.[46] In the United States, the cost of qualification in the wake of a steady decline in practice openings for JD graduates has become a seemingly critical issue for the sector. Law schools are said to have failed to prioritise teaching and been unwilling to engage with the need to better prepare students for practice. American Bar Association (ABA) regulation has been criticised for increasing the costs of legal education by setting high resource thresholds for law schools, and inhibiting experimentation. The remedies proposed by critics have, accordingly, included deregulation, the setting of lower academic salaries and increased teaching loads, and a move to two-year JD programmes.[47]

---

[44] Federation of Law Societies of Canada, 'Task Force on the Canadian Common Law Degree: Final Report' (FLSC, 2009), available at: www.slaw.ca/wp-content/uploads/2009/10/Task-Force-Final-Report.pdf.

[45] Bar Standards Board, 'Review of the Bar Vocational Course: Report of the Working Group' (BSB, 2008), available at: www.barstandardsboard.org.uk/media/1353435/bvc_report_final_with_annexes_as_on_website.pdf; Bar Standards Board, 'Review of Pupillage: Report of the Working Group' (BSB, 2010), available at: www.legalservicesboard.org.uk/what_we_do/regulation/pdf/Annex_B_Pupillage_REPORT.pdf.

[46] See Council of the Inns of Court, 'Burton Pupillage Working Group: First Interim Report with Recommendations for Urgent Action' (COIC, 2012).

[47] See BZ Tamanaha, *Failing Law Schools* (Chicago, University of Chicago Press, 2012); B Garth, 'Crises, Crisis Rhetoric and Competition in Legal Education: A Sociological Perspective on the (Latest) Crisis of the Legal Profession and Legal Education' (2013) 24 *Stanford Law & Policy Review* 503, available at: www.ssrn.com/abstract=2166441. The ABA responded by creating a new Legal Education Task Force, which reported in January of this year with recommendations for redesigning the financial model used by law schools, revising regulation to permit more experimentation and innovation and expanding opportunities for delivery of legal services by non-attorneys; see American Bar Association, 'Report of the Task Force on the Future of Legal Education' (ABA, 2014), available at: www.americanbar.org/groups/professional_responsibility/taskforceonthefuturelegaleducation.html.

A second development of globalised higher and professional education has been the emergence of a discourse and debate about standards. In the move to what some call an 'audit society',[48] the formulation of standards has been a growing feature of regulation across the board. As lawyers and their regulators have reacted to the increasing interests of government and lay bodies, so their perception grew of the importance of stated standards in maintaining the authority of professionalism, the independence of a professional cadre and in maintaining some degree of market control, and market differentiation from an encroaching unregulated sector.[49] We can see this approach developing in the US MacCrate Report 1992,[50] and in the changing discourses of the Anglo-Welsh reports which preceded the LETR from 1971 to 2008.

The 1996 Report of the Lord Chancellor's Advisory Committee (ACLEC) was in many respects pivotal, and prefigures many of the debates that are still taking place around the LETR. In its first two chapters the ACLEC Report articulated the rapid changes occurring in the legal services sector and higher education. The Committee argued legal education and training had become critical to enhancing 'both the quality and the efficiency of the provision of legal services to the public'.[51] In an era of greater professional accountability, ACLEC took the view that an effective professional education and training system is one that can demonstrably assure quality without sacrificing flexibility and responsiveness to a rapidly changing market.[52] What it also articulated, albeit rather less clearly, is the extent to which there is a link between making professional competence demonstrable and the use of competence-based systems, as opposed to systems that rely on prescriptive content regulation or largely unarticulated assumptions about professional socialisation.[53]

ACLEC was undoubtedly influenced in this regard by the work done in developing new vocational training programmes in Canada, Australasia and the United Kingdom in the 1980s, and by the growing emphasis on competences more generally in the development of further, higher and professional education in the 1990s. The broad acceptance of an outcomes

---

[48] M Power, *The Audit Society: Rituals of Verification*, 2nd edn (Oxford, Oxford University Press, 1999).

[49] One of the interesting consequences of the LSA reforms has been to foster professionalism in, and a desire to achieve market differentiation and a degree of market closure by, groups that previously lacked a formal identity as independently regulated occupations—legal executives, licensed conveyancers and costs lawyers.

[50] American Bar Association, Section of Legal Education and Admissions to the Bar, 'Report of the Task Force on Law Schools and the Profession: Narrowing the Gap' (ABA, 1992).

[51] Lord Chancellor's Advisory Committee on Legal Education and Conduct (ACLEC), 'First Report on Legal Education and Training' (ACLEC, 1996) para 1.17, available at: www.ukcle.ac.uk/resources/he-policy/aclec.

[52] ibid, para 2.2.

[53] See particularly the discussion of 'outcomes', ibid, paras 4.16–4.17.

approach by respondents to ACLEC, and by the Committee itself, set down a significant marker for future developments, and particularly the work of the Law Society's Training Framework Review Group (TFRG).[54] The TFRG also sought, with some success, to put outcomes at the centre of its regime for the education and training of solicitors, and more recent initiatives in Canada, Australia, Scotland and the United States[55] have extended the range of competence approaches and appear consistent with a more general 'transition from content-focused to outcomes-focused instruction ... underway in legal education'.[56]

Continuing tensions around vocationalism also lie not far below the surface of most of the recent debates in, for example, Canada,[57] the United States[58] and the United Kingdom, and this inevitably brings us back to the contested relationship between liberal legal education and legal practice that has hovered like a malign spirit over much legal education discourse.[59]

While it might be argued that critics like Margaret Thornton have taken an unduly bleak view of the current decline of liberalism,[60] the professions undoubtedly played a key role historically in England and Wales in bankrolling, and to an extent legitimating, the expansion of university legal education in the late nineteenth and early twentieth century. Particularly in jurisdictions like Australia and the United Kingdom, professional training has become less relevant to academic legal education, as the professions have ceded a large part of their control over the production of lawyers to the universities, and the proportion of students progressing into practice has fallen towards, or even below the 50 per cent mark. The capacity of our complex system of multiple stakeholders and shifting alliances to deliver effective cooperation rather than mere coexistence has been questioned and tested in numerous skirmishes over the years.[61] Today, we are no closer to resolving those differences. Indeed some might argue that the intellectual

---

[54] A Boon and J Webb, 'Legal Education and Training in England and Wales: Back to the Future?' (2008) 58 *Journal of Legal Education* 79.

[55] See further the Legal Education and Training Review, 'Setting Standards' (n 6) ch 4.

[56] R Stuckey, *Best Practices for Legal Education* (Columbia, Clinical Legal Education Association, 2007) 45.

[57] R Devlin et al, 'Response to the Consultation Paper of the Task Force on the Canadian Common Law Degree of the Federation of Law Societies of Canada, Canadian Association of Law Teachers/Canadian Law and Society Association' (2008) *Canadian Legal Education Annual Review* 151, available at: papers.ssrn.com/sol3/papers.cfm?abstract_id=2102596.

[58] WM Sullivan et al, *Educating Lawyers: Preparation for the Profession of Law* (San Francisco, Jossey-Bass, 2007), available at: www.carnegiefoundation.org/publications/educating-lawyers-preparation-profession-law.

[59] See, eg, in the LETR context, J Guth and C Ashford, 'The Legal Education and Training Review: Regulating Socio-Legal and Liberal Legal Education?' (2014) 48 *The Law Teacher* 5.

[60] Thornton, *Privatising the Public University* (n 32).

[61] See, eg, F Cownie and R Cocks, *'A Great and Noble Occupation!': The History of the Society of Legal Scholars* (Oxford, Hart Publishing, 2009) *seriatim*—but most notably perhaps in the arguments about the academic 'core subjects' that followed the Ormrod Report (n 4) 129–34.

battle lines are being drawn increasingly sharply (at the extremes) between those academics who tend to see engagement with practice and employability skills as anti-academic and inconsistent with the liberal ideal,[62] and those judges and practitioners who have been vociferously critical of the more theoretical and abstract drift of legal scholarship and law teaching.[63]

Education and training review processes have tended to constitute interesting spaces within which these contests are (or are not) addressed. In simple institutional or structural terms, the prime movers in creating such reviews have tended to be the professions or the state, not the law schools. Inevitably it has been those institutions which have therefore determined the scope of the game and selected the key players. In England and Wales the pendulum has, since 1971, swung between relatively autonomous (state-sponsored) and profession-sponsored events—from Ormrod to Marre to ACLEC to the Law Society's TFRG and the more narrowly focused Bell Working Group for the Bar.[64] Ormrod and ACLEC represent one side of the equation. They were both in the relatively autonomous camp, though the professions still retained a substantial share of the membership. Ormrod was foundational in carving out a space for university legal education as a liberal education, but it also pushed for a university legal education to be the normal first stage in professional education and training, and sought greater planning and integration of the whole structure of education to training. To that extent it sowed the seeds of many of the tensions that are still being addressed today. ACLEC, with its message to trust the universities[65] may yet emerge, in retrospect, as a high point for liberal legal education, though it too did not seek fundamentally to disrupt the basic Ormrod settlement. It ultimately failed, however, because it neither succeeded in gaining the confidence and support of the legal professions, nor adequately assessed the likelihood of its recommendations being adopted in the difficult political and economic contexts of the then legal services and higher education markets.[66]

---

[62] Notably A Bradney, *Conversations, Choices and Chances: The Liberal Law School in the Twenty-First Century* (Oxford, Hart Publishing, 2003).

[63] Though the complaints have on the whole been louder, or at least more public, in North America: see, eg, HT Edwards, 'The Growing Disjunction between Legal Education and the Legal Profession' (1992) 91 *Michigan Law Review* 34; M Bastarache, 'The Role of Academics and Legal Theory in Judicial Decision-Making' (1999) 37 *Alberta Law Review* 739.

[64] Technically the TFRG process was taken over by the SRA, and the work of the Bell Working Group ultimately fed into a further review of the (then) Bar Vocational Course conducted by the BSB. Work on the BVC differed from the TFRG in that it was not framed by an agenda for radical change and largely confirmed the existing direction of travel for Bar training, while attempting to restore a higher degree of supply control: Boon and Webb, 'Legal Education and Training' (n 54) 101.

[65] ACLEC, 'First Report' (n 51) paras 4.14, 4.19.

[66] See HW Arthurs, 'Half a League Onward: The Report of the Lord Chancellor's Advisory Committee on Legal Education and Conduct' (1997) 31 *The Law Teacher* 1.

On the other hand it is tempting to view Marre[67] and the Law Society's TFRG[68] as attempts by the profession to maintain control of territory which it had in reality already lost. Legal education was largely a sideshow in Marre, which was much more the profession's attempt to occupy the high ground in their fight with the government over professional monopolies and self-regulation. It largely affirmed the Ormrod 'settlement', stressed the importance of ethics and an ethos of public service and gave its imprimatur to a greater focus on skills at the academic and vocational stages. The Law Society's TFRG, however, sought to be genuinely radical, but by focusing heavily on 'Day One outcomes' and centralised assessment, while proposing to relax control over content and processes, it scared the more conservative members of the profession, alienated vocational training providers and still looked to academics like an attempt—perhaps even a last ditch attempt—to reassert professional control over education and training before the Clementi reforms fundamentally changed the rules of the game.[69] In fact what the failure of the TFRG demonstrated above all else was the extent of the fracturing and segmentation of interests between the Law Society, vocational providers and the profession.

These developments thus set the stage for the LETR. The stakes were inevitably high: it was yet another review, taking place in a complex and rapidly changing environment and in the shadow of a recent pantheon of failures—heroic and otherwise.[70] Whether or not the LETR is ultimately a game changer, let alone a success, remains to be seen, and it will be for a more neutral observer to judge whether it has, as intended, turned the dialogue between increasingly fragmented professions and the law schools into a new triadic conversation between legal educationalists, the professions and their regulators, or yet another cacophony of competing interests.

II. THE LETR REPORT: ASSUMPTIONS, PROCESSES, KEY MESSAGES AND RECOMMENDATIONS

Work on the first phase of the LETR, leading up to the publication of the LETR Report in June 2013, commenced in May 2011.

---

[67] Committee on the Future of the Legal Profession, 'A Time for Change. Report of the Committee on the Future of the Legal Profession' (Bar Council/Law Society, 1988) (Marre Report).

[68] See Boon and Webb, 'Legal Education and Training' (n 54) 102–05, 109–16.

[69] This appears to be a strategy the Law Society still wants to pursue in its response to the government's consultation on the review of legal services regulation, where it calls for training, authorisation to practise and standard setting to become the direct responsibility of the professional body—see Law Society, 'The Ministry of Justice's Call for Evidence on the Regulation of Legal Services in England and Wales: The Law Society Response' (Law Society, 2013) 1, available at: www.lawsociety.org.uk/representation/policy-discussion/regulation-of-legal-services.

[70] Compare Arthurs' description of ACLEC as deserving of a place of honour in a pantheon of 'brave—but unavailing—contributions to the cause of legal education', Arthurs, 'Half a League Onward' (n 66) 1.

A. Assumptions and Processes

This first phase was shaped around a number of baseline assumptions and processes. First, the review was to be fundamentally evidence based. The primary function of this phase was thus to inform the regulators as well as to make recommendations based on the evidence. A meta-analysis of existing research and literature was therefore undertaken, supported by a range of fresh empirical research that was agreed as part of the contract specification.[71] Second, there was a commitment on all sides that the review should progress in a way that was, so far as possible, transparent. A consultation and reporting structure was created,[72] website and communication protocols designed and (given the size of the research team) an ambitious plan of interim publications agreed.[73] Third, it was also accepted that the primary focus of the review was on the regulated legal services sector; although a review of the (limited) literature on unregulated legal services was undertaken, and some exploratory, primarily qualitative, work conducted, this was not sufficient to ground substantive recommendations. Fourth, it follows that the review was largely shaped by the LSA framework and 'ethos': this meant not only its regulatory and market liberalisation objectives, its focus on education and training as a regulatory tool and its concern with 'effectiveness'—the competence to deliver legal services,[74]— but also the risks and limitations that may flow from the principle of regulatory

---

[71] The empirical work was predominantly qualitative, comprising interviews and focus groups with key stakeholder and representative groups, individual practitioners, law teachers and students/trainees. Interviews and meetings were also held with representatives of all the Approved Regulators, the Legal Services Board and Legal Services Consumer Panel. There were also two substantial quantitative elements: a workforce projection study conducted by Professor Rob Wilson of Warwick Institute of Employment Research, and an online survey which was designed by the research team. The survey produced both quantitative data, analysed using SPSS, and qualitative comments. The latter were analysed as part of an NVivo database which also included the transcripts from interviews and focus groups, and the written responses received to LETR Discussion Papers. Taking questionnaire and focus group/interview participants together, the research analysed data from over 1600 individual respondents. Draft recommendations were shared with the Consultation Steering Panel and also tested with a group of 'thought leaders' in legal practice and academic and professional education.

[72] The project reported to a 'Review Executive' comprising senior executive officers of the BSB, IPS and SRA, supported by a small project management and liaison team from within the SRA Education and Training Department. An advisory 'Consultation Steering Panel', co-chaired by Janet Gaymer and Mark Potter and comprising representatives of the 'big three' regulators and in excess of 20 interest groups, was also established.

[73] In addition to the final Report, the research team produced a thematic review of the literature, four interim discussion papers, three briefing papers and two interim reports on the fieldwork ('Research Updates'). Two further briefing papers were produced by consultants Richard Susskind and Rob Wilson. All interim papers are archived on the LETR website at www.letr.org.uk/briefing-and-discussion-papers/index.html. The Literature Review is also archived at www.letr.org.uk/literature-review/index.html.

[74] See Legal Education and Training Review, 'Key Issues (1): Call for Evidence' LETR Discussion Paper 01/2012, paras 6–15, available at: www.letr.org.uk/wp-content/uploads/Discussion-Paper-012012.pdf.

competition and the complex network of multiple regulators and representative bodies that has emerged post-Clementi.

The research team came to adopt the term 'legal services education and training' (LSET) to describe the Report's specific focus and as a means of distinguishing it from other aspects of academic and public legal education. As a label, it was felt that LSET had value both in acknowledging the (somewhat) distinct discursive spaces of liberal and public legal education, and in drawing attention to the fact that 'professional' legal education is not just a stage but an ethos of learning geared towards 'the delivery of legal services'.[75]

B. Key Messages and Recommendations

The headline conclusions of the LETR Report can be summarised quite briefly. While the Report found no clear or systematic evidence that the LSET system was not 'fit for purpose', it highlighted the need both to build on existing strengths and address key weaknesses for the future. The Report specifically identified a range of enhancements to the quality, flexibility and accessibility of LSET itself, and to the principles of regulatory design and development that will shape it in the future.

i. Quality

The Report found that not enough had been done to assure quality and competence across the sector. It therefore called for the development or reformulation of 'day one' learning outcomes for prescribed qualification routes into the regulated sector, based on a common threshold level of competence.[76] These it argued would form the basis of a more consistent, robust and flexible system. Further, the Report highlighted a number of broad knowledge and skills gaps and recommended strengthening requirements for education and training in legal ethics, values and professionalism at all stages in training,[77] though it stopped short of recommending that legal ethics itself become a foundation subject for the academic stage. It called for more targeted assessment of legal research and writing skills on the LLB and Graduate Diploma in Law (GDL),[78] and stressed the need to ensure that the development of management skills, and equality and diversity

---

[75] Legal Education and Training Review, 'Setting Standards' (n 6) para 1.11.
[76] Legal Education and Training Review, 'Setting Standards' (n 6) ch 7, Recommendations 1 and 3.
[77] ibid, Recommendations 6–7.
[78] ibid, Recommendation 11.

awareness training, were undertaken at appropriate career points.[79] It also identified a lack of reliable standardised assessment, particularly at the vocational stage, as a further weakness of the system.[80]

A distinctive feature of the LETR, when compared with Ormrod or ACLEC, has been the attention paid to CPD. There was widespread agreement in the research phase that something had to be done about CPD and, as noted, the Bar Standards Board (BSB), SRA and ILEX Professional Standards (IPS) had already taken steps to research, review and/or reform their CPD systems. The LETR therefore built substantially on that work. It can be argued that there has been a relative imbalance in regulation, so that the regulator has tended to duplicate existing quality assurance functions at the academic stage, while doing very little to assure continuing competence post-qualification. The LETR Report therefore called for the introduction of systems of continuing professional development that require practitioners more actively to plan and demonstrate the value of continuing learning,[81] and strongly emphasised the importance of (developmental) monitoring at an appropriate level, backed up by regulatory audit.[82]

The Report was also generally critical of widespread research and information gaps which threatened the ability of providers to make informed decisions about what worked, and of regulators to undertake coherent evidence-based policymaking in respect of LSET.[83] It highlighted, overall, the historic lack of coordination between regulators in setting and assuring standards.[84] Last, in the only recommendation delivered specifically to the LSB, the Report also called on the Board to work with paralegal representative bodies in exploring the development of a voluntary quality assurance scheme for independent paralegals working outside the regulated sector.[85] This was seen by the research team as a means of 'bootstrapping' quality enhancement in the unregulated sector.

ii. Flexibility

An important criticism emerging from the research concerned the relative inflexibility of the LSET system. Greater flexibility was required, not

---

[79] ibid, Recommendation 9.

[80] ibid, Recommendation 2.

[81] At the time of the Report only the Chartered Institute of Legal Executives (CILEx) had instituted this kind of cyclical/developmental CPD framework, though they are widespread in other professional settings—see Legal Education and Training Review, 'Setting Standards' (n 6) paras 6.80–6.90 and Literature Review, ch 5.

[82] Legal Education and Training Review, 'Setting Standards' (n 6) paras 5.180, 6.94–6.95 and ch 7, Recommendations 17–19.

[83] See ibid, paras 3.61, 3.107, 3.126–3.127, 4.54, 5.23, 5.63, 5.73, 5.117, 6.20–6.24 and 6.59.

[84] ibid, paras 2.116–2.124, 4.111, 4.119–4.121 and ch 7, Recommendations 4 and 5.

[85] ibid, Recommendation 23.

as an end in itself, but primarily as a means to enable competition and innovation, increase responsiveness to change and enhance access and diversity. The Report recognised that the larger regulators had taken some steps to reduce bureaucracy and permit some innovative training variations, and it strongly supported continued work on merged LPC/training contracts and work-based learning approaches.[86] These were seen as positive disruptions to the education and training market, but change to the system could not continue to be driven by a system of exceptions; regulatory space was needed for innovation to become the norm. The two major planks in the LETR's 'flexibilisation' strategy were the recommended move to outcomes, to reduce the regulatory burden and create space for developing innovative learning processes and the proposal to remove minimum or normal periods of 'time served' under supervised practice and replace them with an expectation of evaluation against outcomes.[87] Other recommendations focused on adapting elements of the existing training regime: relaxing the expectation that the seven 'Foundations' at the academic stage should be equally weighted;[88] enabling greater specialisation and reducing the breadth of LPC coverage[89] and, as noted, encouraging further experimentation with 'blended' classroom and workplace training.

iii. Accessibility

Third, in looking at accessibility, the research identified a range of evidence demonstrating that, despite the massification of higher education, access to the traditional legal professions was becoming more socially exclusive and elitist. Increased training costs, selection biases and growing reliance on unpaid internships all acted as forms of attrition against under-represented groups in the professions.[90] The research also highlighted the risk of negative equality and diversity effects in restricting transfer and mobility between the smaller and larger professions, and between paralegals and the regulated occupations. The Report acknowledged that such access barriers are often deeply structural and difficult to address 'head-on'. It therefore focused more on seeking to ameliorate their effects at particular pinch points.

The Report therefore highlighted the need to develop a single source of high quality and accessible information on the range of legal careers and the realities of the legal services job market.[91] This sought to address

---

[86] ibid, Recommendation 12.
[87] ibid, Recommendation 15.
[88] ibid, Recommendation 10.
[89] ibid, Recommendation 12.
[90] ibid, paras 6.11–6.15, 6.25–6.34.
[91] ibid, ch 7, Recommendation 25.

widespread concerns about the absence or relative invisibility of current information. It also recommended that regulators establish professional standards and guidance for internships and work experience;[92] create more flexible access and transfer points into and between professional pathways/titles[93] and support the development of higher legal apprenticeships as a non-graduate pathway into the regulated sector.[94] The report also called for better internal quality assurance (ie, within regulated entities) and audit regarding supervision, training and development of paralegals.[95]

C. Regulatory Reform

The significance and complexity of the regulatory environment has been underplayed in previous reviews which have tended thereby to decontextualise legal education from much of its regulation. Ultimately, however, that environment needs to be taken seriously, particularly as the LSA has served to make it even more complex. It matters both for technical reasons (trying to get regulation 'right'), and because setting the regulatory infrastructure and architecture is also a critical political decision. As Winner explains:

> Because choices tend to become strongly fixed in material equipment, economic investment, and social habit, the original flexibility vanishes for all practical purposes after the initial commitments are made ... For that reason the same careful attention one would give to the rules, roles, and relationships of politics must also be given to such things as the building of highways, the creation of television networks, and the tailoring of seemingly insignificant features on new machines.[96]

In seeking to address this challenge, the research team, following Christine Parker and others, advanced a case for 'meta' or 'multi-modal' regulation,[97] which it contrasted with the heavy emphasis on content specification and the regulation of processes that has dominated LSET regulation to date.

Meta-regulation describes the idea that: [A]ll social and economic spheres in which governments or others might have an interest in controlling already have within them mechanisms of steering—whether through

---

[92] ibid, Recommendation 20.
[93] ibid, paras 5.74–5.81; see also Recommendations 1–5.
[94] ibid, Recommendation 21.
[95] ibid, Recommendation 22.
[96] L Winner, *The Whale and the Reactor: A Search for Limits in an Age of High Technology* (Chicago, University of Chicago Press, 1986) 29.
[97] Legal Education and Training Review, 'Setting Standards' (n 6) Literature Review, ch 3, paras 39–55; see C Parker, *The Open Corporation* (Cambridge, Cambridge University Press, 2002); J Braithwaite, 'Meta Risk Management and Responsive Regulation for Tax System Integrity' (2003) 25 *Law & Policy* 1; C Scott, 'Regulating Everything' (2008) UCD Geary Institute Discussion Paper Series WP/24/2008, available at: www.ucd.ie/geary/static/publications/workingpapers/gearywp200824.pdf.

hierarchy, competition, community, design or some combination thereof'.[98] Such a multi-modal approach requires a regulator to adopt more of an oversight and incentivising role, devolving day to day regulatory functions to the regulated community, so that it becomes the regulator's job to 'steer rather than row'.[99] It requires the regulator to have a varied toolbox, moving beyond conventional 'command and control' (hierarchical) and 'market' (competition) regulation by emphasising the importance of 'community' and 'design'. Community here is not intended to signal a return to self-regulation, but it does recognise the importance of deliberative regulatory procedures and stakeholder engagement. 'Design' is also sometimes used narrowly to focus on architectural and technological approaches to regulation, for example, the use of automatic barriers to control platform access at a railway station, traffic management measures, or hardcoding content filters into search engine technology.[100] However, design can be (and in the LETR is) understood more generally to encompass the design and installation of what might be called the 'infrastructural conditions' for LSET: getting the organisational structures, tools, technologies and people in place to enable the system to work in the manner intended.

In adopting a multi-modal approach, the LETR Report thus endorsed some features of 'command and control' and marketisation as a way of introducing flexibility[101] and controlling cost and quality, but it was wary of using either as a primary regulatory tool, even in the context of a vocational training environment that is already heavily privatised. A critical, continuing, design risk of the LSET system, particularly if the current multiple regulator structure is retained, is that it may operate as a set of silos within silos. That is, each regulator largely designs and delivers its own system of training, with limited regard to other (sub-)systems across the sector; this silo tendency may then be exacerbated within each system if course providers in turn deliver silo-based programmes of study, with limited engagement with other parts of the system. Such an environment is potentially problematic:

— It benefits providers at the expense of other stakeholders—notably students and the general public who directly or indirectly pay for the cost of training.

---

[98] Scott, 'Regulating Everything' (n 97) 27.

[99] R Baldwin, M Cave and M Lodge, *Understanding Regulation*, 2nd edn (Oxford, Oxford University Press, 2012) 147.

[100] K Yeung, 'Towards an Understanding of Regulation by Design' in R Brownsword and K Yeung (eds), *Regulating Technologies: Legal Futures, Regulatory Frames and Technological Fixes* (Oxford, Hart Publishing, 2008) 79.

[101] Thus: '[t]here should be a presumption that new, flexible approaches should be encouraged and that the burden should be on the regulator, adopting a risk-based approach, to identify why a pathway should not be permitted'—Legal Education and Training Review, 'Setting Standards' (n 6) para 7.71.

— It encourages providers to treat their learning tools and resources as proprietary private goods. This is inefficient and discourages cost spreading through resource sharing, and the harnessing of open educational resources.

— It risks creating systems of regulation that are unduly complex, expensive to administer and enforce, prone to regulatory capture, and which potentially encourage the regulated community to focus on minimum standards rather than quality enhancement.[102]

— A culture of top-down control reduces the responsibility of providers and teachers for developing their own educational practice and professionalism. Regulation can, in effect, infantilise those being regulated, so that the attainment of a short-term regulatory achievement (a course rated 'excellent', rather than 'satisfactory') becomes an end in itself.[103]

Additionally (on the basis that it has the above effects) silo-based regulation is unlikely to support the regulators themselves in delivering an LSET system that operates in the public or consumer interests nor in maintaining an independent, effective and diverse legal profession. Specifically, given the complexity of the LSA regulatory settlement, the Report was sceptical of the ability (and possibly the will) of the range of approved regulators to coordinate information needs, deliver reliable, clear and accessible information and support the research and educational evaluation that will be necessary to develop LSET into the future.

A primary aim of the LETR Report was thus not to engineer new regulations or get buried in the detail, but to focus on creating for the longer term a 'set of structures and relationships which will work to deal with difficulties in the system in a much more co-operative, co-regulatory way'.[104] This strategy was reflected in three key strands in the Report. First, the adoption of outcomes itself was seen as critical to opening up the regulatory system to innovation while reducing complexity and the culture of compliance. Second, the move to outcomes, the review of learning pathways and transfer arrangements between occupations and the flexibilisation of CPD regimes would also reduce the silo tendencies latent within the existing LSET system. Third, the Report asserted that a key function of regulation

---

[102] See Baldwin, Cave, and Lodge, *Understanding Regulation* (n 99) 134.

[103] As Richard de Friend has observed, this was the case with the Bar Vocational Course. Despite the fact that 'over the last ten years the BVC has been subject to almost constant external scrutiny', it was still extensively criticised by the 2008 Wood Report for the BSB: see R de Friend, 'The Wood Review: Tough Love for the BVC' *The Barrister* (London, undated) 32, available at: www.barristermagazine.com/archive-articles/issue-44/the-wood-review-tough-love-for-the-bvc.html. It is interesting also to speculate whether the disappointing level of institutional responses from vocational providers to the LETR research phase was strategic, or simply indicative of a community of training providers that has got used to being told what to do, rather than proactively seeking to influence the direction of travel.

[104] Legal Education and Training Review, 'Setting Standards' (n 6) para 7.5

should also be to create a 'shared space' for legal education.[105] This was used as shorthand for community building, norm strengthening and culture transforming practices. It thereby sought to recognise that governance requires a space for 'negotiated moral communities and common pool resources'[106] as well as the market. To further this end the Report proposed the creation of a collaborative 'hub' overseen by a new Legal Education Council.[107] This would particularly assist the regulators, and the sector at large, in gathering and disseminating information on LSET (for example, diversity and careers data), conducting and evaluating research, disseminating effective practice, and engaging in 'regulatory conversations'[108] about LSET. Such initiatives, it was argued, have the potential not just to make regulation more of a shared activity, but to increase trust in and thence legitimacy of the regulators.[109] The fate of this and the other LETR recommendations now falls to be considered.

III. 'THE NEXT DAY: WHERE ARE WE NOW?'[110]

The LETR Report was published to a mixed reception; broadly welcomed by the LSB and its commissioning regulators, initial responses from elsewhere, particularly from the trade press were muted—or as legal market commentator and journalist Neil Rose put it, a 'collective meh'.[111] As an assessment that is not entirely unfair. The challenge for both the research team and the regulators was that the exercise largely confirmed what sensible commentators would have already suspected: across the sector there was neither strong stakeholder support for change, nor much agreement about the direction of change, and the existing research base was too weak by itself for an evidence-based report to ground a case for radical root and branch reform. As Richard Moorhead observed, the Report essentially tells us that:

> We do not know anywhere near enough and the system is so complex that it requires a concerted process of engagement and leadership to move things forward. Top down imposition of Grand Plans, if you like, works as well in the legal education and training system as it does in the National Health Service ... The

---

[105] ibid, para 6.158.
[106] G Room, *Complexity, Institutions and Public Policy* (Cheltenham, Edward Elgar Publishing, 2011) 243.
[107] Legal Education and Training Review, 'Setting Standards' (n 6) ch 7, Recommendation 25.
[108] J Black, 'Regulatory Conversations' (2002) 29 *Journal of Law and Society* 163.
[109] See further, Legal Education and Training Review, 'Setting Standards' (n 6) Literature Review, ch 3.
[110] With due acknowledgments to David Bowie and Richard Young.
[111] N Rose, 'Resolving the Impasse' *Legal Futures* (28 June 2013), available at: www.legalfutures.co.uk/blog/resolving-impasse.

research stands as an astute reminder that this is the reality: implementation is everything. This will require resources (knowledge, skills, bodies, money) and it will need mechanisms for change.[112]

At the same time, it is arguable that the full potential of changes such as the move to outcomes and removing the 'time-served' element of professional qualification may not have been fully understood by some commentators, and some quite radical proposals—the restructuring of CPD, development of non-graduate pathways and work on a licensed paralegal scheme—also appear underplayed.

Early concerns were expressed about the ability and willingness of the regulators both to collaborate and hold the line on the key changes proposed by the Report.[113] Interestingly, the LSB also had concerns that the frontline regulators might proceed down radically different paths, and so, in September 2013, the Board announced its intention to issue statutory guidance[114] to the regulators to ensure they adopted a sufficiently flexible approach to legal education and training. Despite objections from most of the regulatory and representative bodies, the Board's final guidance was published in March 2014.[115] Although largely consistent with the Report's direction of travel, the LSB guidelines do go further than the LETR in requiring the regulators to consider the case for formal re-accreditation of practitioners on the basis of risk.[116] The LETR Report did not irrevocably dismiss this option, but it was unconvinced that the case for compulsory re-accreditation could be made out at this time, given the marked lack of evidence as to its effectiveness in a field like law, and without having first attempted substantial reform of the CPD scheme. Since the Report's position on re-accreditation was endorsed by the commissioning regulators, it will be interesting to see how they respond to the LSB's guidance in this, and possibly other, respects. In the interim, the SRA and BSB responses to the LETR—and to their critics—began to take shape.[117] Both had, in

---

[112] R Moorhead, 'LETR: Why Everyone is Happy and No-One is Smiling' *Lawyer Watch* (26 June 2013), available at: www.lawyerwatch.wordpress.com/2013/06/26/letr-why-every-one-is-happy-and-no-one-is-smiling.

[113] ibid; D Bindman, 'Regulators Accused of Failing to Collaborate over LETR Responses' *Legal Futures* (10 October 2013), available at: www.legalfutures.co.uk/latest-news/regulators-accused-failing-collaborate-letr-responses.

[114] Under powers in the Legal Services Act 2007, s 162.

[115] Legal Services Board, 'Guidance on Regulatory Arrangements for Legal Education and Training Issued Under Section 162 of the Legal Services Act 2007' (LSB, 4 March 2014), available at: www.legalservicesboard.org.uk/what_we_do/regulation/pdf/20140304_LSB_Education_And_Training_Guidance.pdf. Para 10 sets five headline objectives: the need to move to outcomes at the point of authorisation; to give providers flexibility in determining how to meet the outcomes; to balance both initial and continuing, and individual and entity obligations; and to place no inappropriate restrictions on the numbers entering the profession.

[116] ibid, Outcome 3(g).

[117] IPS has yet to make any formal announcement in terms of its plans. In some respects IPS and CILEx face a rather different problem from the SRA and BSB, in that much of their work

October 2013, published their broad plans for LETR implementation. The BSB identified six core work programmes.[118] Four of these directly reflect key LETR priorities: (i) developing a competency framework for the Bar; (ii) adopting an outcomes-focused approach to CPD; (iii) improving access routes to the Bar; and (iv) sharing data to support the 'regulatory objectives in education and training'. Two others are perhaps more incidental, committing the BSB to (i) working collaboratively with the SRA to revise Academic Stage regulation and more generally (ii) 'aligning the Bar Training Regulations to modern regulatory standards'.[119] At this stage there is still very little public detail as to what these programmes will actually involve 'on the ground'.

The SRA has similarly committed itself to developing a competency framework based on 'day one' outcomes, and an outcomes-focused CPD scheme.[120] Its 'Training for Tomorrow' programme also promises 'an end to the historic "one size fits all" approach to the solicitors' qualification' with opportunities for tailored qualification pathways, a more flexible approach to assessing and demonstrating competence, and a more general 'bonfire of regulations' as the Authority reviews the full range of its education and training regulations. Training for Tomorrow also makes a particular point of focusing on the need for robust assessment of competences.

Work has already begun on three areas of activity relating to the academic stage, the devising of a competence framework, and the reform of CPD.

A. Changes to Regulation at the Academic Stage

As an initial move in reducing regulatory duplication, the regulators have abolished the Joint Academic Stage Board (JASB), through which they have quality-assured the qualifying law degree (QLD) and graduate conversion courses (CPE/GDL), and replaced it with an obligation on providers to self-certify their compliance with the Joint Statement and Quality Assurance Agency for Higher Education (QAA) standards and quality

---

was judged to be travelling in the direction that the Review was taking, particularly regarding work-based learning, the development of cyclical CPD requirements and widening access, including work on developing apprenticeships. Nonetheless, this also leaves a number of substantial questions unanswered, notably regarding the ability of IPS to move to a (harmonised) fully competence-based training framework, the implications of that for the CILEx assessment model, its plans for data sharing, etc.

[118] Bar Standards Board, 'Education Strategy Framework' (BSB, 2013), available at: www.barstandardsboard.org.uk/regulatory-requirements/changes-to-regulation/legal-education-and-training-review/education-strategy-framework.

[119] ibid.

[120] Solicitors Regulation Authority, 'Policy Statement: Training for Tomorrow' (SRA, 2013), available at: www.sra.org.uk/sra/policy/training-for-tomorrow/resources/policy-statement.page.

assurance requirements. No decision has as yet been made regarding the future of the Joint Statement itself, and the SRA's latest draft Training Regulations (2014)[121] continue to make reference to the Statement, so that it is likely to remain in place in its current form, at least for the time being.

In this context there is also uncertainty as to the future role of the QAA benchmark statement,[122] and whether this is likely to take on a larger part in regulating law degrees post-JASB. A number of concerns were expressed in the LETR Report regarding inconsistencies of language and scope between the Joint Statement and the QAA benchmark statement,[123] and, again, it is not yet apparent whether, and if so, how these will be addressed. It is understood that the QAA is looking again at the benchmark. This seems both necessary and desirable. The current benchmark has been in place since 2000, with only a very minor amendment in 2006; in some respects it may benefit from updating. It is questionable, for example, whether, in the wake of the LETR, it places sufficient emphasis on legal values, law in context, student self-management, including reflection and resilience,[124] and a broader and more up to date range of IT skills. Moreover, by contrast with a number of the other subject benchmarks the law statement is dry, technical and minimalist in its approach, as the UK Centre for Legal Education (UKCLE) observed at the time of the last revision:

> There is no attempt made to place the study of law within its context or to convey to intending students, employers or other interested parties what is distinctive and intellectually exciting about the discipline of law. This is a pity since benchmarks are public documents, intended to be of interest to a range of audiences as well as a tool for law schools. It is important that as such the significance of law as a topic of academic study is adequately conveyed.[125]

It must also be recognised that any review of the benchmark is taking place in a context where there is still very little collective ownership of the

---

[121] See Solicitors Regulation Authority, 'Training for Tomorrow: Regulation Review' (SRA, 2013), available at: www.sra.org.uk/sra/consultations/education-training-regulations.page. Consultation closed, 25 February 2014.

[122] The text of the current (2007) benchmark is available from the QAA website at: www.qaa.ac.uk/en/Publications/Documents/Subject-benchmark-statement-law.pdf.

[123] Legal Education and Training Review, 'Setting Standards' (n 6) paras 4.100–4.103 and ch 4, Annex III.

[124] ibid, paras 4.83–4.90. cp in this regard the Australian threshold learning outcomes for law degrees: S Kift, M Israel and R Field, *Bachelor of Laws: Learning and Teaching Academic Standards Statement* (Strawberry Hills NSW, Australian Learning and Teaching Council, 2010), available at: www.cald.asn.au/assets/lists/Education/KiftetalLTASStandardsStatement2010%20TLOs%20LLB.pdf. See also A Huggins, 'The Threshold Learning Outcome on Self-Management for the Bachelor of Laws Degree: A Proposed Focus for Teaching Strategies in the First Year Law Curriculum' (2011) 2 *The International Journal of the First Year in Higher Education* 232, on the links between values, ethics and self-management.

[125] UK Centre for Legal Education, 'Revised Law Subject Benchmark Statement: UKCLE Response' (UKCLE, 2006), available at: www.ukcle.ac.uk/about/reports/qa.

standard, or knowledge or understanding across the discipline of how the statement has actually been used. For this reason, as well as on grounds of legitimacy, it is to be hoped that there may be greater user engagement and community building than in the previous drafting exercises.[126]

Last, the SRA has been the first of the frontline regulators to move on amending its regulations to permit prospective trainees to satisfy the academic stage without necessarily completing a QLD or CPE/GDL. A new regulation 2.2 has been proposed that would allow for the completion of the academic stage 'by equivalent means'.[127] This would finally provide the SRA with a regulatory basis for assessing individuals from within the EU who seek to qualify under the 'Morgenbesser' principle,[128] but potentially goes far wider than that in permitting the SRA to assess individuals (whether graduates or not) from within the United Kingdom or any jurisdiction against formal criteria to establish whether they satisfy equivalent outcomes to the academic stage.

B. Common Competences

The development of a common competence framework is a cornerstone of the LETR. Any substantive change to the vocational courses or the Joint Statement has to be contingent on the work done to specify 'day one' outcomes. The SRA and BSB are currently collaborating on this project. The framework is being derived from cross-professional work on competences already undertaken by Stan Lester.[129] The form of the proposed statement

---

[126] John Bell notes that the original benchmark drafting exercise was hampered by legal academics' limited familiarity with outcomes approaches at that time, and by a process which did not allow for the need to educate or build ownership of standards in the community: J Bell, 'Benchmarking in Law' in H Smith, M Armstrong, and S Brown (eds), *Benchmarking and Threshold Standards in Higher Education* (London, Kogan Page, 1999) 154. Compare this with the iterative consultation process adopted in drafting the threshold learning outcomes (TLOs) for Australian law schools, where the project involved collaboration and input from the judiciary, legal profession, regulators, academics, students and recent graduates, and was supported by an international advisory group. See Kift, Israel and Field, *Bachelor of Laws* (n 124) 1.

[127] See Solicitors Regulation Authority, 'Training for Tomorrow' (n 121).

[128] Case C-313/01 *Morgenbesser v Consiglio dell'Ordine degli avvocati di Genova* [2003] ECR I-13467. This requires the competent authority in a host state to examine on a case by case basis whether and to what extent the learning and skills certified by the diploma, qualifications and/or professional experience obtained by an EU citizen in another Member State, may satisfy, even in part, the conditions necessary for access to a professional title/activity.

[129] See S Lester, 'Professional Competence Standards and Frameworks in the United Kingdom' (2014) 39 *Assessment & Evaluation in Higher Education* 38. The methodology adopted for developing the competences appears to be a kind of Delphi technique: using an expert panel and wider group of stakeholders to draft and refine competences before submitting the framework to further qualitative and, possibly, quantitative testing. How this methodology will ensure that input is obtained across a range of practice settings and experience levels

follows most UK professional competence frameworks in adopting what Lester calls an 'activity-based approach', focusing on outputs and standards of action rather than identifying the knowledge, skills and attributes required of the individual practitioner (an 'individual' or 'internal' approach). Although most UK competence frameworks adopt the former, law has tended in the past to take an internal approach,[130] so this suggests, at least, that a culture change is on the way for the sector.

Does it matter? While the LETR Report recommendations focus on 'knowledge, skills and attributes', the Report did not expressly take a position on whether an activity-based or internal approach should be adopted. Both have their strengths and weaknesses. The latter tends to be programme/learner centred, and is useful where actual application cannot be readily assessed. As noted in the LETR Report, the internal approach may also be better at identifying and assessing future capability than the activity-based approach, and it arguably places greater explicit emphasis on the underlying moral understanding and affective capacities relevant to ethical action.[131] On the other hand, Lester argues that '[i]ts usefulness for judging ability to practise is more limited, as it does not indicate whether the person is able to draw together the various attributes and use them intelligently to produce competent performance'.[132]

By contrast, the activity-based approach has been developed to assess workplace competence, and in that regard may offer a more logical fit to a set of 'day one' outcomes. The approach, particularly in its original 'NVQ' form[133] has been heavily criticised for its rigidity, 'checklist' behaviourist approach, and limited capacity to reflect the complexities of professional performance.[134] Much of that criticism is quite dated, and modern UK

(so as to ensure input from in-house lawyers and new practitioners, for example) and whether a consumer perspective will be sought has not yet been made public.

[130] See, eg, the SRA's current 'day one' outcomes which were developed out of the Training Framework Review and are currently adopted by the Qualified Lawyers Transfer Scheme: www.sra.org.uk/solicitors/qlts/day-one-outcomes-table.page. See similarly the PEAT1 and 2 outcomes in Scotland: www.lawscot.org.uk/media/561669/peat%201%20guidelines.pdf.

[131] Legal Education and Training Review, 'Setting Standards' (n 6) para 4.46.

[132] Lester, 'Professional Competence Standards' (n 129) 40. This seems contestable, however, from the use of 'internal' outcomes in a sophisticated assessment environment like the QLTS where a range of outcomes can be assessed in a realistic and contextualised setting: see E Fry, J Crewe and R Wakeford, 'The Qualified Lawyers Transfer Scheme: Innovative Assessment Methodology and Practice in a High Stakes Professional Exam' (2012) 46 *The Law Teacher* 132; P Maharg, M Gill and J Rawstorne, 'Qualified Lawyer Transfer Scheme (QLTS): Client-Centred Assessment of Qualified Lawyers' (Learning in Law Conference, Coventry, January 2011), available at: www.ukcle.ac.uk/resources/assessment-and-feedback/maharg-2.

[133] Ie, 'National Vocational Qualifications', a set of technical competence-based awards that were first developed in the 1980s and were the predecessors of the current National Occupational Standards (NOS).

[134] R Barnett, *The Limits of Competence: Knowledge, Higher Education and Society* (Buckingham, SRHE/Open University Press, 1994); M Eraut, *Developing Professional*

competence schemes have evolved to become more sophisticated in their ability to reflect complex areas of work, including those that place a premium on professional judgement and ethical behaviours.[135] The overall approach to the competences has been discussed at a number of 'road-shows' organised by the SRA.[136] A view has emerged from these events— rightly it is submitted—that finding the right balance requires both further research and a commitment to continuing dialogue between the SRA, practitioners and educators.

The SRA is developing its assessment framework in tandem with work on the competence statement, using broadly the same methodologies. It follows that it will be outcomes based, focused on what practitioners need to be able to do. The SRA plans to have its competence and assessment framework completed in 2016, though signs are that the BSB is not wedded to that timeline. It is to be hoped that the SRA and BSB will ensure that their timetable allows for substantial and meaningful consultation on the drafts.

C. Continuing Competence and CPD

The other main area of work for the regulators so far has been in relation to CPD. As noted above, by the time the Report was published the commissioning regulators had already undertaken a considerable amount of work on CPD, most of it pointing away from the retention of traditional hours-based CPD schemes.

A revised BSB scheme is expected to go out to consultation later this year, with a view to piloting in 2015 and full implementation in January 2016. In the interim the BSB has amended its monitoring processes so that practitioners are currently not required to make an annual CPD return, but are subject to randomised 'spot checks'. Annual CPD records are required to be kept for this purpose for two years only. It is tempting to see this as sending out the wrong message, by prioritising the basic policing function over any longer-term interest in the developmental role of CPD.[137] Whether this will change at all with any new scheme is moot.

Knowledge and Competence (London, Routledge Falmer, 1994) chs 9–10. In the legal education context, see also C Maughan, M Maughan and J Webb, 'Sharpening the Mind or Narrowing It? The Limitations of Outcome and Performance Measures in Legal Education' (1995) 29 *The Law Teacher* 255.

[135] See Lester, 'Professional Competence Standards' (n 129) 51; A Wolf, 'Competence-Based Assessment' in J Raven and J Stephenson (eds), *Competence in the Learning Society* (New York, Peter Lang Publishing Inc, 2001).

[136] See summaries available on the Solicitors Regulation Authority 'T4T Blog' at: www.sra. org.uk/sra/policy/training-for-tomorrow/tomorrow.page.

[137] The point being that CPD arguably ought to form part of a three to five-year personal development planning cycle, rather than be treated as an annual fix.

The SRA is currently consulting over its own proposals for a revised CPD scheme.[138] It acknowledges the criticism, made in the LETR Report, that the current regime can degenerate into a 'tick box' exercise with little attention to the quality or developmental benefit of the training undertaken.[139] It is therefore consulting on three variant models. These are: (i) a 'competence-based' approach which removes all existing CPD training obligations and enforces CPD through existing (conduct of business) regulation which obliges entities and individuals to deliver competent services, and to train and supervise their staff. This would be supported by non-mandatory guidance to assist practitioners in reflecting on current practice, identifying training needs, and undertaking relevant activities. (ii) Option two also moves CPD onto an outputs-based system, but uses regulations to require practitioners to evidence their planning and recording of CPD activity, but with recording and monitoring conducted at the entity level, rather than requiring individual reports to the SRA. (iii) The final option retains in large part the present inputs-led and hours-based system with some modifications, namely, requiring practitioners to demonstrate that CPD activities relate to their current or anticipated area of practice, and extending the range of activities to count, including recognition of 'on the job' learning.

While (i) and (ii) both move the SRA closer to a flexible system capable of taking continuing competence more seriously, it is notable that option two is the approach most consistent with the LETR recommendations, and probably the less high risk for the regulator, whereas the SRA has indicated its preference for option one. The inclusion of option (iii) seems something of a hostage to fortune, particularly in the light of the LSB's statutory guidance and a critical response from the Legal Services Consumer Panel, which describes option (iii) as seeking to 'continue a discredited model that is out of step with good practice'.[140]

The consultation does not discuss how these obligations might operate in terms of lawyer discipline and the scale of sanctions for breach—whether by entities or individuals. Historically, the disciplinary approach

---

[138] Solicitors Regulation Authority, 'Training for Tomorrow—A New Approach to Continuing Competence' (Consultation Closed, SRA 2014), available at: www.sra.org.uk/sra/consultations/t4t-continuing-competence.page.

[139] Legal Education and Training Review, 'Setting Standards' (n 6) paras 2.152, 2.159–2.163. See also J Ching, 'Solicitors' CPD: Time to Change from Regulatory Stick to Regulatory Carrot?' (2011) *Web Journal of Current Legal Issues*, available at: irep.ntu.ac.uk/R/?func=dbin-jump-full&object_id=205940&local_base=GEN01.

[140] Legal Services Consumer Panel, 'Consultation Response: SRA: Training for Tomorrow—A New Approach to Continuing Competence' (Legal Services Consumer Panel, 2014) para 32, available at: www.legalservicesconsumerpanel.org.uk/publications/consultation_responses/index.html. The Consumer Panel also favours option two. It considers option one a step too far at this stage in the development of CPD, in that (among other things) it underplays the need for individual accountability, and raises concerns as to how (readily) the SRA might identify poor quality work such as to trigger monitoring or enforcement action.

has been quite lenient, treating the breach of CPD requirements essentially as an administrative matter, to be admonished or dealt with by a small fine. Does this accord with an approach that seeks to link CPD far more closely to the core professional duties of maintaining a competent workforce? Is it consistent with the underlying ethos of the LETR which was to develop the use of training as a regulatory tool to enhance quality and standards? At the very least, the SRA needs to be wary of sending out mixed messages.

D. And the Rest?

If the regulators are clearly moving on some of the 'big issues', the extent to which we are likely to see progress across the range of LETR recommendations remains unclear; to that extent the LETR is still very much 'in the post' and unlikely to be delivered for some time. If, as the resurrection of the SRA's CPD option (iii) suggests, the regulators are willing to dust off and debate options which the LETR Report had already rejected, then the LETR isn't just in the post, it is still being (re-)written.

In terms of other developments, a number of points are worth making, regarding ethics and professionalism, the reform of vocational stage training and workplace learning more generally, apprenticeships and the complex access and diversity agenda.

The LSA regulatory objectives highlight the constitutionally and ethically distinctive contribution of regulated legal services providers to society. The research team accordingly committed to putting ethics and professionalism at the heart of the review, by strengthening requirements for education and training in legal ethics, values and professionalism throughout the continuum of education and training. It is not yet clear whether this message has been understood by the regulators, and a clearer statement of their intentions in this regard would be helpful.

Anecdotally, it appears that a number of law schools are already looking at their approach to legal values and ethics, and some are moving ahead with introducing an element of professional legal ethics at the academic stage, even though that is not a 'LETR requirement' as such. Enhancements in this area at the vocational stage were left largely undefined by the Report, though it did comment positively on the steps taken to make professionalism more central and pervasive in the Scottish PEAT1 programme; there appears to have been little debate about what this might look like in England and Wales. The Report's suggestion that ethics and professionalism should be a core CPD requirement did not form part of the SRA's recent 'continuing competence' consultation, which focused purely on the larger design and monitoring questions. Ethics is already a constituent part of the BSB's New Practitioner Programme; hopefully the Board's intentions regarding established practitioners will also become apparent in its forthcoming consultation.

The Report said relatively little at the level of detail about changes to the vocational stage for solicitors and barristers. To an extent, that was necessitated by the overriding intention to move to a reformulated set of 'day one' outcomes. The contents of the vocational stage need to be reverse engineered from those outcomes, so it would have been illogical and unhelpful of the LETR to put that particular cart before the horse. The key issue for the vocational stage, however, is 'flexibilisation'. Flexibility is seen as a way of reducing the cost and possibly duration of training, enhancing access and narrowing the gap between classroom and workplace. The SRA has already shown its willingness to permit experimentation and adaptation of the LPC–training contract continuum, so further developments may already be possible ahead of regulatory reform; change will be more difficult for the BSB in the context of a Bar Professional Training Course that is in many respects so standardised that it offers limited opportunities for structural experimentation. However, substantial change, which must flow from a move to an outcomes-led system, is going to require deregulation in terms of both a reduction in structural constraints on the form and duration of courses and, ultimately, the removal of time-served requirements for qualification. The latter is clearly anticipated by the LSB's statutory guidance, but we are not there yet.

The development of apprenticeships has not really been a regulatory problem so far, as schemes have managed to map onto existing qualification pathways. Level three advanced and level four higher[141] apprenticeships in legal services were launched in 2013, with CILEx as the lead awarding body. A conveyancing apprenticeship approved by the Council of Licensed Conveyancers also launched this year. A second phase of higher level apprenticeships was announced in March 2014 as part of the government's new 'Trailblazer' initiative.[142] These are likely to be more challenging in qualification terms, as they would enable apprentices to qualify as solicitors through a work-based learning pathway. The standards for the new apprenticeship qualifications ('Apprentice Trainee Solicitor' and 'Apprentice Trainee Lawyer') are currently being devised by an employer-led consortium of national law firms, alongside the SRA, CILEx, BPP and the University of Law.

Apprenticeships had been largely welcomed by stakeholders during the research phase, and offer a potentially useful model for the development of new 'access-friendly' pathways into the solicitors' profession, alongside

---

[141] ie, equivalent to the completion of first-year undergraduate studies.
[142] See Solicitors Regulation Authority, 'News Release: SRA Signs up for Trailblazers Apprenticeship Scheme' (SRA, 2014), available at: www.sra.org.uk/sra/news/press/trailblazer-apprenticeships.page.

the traditional and relatively little used CILEx route. It is still too early to say whether they will make a significant difference either numerically or in diversity terms to the make-up of the profession. The research team had its doubts, which is why it called for specific research into and diversity monitoring of legal apprenticeships. Whether apprenticeships should ultimately be the main game in town is also an important question for the sector, given their current dependency on government support and funding; the risk is that other (non-graduate) alternatives may not be explored before government funding (eventually) dries up.

This leads us more generally to the recommendations of the LETR Report on access and diversity. The BSB has, as noted, indicated that it will be examining access as one of its six work programmes; the SRA has similarly in its 'Training for Tomorrow' policy statement highlighted the need to enhance access, but at present we have no indication in detail of what that means for either regulator.[143] This leaves us with three very specific questions.

First, and most importantly, in the light of the considerable information asymmetry that the Report identified in the market for LSET, what coordinated steps will the regulators or representative bodies take to enhance the accessibility, comparability and comprehensiveness of training and careers information for the legal services sector?[144] There is a danger that the regulators will assume that if they deliver flexible alternatives, students will come. However, without more and better information this risks, as Melissa Hardee observes, overestimating the ability of students to make an informed choice about career options and/or the available pathways to achieve different careers.[145]

Second, since information is also an important regulatory tool, are the regulators committed to developing data that will better inform their ability to meet the diversity limb of the regulatory objectives? Current and arising priorities were identified in the Report, including diversity monitoring of apprenticeship routes, the GDL and LPC, the need for improved diversity data on the BPTC, as well as longitudinal analysis of the diversity impact of the Bar Course Admission Test (BCAT).[146]

Third, are they, and particularly the SRA, planning to issue guidance to entities on the design and offering of internship and work placement programmes, as these are now primary determinants of access to the profession? Again, for the present, it seems we must wait and see.

---

[143] Read literally 'Training for Tomorrow' seems to limit accessibility reforms to developing apprenticeships and other new pathways and removing unnecessary regulatory barriers to access.

[144] See Legal Education and Training Review, 'Setting Standards' (n 6) paras 7.63–7.67.

[145] M Hardee, 'To Prescribe or Not to Prescribe? That Is the Question' (2014) 48 *The Law Teacher* 69.

[146] Legal Education and Training Review, 'Setting Standards' (n 6) paras 7.49, 7.51, 7.54.

IV. LEGAL EDUCATION LOOKING FORWARDS

Thus far this chapter has examined the complexity of the environment into which the LETR was born and to which it has sought to respond. It has identified the work plans of the largest regulators and some key steps that have already been taken. It also highlights how much remains to be done, and the existence of some significant areas of uncertainty. In this final section it steps back to consider some of the potential consequences of the LETR for the legal academy.

A. A First Word, Not the Last

The LETR Report was never going to be the last word, even on LETR. As we have seen the project was not designed on that basis, and the research that was possible within the constraints of the design and the time frame meant that the Report has in many respects been better at raising questions than providing answers. It would be excellent news if it was to be the last substantial review for at least another 40 years, but that is unlikely unless the key stakeholders in LSET are prepared to put time and resources into making it so. There is also much of legal education that falls outside the LETR remit: legal education in schools; public legal education, postgraduate academic legal education, law for non-lawyers; legal and socio-legal research. Questions of training for the unregulated sector also appear to be a grey area. Some of these (legal education in schools, public legal education and the unregulated sector in particular) may, in access to justice terms, become increasingly critical in the next few years. The profession-centric nature of reviews such as the TFR and LETR means that these other aspects of legal education, for good or ill, continue to be largely overlooked and under-researched.

The LETR, of course, is also not the only game in town. In terms of a political economy of legal education, it is widely recognised that the law school is sandwiched, often uncomfortably, between the state, the university and the profession. It follows from what has already been said that, in the context of an increasingly marketised and competitive higher education system, some of these tensions are likely to increase rather than decline, and there may be little that the LETR (as currently defined) can do to prevent that. It is more than possible that the academy may become more fragmented, that upward pressures on costs and numbers will continue to be difficult to control and tensions between the liberal and vocational aims of legal education will continue to dominate the debate, but equally these are not inevitable outcomes.

B. The LETR and the Economics of Legal Education

Little has been said so far about the massive changes to higher education funding, particularly those that are creating an increasingly competitive environment for both student numbers and research. The LETR is unlikely to be a major driver of change in this regard, but it may have some effect.

Changes to student funding in particular have increased both the marketisation and potential fragmentation of legal education. Student numbers for law, even in the context of £9000 fees, have remained relatively buoyant, but that likely disguises significant movements of students across the sector. HEFCE data in general shows that the creation of a competitive market in high A level tariff students (those that fall outside protected 'core' funding) is in general starting to skew recruitment patterns, with recruiters geared to mid to low tariff students 'more' likely to have experienced a 10 per cent plus fall in undergraduate numbers over the last three years.[147]

The creation of a market for high tariff students is encouraging some law schools, particularly in the pre-1992 sector, to implement significant expansion plans. Consequently, it is likely that a number, particularly of post-1992 institutions, will experience increased difficulty in meeting undergraduate recruitment targets. As noted, LPC providers are also continuing to have a difficult time, with some courses (for example, at Plymouth and Oxford Brookes) having already closed, and many others at around 50 per cent to 60 per cent capacity. Given that the majority of public institutions offering the LPC are also post-1992 institutions, the combination of funding threats is likely to cause some turbulence. This will not be unique to law: 'most commentators are assuming that there will be a good deal of institutional restructuring in the form of takeovers, mergers, strategic alliances and the like, and indeed this is the preferred scenario in the Browne Report',[148] but the particularities of the legal education market will bring its own pressures. If the LETR succeeds in creating a more flexible training regime it may in fact increase the challenge for parts of the university sector by potentially enhancing competition between the law schools and both non-graduate (for example, apprenticeship, CILEx) and international access. The risk that a small number of departments may become vulnerable to closure cannot be discounted.

---

[147] Higher Education Funding Council for England, 'Higher Education in England 2014: Analysis of Latest Shifts and Trends' (HEFCE, 2014), available at: www.hefce.ac.uk/heinengland/2014.

[148] R Brown, 'After Browne: The New Competitive Regime for English Higher Education' (2011) *Centre for Studies in Higher Education UC Berkeley* 8, available at: www.escholarship.org/uc/item/9569q5n5.

These financial pressures may create new quality risks in some institutions, and may also hasten the process of market differentiation and possibly fragmentation of the law school sector. Many lower tariff law schools already play only a marginal role in (traditional) professional formation, with the great majority of their students going into paralegal or non-legal careers. We may see moves by some institutions to try to differentiate their offerings from 'competitors' by adopting new pedagogies (such as problem-based learning) while others seek to capitalise on the perceived 'vocationalisation' of the curriculum by adding placements, or professionally related modules to undergraduate programmes, or creating paralegal pathways, or new exempting degrees. Again, if the LETR makes some of these processes easier, it may hasten the increase in vocationalism, or at least a greater blurring of lines between academic and vocational programmes. Conversely, in some more extreme instances significant financial pressure may well have a chilling effect on innovation.

Whether the LETR will do much to reduce the costs of vocational training is uncertain. There is relatively limited price variation across the market, and the decline in student numbers has not seen prices fall significantly; indeed in most providers they have continued to rise year on year. While this may seem counter-intuitive, factors such as the incidence of sponsorship (which likely reduces the elasticity of demand) and possibly the narrowness of profit margins[149] may well help sustain the price of training, though experimental economics does also demonstrate that higher prices and the emergence of 'collusive' behaviour without explicit negotiation may actually be more likely, under certain conditions, in a shrinking market, as suppliers seek to maintain profitability.

C. The Numbers Game

The continuing growth in student numbers at the academic stage and the excess of LPC and BPTC graduates over training places was a recurrent concern among respondents to the LETR research. The LETR Report did not recommend any attempt at direct control of numbers. Imbalances in supply and demand are to be expected in a market system; they are cyclical and therefore tend to be (relatively) temporary. Any attempt at number control thus is difficult, and potentially unreliable. Number control would likely also be deemed anti-competitive. It can be regarded as a form of rent seeking or monopolistic behaviour as it may serve artificially to maintain

---

[149] This point is entirely anecdotal as the research team was unable to undertake any meaningful analysis of cost and profit data as the majority of vocational providers either did not respond or declined to disclose requested financial information—even on a confidential basis—on grounds of commercial sensitivity.

higher prices for legal services. Ultimately, as Richard Abel rather bluntly observes, 'the legal profession exists to serve the public, not its own members'.[150] The wider view, outside the bubble of the legal profession, is thus likely to be that, while high numbers of lawyers tends to be a problem for lawyers, it is not necessarily so for the public at large.

Within the confines of that reality the LETR Report has sought to reframe the problem: what if it is not too many lawyers per se, but too many seeking to be trained in the same way to do the same thing(s)? The question then becomes, how do we reconstruct LSET to deliver a greater diversity of roles, and support aspirants to prepare for a market in which 'alternative careers' are more centre stage, and retraining for changes of direction may of necessity become more commonplace? The answer from the Review has been to provide more careers information, and to develop flexible pathways and 'off and on ramps' to facilitate career transition. This acknowledges that the problem is not just one of supply for a particular route exceeding demand, but a more structural problem for LSET in general. The question is whether those in the existing professional, academic and regulatory silos will be prepared to invest in preparing people for a future in which those stakeholders may play a different or smaller part?

D. Building New Structures and Relationships

A critical variable throughout the reform process will be the attitudes of the various actors. Are the regulators really up for the job? What about the academics and the professional representative bodies? Just how willing will the regulators be to disrupt existing structures in the face of determined resistance? To what extent are they prepared to invest time and resources in research? Do they have the authority, skills and resources to step beyond the limits of conventional stakeholder consultation and develop proper evidence-based policymaking?

The quality of the regulatory interface with the profession, the academy, and other regulators will be crucial. At present those relationships seem to fall short of the co-regulatory ideals anticipated by Clementi. In practice, the frontline regulators seem caught (at various times and to varying degrees) between strategies of command and control and a level of partnership that appears, to an outsider at least, close to regulatory capture.[151] The SRA in

---

[150] RL Abel, 'What *Does* and *Should* Influence the Number of Lawyers?' (2012) 19 *International Journal of the Legal Profession* 131, 142.

[151] See N Rose, 'Brothers in Arms' *Legal Futures* (13 December 2013), available at: www.legalfutures.co.uk/blog/brothers-arms (on the LSB investigation into the relationship between the Bar Council and Bar Standards Board). By contrast, note the various calls to the Ministry of Justice's legal services regulation review (including from the LSB, SRA, Council of Licensed Conveyancers and Legal Services Consumer Panel) for frontline regulators to have 'greater'

particular is still struggling to win the trust of the profession,[152] the LSB perhaps even more so.[153] The LETR in this regard may well prove a significant test of the current regulatory settlement, and of the ability of the front line regulators to work together to make the overly complex web of regulatory relationships created by the LSA actually work.[154] The reduced likelihood of further regulatory reform by government[155] at least limits the risk that the implementation process will be delayed or derailed by wider reforms, though a simplified regulatory structure could equally facilitate some of the more radical options discussed in the Report, such as a move to activity-based authorisation.[156]

The relationship with academic and vocational teachers of law may in some respects be even more challenging, albeit for different reasons. The primary focus of the review on professional 'training' may lead many to assume it is irrelevant to their concerns; more may need to be done to engage this community in the debate. Certainly the limited amount of formal engagement by the law teaching community (including vocational stage academics) with the LETR first phase should be a matter of some concern to all.[157] Not only is legal education our core business, our silence arguably

independence from their representative bodies—see, eg, J Webb, 'Legal Services Regulation Review: The Battle-Lines are Being Drawn *hEaD space* (10 September 2013), available at: legaleducation.wordpress.com/2013/09/10/legal-services-regulation-review-the-battle-lines-are-being-drawn.

[152] See, eg, N Rose, 'Law Society Makes SRA Power-Grab' *Legal Futures* (4 September 2013), available at: www.legalfutures.co.uk/latest-news/law-society-makes-sra-power-grab in addition to ongoing antipathy to ABSs and OFR.

[153] See, eg, Bar Council, 'Response to the Ministry of Justice Consultation Paper: Review of the Legal Services Regulatory Framework' (Bar Council, 2013), available at: www.barcouncil.org.uk/for-the-bar/consultations/responses-to-external-consultations; Law Society, 'The Ministry of Justice's Call for Evidence on the Regulation of Legal Services in England and Wales: The Law Society's Response' (Law Society, 2013), available at: www.lawsociety.org.uk/representation/policy-discussion/regulation-of-legal-services; and Webb, 'Legal Services Regulation Review' (n 151). Note however that there was general acceptance at the Board's 2012 Triennial Review that the LSB had a continuing role to play in providing oversight regulation, though more critical views were expressed concerning the way in which it interpreted and developed its functions: Ministry of Justice, 'Triennial Reviews: Legal Services Board and Office for Legal Complaints. Combined Report on Stages One and Two' (MOJ, 2012), available at: consult.justice.gov.uk/digital-communications/review-lsb-olc.

[154] It is almost axiomatic at this point to refer to the quality assurance of advocates scheme (QASA) as 'the most wretched example' of cross-professional collaboration imaginable: see R Moorhead, 'Precarious Professionalism—Some Empirical and Behavioural Perspectives on Lawyers' (2014) HLS Programme on the Legal Profession Research Paper 17/2014, available at: papers.ssrn.com/sol3/papers.cfm?abstract_id=2407370.

[155] See J Hyde, 'MoJ Puts Regulation Shake-Up On Hold' *Law Society Gazette* (London, 9 September 2013), available at: www.lawgazette.co.uk/law/moj-puts-regulation-shake-up-on-hold/5037458.article.

[156] See Legal Education and Training Review, 'Setting Standards' (n 6) paras 5.6–5.23.

[157] Aside from submissions from the Association of Law Teachers, Committee of Heads of University Law Schools and the Society of Legal Scholars, formal submissions to Discussion Papers were received from eight law schools, including three private sector providers, and five individual law teachers. No collective submissions were received from BPTC providers or

sits uncomfortably with what many, though perhaps not all, would see as a core social responsibility of the university to engage in public debate, and to speak truth to power.[158] For legal academics such as Harry Arthurs this translates as a necessary commitment to maintain a critical distance from practice, but not so much to disregard it, as to better engage with and shine a critical light on the work and values of the profession.[159]

Particularly given these concerns about effective engagement, is there a need for some forum in which to continue researching, debating and fine-tuning the process of educational reform? The LETR Report itself recognised the infeasibility of making sweeping changes under current conditions of what Ron Barnett has called 'supercomplexity'.[160] This is why, in Recommendation 25, it called for the setting up of a Legal Education Council to coordinate research and evaluation and inform continuous regulatory reform, thereby seeking to reduce the prospect of another LETR 5 or 10 years down the line. In this regard the Report was by no means unique. The lack of established structures for effective engagement between the professions and the academy has been a recurrent complaint of every review of legal education in England and Wales since 1934.[161] Indeed, the LSB's David Edmonds has himself argued the need for '[A] constant

---

the Association of LPC Providers (though both groups were represented on the Consultation Steering Panel). Responses to the online survey were received from 64 public sector law teachers (5.7% of survey respondents) and 17 (1.5%) from the private sector. A total of 53 academics/vocational stage teachers agreed to take part in focus groups/interviews out of a total of 307 respondents (17.3%)—see Legal Education and Training Review, 'Setting Standards' (n 6) Appendices A and D (Tables D.1 and D.2).

[158] N Chomsky, 'The Responsibility of Intellectuals' *New York Review of Books* (23 February 1967), available at: www.chomsky.info/articles/19670223.htm; E Said, *Representations of the Intellectual* (New York, Vintage Books, 1994) x and 76.

[159] '[T]he scholarly enterprise of law can flourish neither divorced from the profession, nor in its close embrace, nor in hand-to-hand combat with it. Its best prospect for growth and development is therefore to take up a position within the law faculties as a distinct and separate endeavour, with its own goals, standards and basis of legitimacy. Only such a stance will at once stimulate energies, promote sensible interdisciplinary cooperation and provide a free and equal basis for exchange between scholars and practitioners': Social Sciences and Humanities Research Council of Canada, *Law and Learning/Le droit et le savoir. Report of the Consultative Group on Research and Education in Law* (Ottawa, SSHRC, 1983) 140 (Arthurs Report).

[160] See, eg, R Barnett, 'Reconfiguring the University' in P Scott (ed), *Higher Education Re-Formed* (London, Falmer Press, 2000) 112.

[161] See Atkin Committee, *Report of the Legal Education Committee* (Cmd 4663, 1934) paras 13–17, 20; The Ormrod Committee's repetition of the Atkin recommendation led to the creation of the (first) Lord Chancellor's Advisory Committee on Legal Education, though this was a profession—rather than government—sponsored body and (from the universities' perspective) rapidly became dominated by professional interests—see Cownie and Cocks, '*A Great and Noble Occupation!*' (n 61) 131. Its successor, ACLEC, proposed creating a Joint Legal Education and Training Standards sub-committee to review the setting and devise ways of improving standards (ACLEC Report, 'First Report on Legal Education and Training' (n 51) para 7.15. The sub-committee did assist Bell's group in the early stages of the law benchmarking process (discussed in the text accompanying Bell, 'Benchmarking in Law' (n 126)), but was then abolished with ACLEC in 1999.

interplay between practice and education, with the two spheres in constant dialogue, each driving improvement and innovation in the other to the broader public good'.[162] The importance of such dialogue has also been acknowledged internationally. The Canadian Bar Association consultation on its 'Futures Initiative' identified 'a resounding sentiment that there needs to be a permanent conversation about the future of the profession—from broad and creative imaginings of future business structures, to assessing emerging technologies, to pedagogical reform in the training of lawyers'.[163] In the United States, the recent ABA Task Force report moreover has expressly called on the ABA to establish a centre 'or other framework' to engage in continuous evaluation and improvement of legal education.[164] This has been echoed publically here in the United Kingdom by William Twining's call for a 'national institute for legal education and training' as a cross-sector meeting ground and as a centre for legal education research and development,[165] and less publically (so far) by the efforts of the new Centre for Legal Education at Nottingham Trent University to create and coordinate a network of legal educators and trainers to take the information sharing and collaboration agenda forward. That the regulators appear to have dismissed Recommendation 25 on the (untested) assumption that the work can be achieved within existing structures is disappointing, and a failure not just of imagination but responsibility.[166] If the ABA goes ahead, by doing nothing we risk not only missing an opportunity for ourselves, but also handing a large slice of competitive advantage in the development of education and training to our closest rival in the market for global legal services. There is a real risk that in this regard, perhaps above all others, the response to the LETR and not the LETR Report itself will be the missed opportunity.

V. CONCLUSION

The LSA has emphasised the centrality of LSET to maintaining a competent workforce, in enhancing understanding of legal ethics and values and developing 'ethical infrastructures' and to fostering a culture of innovation. The LETR has responded by offering the means to complete the work of

---

[162] Edmonds, 'Training the Lawyers of the Future' (n 3) 6 (emphasis added).

[163] Canadian Bar Association, 'Legal Futures Initiative: Report on the Consultation' (CBA, 2014), available at: www.cbafutures.org/The-Reports/Report-on-The-Consultation.

[164] American Bar Association, 'Report of the Task Force' (n 47).

[165] W Twining, 'LETR: The Role of Academics in Legal Education and Training: 10 Theses' (2014) 48 *The Law Teacher* 94.

[166] It is notable that Edmonds framed the need for constant dialogue as necessary to meet the LSA regulatory objective of ensuring a 'diverse and effective' legal profession, see Edmonds, 'Training the Lawyers of the Future' (n 3) 6.

Ormrod and ACLEC: structurally to align the academic, vocational and continuing stages of LSET, without destroying what is educationally valuable and desirable in a liberal legal education. It seeks to put ethics and values more centre stage; it creates an opportunity to transform 'competence' from a relatively static, passive, state, to one that is both active and continuing, and to support the opening up of new, flexible, qualification pathways and careers within the legal services sector. It is also not without risks. Paradoxically, perhaps, it may liberalise too much or further bureaucratise learning, open up opportunities to train or create divisions between first and second-class pathways and create new access problems without adequately resolving existing ones. It is clear, in sum, that the ink on this LETR is barely dry.

Much will also depend on the delivery; to sustain the postal metaphor, will it be more pony express or third-class mail? Are the regulators committed to delivering it intact, or will yet further rounds of debate and consultation reduce it to a 'smorgasbord' of ideas that rob the recommendations of their underlying coherence and impact? Will it be lost in the post? Stolen away by hostile interests in the academy and/or professions, or hijacked to a particular regulatory agenda, say, around re-accreditation or activity-based authorisation? Will it be so delayed that it simply becomes old news, overtaken by the pace of change in the marketplace?

The portents at the moment are mixed. While there are some encouraging early signs from the SRA and BSB, the lack of timetable, and of specific responses to numerous of the LETR recommendations is a matter of some concern; the relative lack of academic engagement likewise. Ten months after the publication of the LETR Report, I find myself empathising with Sir Roger Ormrod who, in noting the relative lack of response to, and analysis of, his report, observed:

> I wonder whether we are sitting in the eye of the storm or whether we have achieved nothing, or whether inconceivably, everyone agrees with us! Which it is I do not know and I am waiting with interest to see what reaction we produce.[167]

After so many missed opportunities in the last 45 years, procrastination and continuing uncertainty will show neither the regulators, nor the profession, nor the academy, in a good light. Doing nothing is, on this reading, the worst option. On the other hand, if the LETR really is to succeed, even on its own relatively pragmatic terms, it will require a level of coordination, commitment and openness to change that is probably unparalleled in the history of English legal education. The question is, are we, collectively, willing to meet that challenge?

---

[167] R Ormrod, 'The Reform of Legal Education' (1971) 77 *The Law Teacher* 5.

7

Poor Thinking, Poor Outcome? The Future of the Law Degree after the Legal Education and Training Review and the Case for Socio-Legalism[1]

ANDREW SANDERS

T HIS CHAPTER IS concerned with two questions. First, what should be the central elements of all law degrees in England and Wales? This intellectual and pedagogical question is part of a wider debate about the increasing commodification of knowledge through the growth of corporatism in Western universities. Second, what educational principles and values should underpin the education and training of entrants to the legal profession in England and Wales? This question has to be answered with reference to the relatively new regulatory framework established in 2007.[2] In 2011, the three 'front line' legal regulators in England and Wales initiated a Legal Education and Training Review (LETR), including the commissioning of a research report[3] to tackle the second question. This chapter explores the way the Report tackled these questions, what answers

---

[1] I am hugely indebted to Julian Webb, who commented on this chapter when I delivered a short version of it at the WG Hart Workshop at IALS in June 2014; Imogen Jones (the Birmingham Law School expert on the relationship between criminal law and evidence); Hilary Sommerlad, Steven Vaughan and Richard Young, whose varied insights and expertise enabled me to eradicate the chapter's worst faults, and enhance my arguments immeasurably; and Tina Martin who found innumerable references for me. I should declare that, as a member of the Bar Standards Board (BSB) and Chair of its Education and Training Committee, I am one of the regulators to whom I partly address this chapter. However, the chapter is written in my capacity as an academic, and does not represent the policy of the BSB.

[2] Legal Services Act 2007.

[3] Legal Education and Training Review, 'Setting Standards: The Future of Legal Services Education and Training Regulation in England and Wales' (SRA, BSB and CILEX, 2013), available at: www.letr.org.uk.

it gave, and what the answers should have been. I shall argue that the LETR Report is seriously flawed in its thinking and therefore in some of its recommendations. In particular, it misunderstands the nature and importance of socio-legalism, and fails to take into account some of the statutory criteria in the Legal Services Act 2007 (LSA). In consequence, it neglects the way that legal education and legal services fail the least well off in the United Kingdom. I offer an alternative—intellectual and critical—vision that resists commodification and corporatism.

The LETR Report looked in far more detail at the vocational, training and post-qualification stages of legal education than it did at law degrees. And it did not look at issues such as the desirable length of law degrees or the implications of the growth of private law degree providers. But it did suggest that all stages of legal education and training be designed by working back from legal professional 'day one outcomes'.[4] The implications for law degrees could be profound given that this appears to put university legal education at the service of the legal profession. Law degrees could drift into a narrow vocationalism either by default or, worse, because vocationalism comes to be seen as the main principle underlying academic legal education.[5] This would be the kind of commodification of knowledge about which commentators such as Margaret Thornton have warned us.[6] It is of especial concern because, as we shall see in section II, the legal 'super-regulator' (the Legal Services Board (LSB)) is fiercely neo-liberal: it seeks minimal education standards for lawyers in the belief that market forces will enable consumers of legal services to secure lawyers who have the training they need to do the job in question. It therefore resists 'gold plated' legal education and training, making the vocational education and training of the late twentieth century appear intellectually indulgent by comparison. We therefore need to consider what academic and intellectual values should shape law degrees in the light of the changing world to which LETR has rightly alerted us. If in the process legal education and research helps to shape the legal profession, so much the better.

One of the criticisms I will make of law degrees is their narrowness. One element of this is their Anglo/Welsh centricity. It is true that law degrees in most jurisdictions are similarly highly jurisdictionally specific. Arguably, this reflects the lack of intellectual ambition underlying most legal scholarship the world over, which is reflected in law degrees the world over. But being part of a crowd does not make one right. However, while I will return

---

[4] ibid, Recommendation 3, xiii.

[5] W Twining, 'LETR: The Role of Academics in Legal Education and Training: 10 Theses' (2014) 48 *The Law Teacher* 94; J Guth and C Ashford, 'The Legal Education and Training Review: Regulating Socio-Legal and Liberal Legal Education' (2014) 48 *The Law Teacher* 5.

[6] See, eg, M Thornton, *Privatising the Public University: The Case of Law* (Abingdon, Routledge, 2012).

to the problem of degrees being intellectually narrow, I regrettably have to acknowledge that this discussion will be almost entirely about English/ Welsh law degrees. However, I will briefly consider conversion courses—ie, the non-law degree route into the profession—at the end. I will also briefly consider how, in the light of my analysis, we should view the proposal by the Solicitors Regulation Authority (SRA) that graduate entry should no longer be the main route to becoming a solicitor.[7]

A final preliminary point concerns legal skills. Many argue that legal education is, or should be, primarily a matter of 'skills': that any legal subject can be learned on one's own if one has a good grounding in legal skills, as long as those skills are taught in relation to some substantive law.[8] This is a strong argument if by 'legal subject' we mean 'the law' in the sense of doctrine; but if legal subjects include subjects that are 'about law', or include the social/economic/political context of those subjects, then the argument changes. To understand the origins and impact of the law, for example, contextual or interdisciplinary work is required. Social, political or economic theory may be required; depending on what it is 'about law' that one is studying. This cannot simply be picked up eclectically and grafted onto a doctrinal core. For gaining that understanding requires a range of skills that go beyond those needed for doctrinal work, plus a systematic grounding in substantive material (be it theory or an understanding of social structure). Skills can, therefore, not replace substance.[9]

I. TWENTIETH CENTURY LAW DEGREES

Entry to the solicitors' or barristers' professions is controlled by their regulatory bodies: the SRA and Bar Standards Board (BSB) respectively. For both professions the route to qualification for the overwhelming majority is:

— Academic stage (law degree; or non-law degree plus conversion course)
— Vocational course
— Training contract/pupillage.[10]

---

[7] Solicitors Regulation Authority, 'Training for Tomorrow' (SRA, 2014), available at: www.sra.org.uk/sra/policy/training-for-tomorrow.page.

[8] R Huxley-Binns, 'What is the "Q" for?' (2011) 45 *The Law Teacher* 341.

[9] It should be observed that Huxley-Binns (ibid) does not advocate replacing substance with skills. However, she does argue that the nature of that substance is irrelevant; and her skills list is entirely doctrinal (with one notable exception, discussed later) despite occasional nods to the value of contextual work.

[10] The Law Society, 'Routes to Qualifying' (Law Society, 2014), available at: www. lawsociety.org.uk/careers/becoming-a-solicitor/routes-to-qualifying; The Bar Council, 'How to Become a Barrister' (Bar Council, 2014), available at: www.barcouncil.org.uk/becoming-a-barrister/how-to-become-a-barrister.

For a law degree to 'count' as satisfying the academic stage it has to be a qualifying law degree (QLD).[11] The regulators made no substantial change to the 'joint announcement' of the former regulators (the Law Society and the Bar Council).[12] This is why this section is headed 'Twentieth Century Law Degrees': they really have not changed much since this scheme was established after the last major review of legal education and training, which reported in 1971.[13] A QLD must cover seven 'foundation subjects', devoting at least one-half of a three-year programme to them. In addition, a further one-sixth must be 'law' of any description. That leaves one-third to the discretion of the academics running the programme. Certain basic legal skills are also prescribed. Finally, the main elements of English legal system and methods need to be covered, either separately or in the course of fulfilling the other requirements.[14]

The foundation subjects are: contract; tort; criminal law; equity and the law of trusts; law of the European Union; property law; and public law including constitutional law, administrative law and human rights law.[15] It is almost entirely up to individual law schools to decide the weight to give different subjects (within the limits set out above), the topics covered within the broad headings, how skills are to be imparted and assessed and so forth. Nothing is said about whether (or not) the knowledge or skills elements should include legal theory, or comparative, historical or social science approaches, or international elements.[16]

So at one level there is a huge amount of freedom. One QLD might focus, in trusts and property, for example, on controversial policy issues such as homelessness or the charitable status of independent schools, while another could be concerned mostly with easements, conveyancing and the rule against perpetuities. Regarding criminal law, one QLD might concentrate on why and how we criminalise some things and not others, while another might dwell on the meaning of 'intention' and the point at which 'property'

---

[11] The Law Society, 'Routes to Qualifying: Qualifying with a Law Degree' (Law Society, 2014), available at: www.lawsociety.org.uk/careers/becoming-a-solicitor/routes-to-qualifying.

[12] See now Solicitors Regulation Authority, 'Completing the Academic Stage of Training Guidance for Providers of Recognised Law Programmes' (SRA, 2011), available at: www.sra.org.uk/students/academic-stage.page.

[13] Committee on Legal Education, *Report of the Committee on Legal Education* (Cmnd 4595, 1971) (Ormrod Report). Indeed the foundation subjects have not changed a lot since the early twentieth century, when university legal education outside Oxbridge had no pretensions other than to provide a service to the professions. And, in the absence of legal aid, the professions overwhelmingly serviced capital.

[14] Bar Standards Board and Solicitors Regulation Authority, 'Academic Stage Handbook' (BSB and SRA, 2014) 4.

[15] The Law Society, 'Routes to Qualifying: What to Expect During your Studies' (Law Society, 2014), available at: www.lawsociety.org.uk/careers/becoming-a-solicitor/routes-to-qualifying.

[16] Bar Standards Board and Solicitors Regulation Authority, 'Academic Stage Handbook' (n 14).

in goods passes from A to B for the purposes of the law of theft. Any one programme might focus on the intellectual or the practical, the doctrinal or the contextual, the UK or the international and comparative. A programme can take one monolithic approach or it can have different modules with different focuses.

At another level this is very restrictive. It is not self-evident that knowledge of trusts and land law is more important than non-foundation subjects like welfare law, family law, criminal justice and international law. This was acknowledged even by conservative doctrinalists like Peter Birks.[17] And giving complete freedom to only one-third of the curriculum limits programme design. 'Criminology' is explicitly included as a law subject, so there is plenty of scope for law/criminology programmes to be QLDs. But depending on how generously law is interpreted, this is not true of law/social policy and law/finance degrees, for example.

In short, the 'joint announcement' originally reflected a compromise: the academic law schools wanted the legal professions to be graduate only and envisaged most graduate entrants having QLDs. But they wanted maximum freedom to design those QLDs as they wished. The professions were happy enough to be primarily graduate only, but wanted to ensure that trainees started vocational legal training with what they perceived to be as solid and comprehensive a foundation of knowledge and techniques as reasonably possible.[18] For many in the solicitors' profession, in particular, this would have included company law and 'commercial awareness', and for the Bar it would have included ethics, evidence and procedure. The compromise was that these subjects would not be required in QLDs, but the foundations on which they could be built (the foundation subjects) would be. The result lacked intellectual coherence or any justification based on what those graduates would do, whether as legal professionals, employees in a wealth of other spheres, or simply as citizens with an understanding of law.

Do law degrees follow a particular pattern? While the foundation subjects are capable of being taught in many different ways, the narrow range of skills required to be taught suggests that doctrinalism dominates. Fiona Cownie accurately sums up doctrinalism as positivist, focusing on what the legal rules are and providing no basis on which to analyse or critique the values on which they are based;[19] nor, I would add, to analyse or critique the way these rules actually work and the power structures they support or challenge. Anthony Bradney viewed doctrinalism in 1998 as 'entering its death throes'.[20] Just a few years later, Cownie found only half of legal

---

[17] Quoted in Huxley-Binns, 'What is the "Q" for?' (n 8).

[18] Twining, 'LETR: The Role of Academics' (n 5).

[19] F Cownie, 'Exploring Values in Legal Education' (2011) 2 *Web Journal of Current Legal Issues*.

[20] A Bradney, 'Law as a Parasitic Discipline' (1998) 25 *Journal of Law and Society* 71, 73.

academics describing themselves as primarily doctrinal, and over half of these said they looked at the law 'in context'.[21] However, Cownie endorses Bradney's view too uncritically. Self-description is not always accurate, and there are many reasons to doubt it both in general (Bradney himself cites the view that 'trait theories of the profession rely too much on the "professionals'" own definition of themselves')[22] and in this instance. The Nuffield Enquiry on Empirical Legal Research reported in 2006: 'Lacking a broad perspective on legal enquiry ... when law graduates who do consider an academic career choose postgraduate courses and topics for doctoral research, they naturally gravitate towards doctrinal topics'.[23] Thus, many papers given at Socio-Legal Studies Association (SLSA) conferences are not socio-legal at all.[24] Many are doctrinal papers with a contextual or policy element. Cownie herself cites some of her respondents who are very critical:

> I went to a 1-day conference a few weeks ago ... I was astounded at what they got away with ... there was one paper which drew very superficially on work in political theory—the person didn't have sufficient background in the subject to use it properly.[25]

Apart from explicitly socio-legal or criminological modules, most modules in all the law schools of which I have been a member or external examiner have been mildly contextual at best. And the same is true of the most popular textbooks, particularly in the foundation subjects.[26]

II. TWENTY-FIRST CENTURY REGULATION OF LAW DEGREES

Independent regulation arrived in the legal world with the LSA. As stated earlier, solicitors and barristers are regulated by the SRA and BSB respectively (the front line regulators). And they (together with other legal regulators with whom this chapter is not concerned) are overseen by the LSB. They all have legal education and training within their remit.[27] We need to be clear about that remit. It is not for regulators to decide or recommend

---

[21] F Cownie, *Legal Academics: Culture and Identity* (Oxford, Hart Publishing, 2004) ch 3.

[22] A Bradney, 'How to Live: Aristocratic Values, the Liberal University Law School and the Modern Lawyer' (2011) 2 *Web Journal of Current Legal Issues*, quoting T Johnson, *Professions and Power* (London, Macmillan, 1972) 25.

[23] H Genn, M Partington and S Wheeler, *Law in the Real World: Improving our Understanding of How Law Works* (London, Nuffield, 2006) para 87.

[24] See section IV of this chapter for a discussion of 'socio-legalism'.

[25] Cownie, *Legal Academics* (n 21) 67.

[26] For an extended example, see section V.A of this chapter. This is truer of some subjects (eg, property, trusts, EU) than others (eg, public law): see generally C Hunter (ed), *Integrating Socio-Legal Studies into the Law Curriculum* (Basingstoke, Palgrave Macmillan, 2012). For a lengthy and nuanced discussion see R Collier, 'We're all Socio-Legal Now?' (2004) 26 *Sydney Law Review* 503.

[27] See Legal Services Act 2007, s 4 for the remit of the LSB.

what kind of legal education and training should be provided. The legal regulators have a duty to regulate legal education only to the extent necessary to achieve their statutory objectives. In pursuing these objectives, all regulators must have regard to the 'better regulation' principles, of which proportionality and targeting are the most important in this context.[28] The regulation of education and training must therefore become highly instrumental. This change reflects a wider social shift towards the control of public services through New Public Management, which is in turn generally conceptualised in terms of the increasing hegemony of neo-liberal values.[29] The result has been that, in general, the freedom to design standards according to liberal intellectual values in abstract, accorded to Ormrod in 1971,[30] has gone.

Section 1 of the LSA sets out eight regulatory objectives in respect of the supply of legal services:

1. Protecting and promoting the public interest.
2. Supporting the constitutional principle of the rule of law.
3. Improving access to justice.
4. Protecting and promoting the interests of consumers.
5. Promoting competition in the provision of services.
6. Encouraging an independent, strong, diverse and effective legal profession.
7. Increasing public understanding of the citizen's legal rights and duties.
8. Promoting and maintaining adherence to the professional principles.

The LSB prioritised them in 2014 as follows:

Legal education and training is directly linked to the regulatory objectives in the [LSA] and, in particular, to the need to protect and promote the interests of consumers and to ensure an independent, strong, diverse and effective legal profession. There is also a clear link to securing the wider benefits of market liberalisation for consumers.[31]

The 'public interest', 'rule of law' and 'access to justice' regulatory objectives are ignored. This may be because the LSB understands these objectives to be directed to what regulation should achieve, rather than to individuals. The 'competition' objective, for example, is a matter of ensuring a market, and is not something any individual lawyer, or his or her education, need

---

[28] ibid, s 3. Now see The Regulators' Code 2014 (BRDO/14/705), published under the authority of the Legislative and Regulatory Reform Act 2006—Better Regulation Delivery Office, 'Regulator's Code' (BRDO/14/705, Department for Business Innovation & Skills, 2014).

[29] See the chapters by Evetts and Webb in this collection. We shall, however, see that the regulatory objectives in the LSA are far less neo-liberal than the LSB appears to favour.

[30] See Committee on Legal Education, Ormrod Report (n 13).

[31] Legal Services Board, 'Increasing Flexibility in Legal Education and Training' (LSB, 2013).

address.[32] However, in order to encourage 'an independent, strong, diverse and effective legal profession' individuals need to be educated to understand what it means to be, and be able to practise being, 'strong, diverse and effective'. That requires them to understand the rule of law in its full sense, what is 'the public interest', and the differential socio-economic impact of the law. This argument will be further developed through the chapter.

Thus, although the LSB is the super-regulator there is no reason why anyone—neither the legal community nor the front line regulators—should adopt the LSB's particular prioritisation of the regulatory objectives. Indeed, there are good reasons not to do so. The stance of the LSB is simply an example of the broader neo-liberal pressures to erode key public values and privilege powerful economic interests, which are pervasive features of the reform of the public sphere.[33]

The LSB's 'statutory guidance' (that is, instructions)[34] to the regulators includes five requirements of regulated legal education and training, including that, 'education and training requirements focus on what an individual must know, understand and be able to do at the point of authorisation'.[35] Another requirement, concerned with the balance between pre-qualification and post-qualification education, is elaborated by the LSB as follows:

a. Education and training requirements should be set at the minimum level at which an individual is deemed competent for the activity or activities they are authorised to do.

b. Requirements beyond the minimum are only in place where they can be justified by the risks. We would expect regulators to review all available evidence to determine the likelihood of the risk occurring and to monitor the impact of any requirements over time. This may lead to an ongoing review cycle with strong links to regulatory supervision functions.[36]

It is therefore no longer open to the front line regulators to argue that the foundation subjects, or any other subjects, 'must' be studied simply because they, the professions or the law subject associations think that these are in some unspecified ways 'a good thing' for prospective lawyers to know. Nor, in the new world of 'outcomes-focused regulation' is it acceptable to specify how long students should spend on any one subject or type of subject: a weak student might need to spend half of his or her study time on

---

[32] See Legal Services Board, 'The Regulatory Objectives: Legal Services Act 2007' (LSB, undated), available at: www.legalservicesboard.org.uk/news_publications/publications/pdf/regulatory_objectives.pdf.

[33] R Shamir, 'The Age of Responsibilization: On Market-Embedded Morality' (2008) 37 *Economy and Society* 1.

[34] Legal Services Act 2007, s 162.

[35] Legal Services Board, 'Increasing Flexibility' (n 31) Outcome 1.

[36] ibid, Outcome 3.

the foundation subjects to grasp them, whereas an excellent student might achieve this much more quickly. For the LSB, the question is simply: what is the minimum that 'day one' trainee lawyers must know, understand and be able to do in order to meet the regulatory objectives?

The limitations of this kind of approach are discussed at length by several commentators. For instance, Thornton relates the turn from critical legal scholarship in the late twentieth century to the marketisation of university education. She argues that narrow vocationalism is overtaking universities, and that this is fundamental to the neo-liberal reconfiguration of the economy, state and public sphere.[37] In opposition to positivist and vocational approaches, William Twining has long argued for an intellectually rooted legal education, and observes that, because the LETR Report argues only for basic competence, its approach is inimical to what high quality universities should aim at.[38] Presumably the LSB response would be that the market will, and should, differentiate adequate education from the best education; thus students and employers can make their choices accordingly; and the job of regulators is not to force them to choose the best education and the best educated, but simply the competent.

This might work for technical trades. But there is a difference between a technician and a professional. Technicians do discrete jobs, while professionals have the potential, at the very least, to (to a greater or lesser extent) shape social practice in the course of their work. It is true that, as other chapters in this book show (for example, those by Evetts, Faulconbridge and Muzio, and Webb),[39] the legal professions (solicitors in particular) are becoming increasingly stratified. Some solicitors increasingly do routinised

---

[37] Thornton, *Privatising the Public University* (n 6). For a flavour of this work more generally see, in the UK context, A McGettigan, *The Great University Gamble, Money, Markets and the Future of Higher Education* (London, Pluto, 2013); R Brown and H Carasso, *Everything for Sale? The Marketisation of UK Higher Education* (London, Routledge, 2013); and S Collini, *What are Universities For?* (London, Penguin, 2012). Note also D Hill and R Kumar (eds), *Global Neoliberalism and Education and its Consequences* (London, Taylor & Francis, 2009); C Morphew and P Eckel (eds), *Privatization of the Public University: Perspectives from Across the Academy* (Baltimore, John Hopkins University Press, 2009); J Currie, B Thiele and P Harris, *Gendered Universities in Globalized Economies: Power, Careers and Sacrifices* (Maryland, Lexington Books, 2002); J Currie and J Newson (eds), *Universities and Globalization* (London, Sage, 1998); A Brooks and A Mackinnon (eds) *Gender and the Restructured University* (Buckingham, SRHE/Open University Press, 2001); V Gillies and H Lucey (eds), *Power, Knowledge and the Academy: The Institutional is Political* (London, Palgrave Macmillan, 2007); S Slaughter and L Leslie, *Academic Capitalism: Politics, Policies and the Entrepreneurial University* (Baltimore, Johns Hopkins University Press, 1997); S Cooper, J Hinkson and G Sharp (eds), *Scholars and Entrepreneurs: The Universities in Crisis* (Melbourne, Arena Publications, 1992); and S Marginson and M Considine, *The Enterprise University: Power, Governance and Reinvention in Australia* (Cambridge, Cambridge University Press, 2000).

[38] Twining, 'LETR: The Role of Academics' (n 5) 97. For an example of his general line of thought see W Twining, 'Pericles and the Plumber' (1967) 83 *Law Quarterly Review* 396.

[39] Evetts, ch 2 in this collection; see also ch 6 by Webb in this collection.

tasks. But as at least some of these move into different strata, or simply become more active in, for example, local law societies and specialist societies; they may confront more complex matters with greater socio-political dimensions. Perhaps plumbers and surveyors can be trained in a technocratic and instrumental way, but professionals need to be educated so they understand the society they help to shape and the values that should underpin that shaping. Identifying, analysing and understanding the implications of different values are key elements of all liberal undergraduate degree programmes, whether in law or other disciplines.[40] This is no new insight.[41] We need to educate people to be good citizens, not just train workers. This idea[42] must surely underpin one of the regulatory objectives that the LSB did highlight, namely, encouraging an independent, strong, diverse and effective legal profession. As Julia Black puts it, '"professionalism" invokes a sense of public duty and responsibility'; it thus requires an ethical dimension as well as expertise, and so cannot be captured by mere 'competence'.[43]

Thus, barristers and solicitors need a broad intellectual education to underpin the more technical training they later receive if we wish them to be professionals and not mere technicians. This can be reconciled with the regulatory objectives in the LSA, for they include the public interest, the rule of law and access to justice. Understanding these objectives, along with how different ways of practising law affect them, and what it means to have an independent, strong, diverse and effective legal profession, is not straightforward. It requires undergraduate-style education. Indeed I shall argue that it requires non-doctrinal education of a kind that the foundation subjects may not, and frequently do not, provide. To sum up the argument so far, a QLD should include, at a minimum:

— Legal methods and skills as set out in law benchmark statements, enhanced on the lines set out in the LETR Report.
— Enough substantive law in any subject to enable students to demonstrate their ability to deploy those skills and methods to a high standard.
— Whatever is needed to satisfy the regulatory objectives in the LSA, or to provide the intellectual foundation that will enable them to be satisfied in the vocational and training stages.

The rest of this chapter will look at the way the LETR Report handled these issues, and how it should have done so.

---

[40] Cownie, 'Exploring Values' (n 19); Bradney, 'How to Live' (n 22).

[41] See, eg, O Kahn-Freund, 'Reflections on Legal Education' (1966) 29 *Modern Law Review* 121; Twining, 'Pericles and the Plumber' (n 38).

[42] Newman's 'Idea of a University' as discussed by A Bradney, *Conversations, Choices and Chances* (Oxford, Hart Publishing, 2003) ch 2.

[43] J Black, 'Regulation, Education and Training' (LETR symposium, Manchester, June 2012) 2, 3.

III. THE LETR RESEARCH REPORT

We have seen that the concept and content of the QLD was a product of a compromise between the liberal yet monopolistic instincts of academics and the interest of the professions in acquiring graduates who knew something about the subjects that they considered important.

In his Lord Upjohn lecture in 2010, David Edmonds, the Chair of the LSB, declared that legal education is 'not fit for purpose', although he failed to cite any evidence for this claim.[44] Nonetheless, the front line regulators established the LETR to investigate the claim and to help plan the way in which legal education and training should adapt to the changing nature of the legal professions. A research team, appointed in 2011, reported in 2013.[45] In addition to desk research, the team conducted interviews and focus groups with 307 academics, practitioners, students etc; and administered an online survey to which 1,128 persons from the same categories responded.[46] These are tiny proportions of these categories, and there was no random sampling. Thus, the data produced by this empirical work needs to be treated with caution.

The LETR Report found that legal education and training is broadly 'fit for purpose'. It concluded that 'it provides, for the most part, a good standard of education and training'.[47] This does not mean that it considered the status quo to be flawless. Indeed, it identified several 'gaps and deficiencies' in legal education and training as a whole. In particular,

> the treatment of professional conduct, ethics and 'professionalism' is of variable quality ... There was general support in the research data for all authorised persons receiving some education in legal values and regulators are encouraged to consider developing a broad approach to this subject rather than a limited focus on conduct rules or principles.[48]

Other gaps identified by the responses included a lack of engagement with equality and diversity, commercial awareness and business and management

---

[44] D Edmonds, 'The Lord Upjohn Lecture, 2010 "Training the Lawyers of the Future—A Regulator's View"' (2011) 45 *The Law Teacher* 5.

[45] Legal Education and Training Review, 'Setting Standards' (n 3).

[46] ibid, x.

[47] ibid, ix.

[48] ibid, xiii. One would hope that everyone involved in, and regulating, legal education would have regard to the broadest possible conception of 'values' (not simply a matter of ethics), such as Bradney shows as underlying the 'neighbour principle' in *Donoghue v Stephenson* and the disappearance of divorce law from the curriculum simply because it is now treated bureaucratically rather than judicially. See Bradney, *Conversations, Choices and Chances* (n 42) 91–98. The latter could be seen as an example of the way legal academics sleepwalk into the mindset of the corporatists identified by Thornton, *Privatising the Public University* (n 6): if it is not the subject of legal business, the academy jettisons it!

skills.[49] However, with the exception of the broad legal values that underpin 'professionalism' (and, one might add, 'law' more broadly) the Report did not see the need for law degrees to incorporate these elements.

The Report agonised over the foundation subjects. On the one hand, it acknowledged that there was some arbitrariness in the list. On the other hand, it saw the foundation subjects as a proxy for the necessary underlying knowledge, which was the gist of many of the responses.[50] One would think it should not therefore matter how much time one spent on them in relation to each other or what is studied under each subject heading. Yet, based on the view that some consistency is desirable (which, like the 'proxy' argument, the Report acknowledges is open to challenge),[51] Recommendation 10 states: 'A broad content specification should be introduced for the Foundation subjects. The revised requirements should, as at present, not exceed 180 credits within a standard three-year Qualifying Law Degree course'.[52]

It is notable that there is (at least) one more type of inconsistency noted in the Report: quality and standards. It is widely believed—not least among many academics—that standards are lower in some institutions than others and that work attracting a certain grade at one institution would secure a higher grade at another institution and a lower one at yet another. The external examining system provides little comfort. This is evident from an interesting natural experiment that took place recently. Students taking the Bar Professional Training Course (BPTC) used to be examined by the eight higher education institutions providing the course. There were eight sets of exams, set and marked by each of the eight institutions. From 2013, the three core 'knowledge' modules have been examined by a central exams board. Pass marks in these subjects dropped significantly for the cohorts from some universities following this change and were out of line with pass marks in the subjects that were still marked in-house.[53] The conclusion that some universities set standards for pass marks and subsequent grades on the BPTC differently is difficult to challenge, and there is no reason to think that would be different in the less regulated QLDs that most of these institutions teach.

One result of the problem of standards is that many recruiters are wary of recruiting from less well-known 'brands', thus entrenching the barriers faced by 'non-normative' (or maybe non-traditional) students. The Report acknowledged these equality and diversity issues but made no recommendations to deal with them.[54] This reflects the influence of neo-liberalism to

---

[49] Legal Education and Training Review, 'Setting Standards' (n 3) xii. Some specific legal skills were also an area for concern, but they will not be discussed here.

[50] ibid, 28, para 2.53.

[51] ibid, para 2.54.

[52] ibid, xv, Recommendation 10.

[53] This knowledge is available to me as a member of the BSB. However, by the time this book is published the data should be publicly available.

[54] Legal Education and Training Review, 'Setting Standards' (n 3) 49, para 2.118.

which we have already drawn attention. There is a rhetorical commitment to fairness but concrete practice—based on instrumentalism and market forces that inevitably disadvantage the socially and economically marginal—is not challenged by the Report. To put it crudely: in the 1970s higher education and professional employment was primarily for the middle classes and a small upwardly mobile section of the working class. Now we have mass higher education, professional employment remains primarily for the middle classes and a small upwardly mobile section of the working class.[55]

Another problem is that there is no point specifying what should be studied in a contract module, for example, if the level at which it is studied and assessed can vary wildly. If there are institutions where standards are very low, their students might as well not have studied the subject at all. Even if this is too apocalyptic a view, we must remember that the purpose of closer specification is to increase consistency. But if institution A teaches at a significantly more superficial level than B, and if it really is important that all QLD holders have a consistent understanding of foundational building blocks, then it might be better for A to spend twice as long on offer and acceptance than B does, and none on mistake, than to require both institutions to devote a certain percentage of the degree programme studying both. That these might be problems was not tackled at all in the Report or in its recommendations (except, in relation to professional courses, in Chapter 4). The same is true of the specification of the foundation subjects in general. To simply characterise them as a 'proxy', without analysing how far their study meets the regulatory objectives, was lazy. And why 180 credits? Presumably because to suggest 'no change' risks offending fewer people than raising, lowering or abolishing the requirement. Surely the essence of the new approach to regulation set out in section II of this chapter is outcomes-focused regulation: consistency in standards has to be more important than consistency of knowledge and time served unless the latter are tied to the LSB's outcome 1: '[E]ducation and training requirements focus on what an individual must know, understand and be able to do at the point of authorisation'.[56] This was a failure by the Report to give effect to the regulatory principles on which it was established.

It is evident from this discussion that the Report mixed discussion of principles (for example, legal values 'should' be a compulsory part of legal education) and empirical data (x per cent of respondents 'think that' legal values should be a compulsory part of legal education). This was necessary in one respect. The Report needed to show the way in which education and training should orient itself to what lawyers 'must know, understand and be

---

[55] L Ashley and L Empson, 'Differentiation and Discrimination: Understanding Social Class and Social Exclusion in Leading Law Firms' (2013) 66 *Human Relations* 219.
[56] Legal Services Board, 'Increasing Flexibility' (n 31) Outcome 1.

able to do at the point of authorisation' (the LSB formulation). The research team aimed to discover this. But the way to do that is not to conduct what amounts to an opinion poll, especially one with huge potential sampling error. There was no attempt to analyse whether what lawyers said was necessary or desirable.

The inconsistencies and lapses of logic in the Report are a product of this incoherent mixture of normative analysis and opinion. The Report was supposed to guide the regulators on how to fulfil their obligations regarding legal education and training. It does not matter how many lawyers, professional or academic, want to include a particular subject or skill set if there is no regulatory reason to do so. This is why specifying a certain percentage of credits for particular subjects no longer makes sense. It is why assuming that the foundation subjects are a proxy, without analysing how far their study meets the regulatory objectives (whether the ones picked out by me or those picked out by the LSB), is unacceptable. It is why the failure to take on board arguments about the value of a liberal intellectual education, in creating a set of liberal benchmarks by which to evaluate the commercialisation of the professions,[57] is a failure to give effect to the regulatory objectives. This is also why the failure to analyse the contribution made to legal education and training by the socio-legal approach is equally unacceptable, as we see in the next section.

IV. RICH PEOPLE'S LAW, POOR PEOPLE'S LAW AND SOCIO-LEGALISM

We have seen that the LETR Report identifies ethics and values as the main gap in most QLDs, and the contexts of legal services (including 'commercial awareness' but also—less assertively—'social awareness')[58] as another, lesser, gap. It uncritically reports its findings that most practitioners regard jurisprudence and socio-legal studies as the least relevant in the curriculum, yet it ignores this finding as far as the ethics and values aspects of jurisprudence is concerned: it analyses the relevance to the profession of ethics and values but not of socio-legal studies (or indeed 'theory' elements of jurisprudence). Jessica Guth and Chris Ashford observe that this is because of confusion about the meaning of 'socio-legal'.[59] We could argue at length about the relevance to professionals of 'socio-legal studies' as a discrete subject, but its value as one of many approaches to any given subject is incontestable.

---

[57] Eg, Bradney, 'How to Live' (n 22); Kahn-Freund, 'Reflections' (n 41) 121; Twining, 'Pericles and the Plumber' (n 38) 396.

[58] Legal Education and Training Review, 'Setting Standards' (n 3) para 4.69.

[59] Guth and Ashford, 'The Legal Education and Training Review' (n 5). It is also because, as noted earlier, it incoherently mixes normative analysis and opinion.

One result of the foundation subject stranglehold is that students receive a foundation in law that primarily relates to corporations and the wealthy: land, equity and trusts, contract, reinforced by the doctrinal focus on appeal cases, which are primarily brought by corporations and the wealthy. The student gaze is directed to the wealthy, reinforcing the tendency of most law students to want to earn high salaries (which almost always means serving the wealthy), and the lack of training contracts in firms and organisations serving the poor. While it is true that public law and EU law, for example, concern the relationship between the citizen and the state, the idea of law serving a broad democratic function, and of the state having duties towards citizens, is subordinated to the idea of law as dispute resolution between legal entities.[60]

Table 3.4 of the LETR Report[61] illustrates the knock-on effects. It shows the proportions of different types of work done by regulated and unregulated providers respectively. The former are largely solicitors and barristers, the latter are semi-professional advisers such as at Citizens Advice. Property ownership and some types of injury matters (for example, relationship breakdown, mortgage, wills, clinical negligence and non-work injuries) were all dealt with twice as often by the former than the latter. The only exceptions were police matters and immigration. By contrast, mental health, homelessness, planning applications, and neighbour disputes were all dealt with twice as often by the latter than the former; the latter dealt more than the former with consumer problems, domestic violence, discrimination, welfare/tax benefits, debt/money problems and issues relating to children too. The point here is that, with the exception of immigration and police matters, regulated providers gave advice overwhelmingly in law relating predominantly to the middle and upper socio-economic groups, while the reverse is true in relation to the lowest socio-economic groups. To put it crudely, lawyers do not do much 'poor law' any more. Cuts to legal aid mean that they are likely to do even less in future. The LETR Report fails to acknowledge the socio-economic implications of this, or the role that the QLD foundation subjects have in creating and perpetuating this.

There is a feedback loop at work here: as Webb notes, students learn mostly about rich people's law and seek employment in rich people's law firms. Legal education and training is perceived to be failing because its preparation of students for the world of rich people's law is—despite this—inadequate. Legal education and training therefore needs to up its game in this respect, whereas its failures in relation to poor people and their law are ignored. This paragraph actually paraphrases part of a paper by a professor of legal education. In this paper, the list of 'intellectual professional legal

---

[60] See ch 10 by Abel in this collection.
[61] Legal Education and Training Review, 'Setting Standards' (n 3) 104, Table 3.4.

skills' that Rebecca Huxley-Binns argues all QLDs should be structured around includes 'legal commercial awareness'. Why?

> [S]tudents on a QLD should be required to show an appreciation of the business context of the legal services sector and an ability to behave appropriately according to context. Profit and loss, top and bottom lines, client relations, strategy, mission: these are terms our students need to know and understand if they are to do well in the new legal services sector, as are firm, limited liability, self-employed, employed, and indemnity to name a few more.[62]

Leaving aside the way this sounds more like knowledge than skills, the passage is striking in several ways. First, this is an argument for contextual or socio-legal work, something we can celebrate even if it is not phrased in this way. But, second, context receives only a couple of throwaway references in relation to non-business material. The idea that vulnerable people or minorities inhabit a context that lawyers should understand (particularly as most lawyers inhabit very different socio-economic contexts) does not arise. Finally, Huxley-Binns' 'employability' strategy, and others like it that embody 'employability skills', do not even seem to achieve their employability goals. Richard Moorhead, for example, discusses a US law school that put various employability strategies into its curriculum, only for its graduates to find themselves less employable, suggesting that employers do not really want students to learn narrow vocational employability skills at university.[63] And in the United Kingdom, large firms and barristers' chambers continue to value Russell Group graduates—with and without QLDs—instead of graduates from universities that incorporate vocational and employability elements. The reasons for this are complex. They include the concern over standards flagged up in section III, and appreciation of the value to them of an intellectual education and the cultural capital brought in by 'Oxbridge' graduates in particular.[64]

The fundamental problem with Huxley-Binns' argument is that an academic education is supposed to challenge the status quo, not simply equip students with the skills to leech off it. Effectively, her argument is for the sort of commoditised and narrowly instrumental education to which Thornton and similarly minded critics object.[65] The intellectual argument for incorporating commercial awareness in law degrees could be that only in this way can we truly understand, for example, research uncovering

---

[62] Huxley-Binns, 'What is the "Q" for?' (n 8) 350, 351.

[63] Lawyer Watch, 'LETR II: Employability May Not be What Employers Really Want' (27 June 2013), available at: lawyerwatch.wordpress.com/2013/06/27/letr-ii-employability-may-not-be-what-really-employers-want.

[64] H Sommerlad, 'Minorities, Merit, and Misrecognition in the Globalized Profession' (2012) 80 *Fordham Law Review* 2482; and H Sommerlad, 'The Commercialisation of Law and the Enterprising Legal Practitioner: Continuity and Change' (2011) 18 *International Journal of the Legal Profession* 73.

[65] See above (n 37).

the way legal disputes are avoided through the use of commercial contract law.[66] I have often heard solicitors say that law students need to be 'uneducated' about contract and commercial law: for example, they need to know that, just because one has a cause of action, it does not follow that there should be a court case. This is not just because parties to disputes usually settle out of court, but is also a matter of maintaining long-term business relationships. An important element of commercial awareness is understanding relationships.[67] But to truly understand relationships one needs to understand power differentials and the role law plays in eroding or maintaining those differentials.

There is an intellectual issue here about the use of law, as well as the fact that commercial law cannot be practised satisfactorily without this understanding. Let us leave aside the fact that this kind of work would be best done within contract, company and commercial law modules (where it is often ignored or marginalised) rather than as a separate commercial awareness module. Exactly the same kind of argument can be made about social awareness. Hilary Sommerlad reports 'radical' lawyers' concern about the complexity of poor people's problems: for example, the 'baggage' accompanying domestic violence; the difficulties some have with lawyers who appear 'high and mighty' or with 'a pound of plums' in their mouth.[68] Cutting through the complexity takes time and skill: 'if you don't have a rapport you can't get the information, and you can't put your client's case forward'.[69]

As with commercial awareness, academic social awareness requires knowledge of substantive material, and skills in interrogating that material, while the social awareness that practitioners need builds on this knowledge and skills base. Some lawyers take it further, becoming 'change agents ... creating an alternative model for the delivery of legal services to traditionally subordinated groups'.[70] This requires a holistic approach:

> Somebody with a lot of complex, poverty-related issues isn't just an ordinary person without money—they're in a completely different place not only economically

---

[66] For the seminal study see S Macauley, 'Non-Contractual Relations in Business' (1963) 28 *American Sociological Review* 55. For follow-on work in the United Kingdom, see H Beale and T Dugdale, 'Contracts Between Businessmen' (1975) 2 *British Journal of Law and Society* 45 and P Vincent-Jones, 'Contract Litigation in England and Wales 1975–1992: A Transformation in Business Disputing?' (1993) 12 *Civil Justice Quarterly* 337.

[67] See, further, section V.C below.

[68] H Sommerlad, 'Socio-Legal Studies and the Cultural Practice of Lawyering' in D Feenan (ed), *Exploring the 'Socio' of Socio-Legal Studies* (Basingstoke, Palgrave Macmillan, 2013) 192.

[69] ibid.

[70] L Trubek and E Kransberger, 'Critical Lawyers: Social Justice and the Structures of Private Practice' in A Sarat and S Scheingold (eds), *Cause Lawyering, Political Commitments and Professional Responsibilities* (New York, Oxford University Press, 1998).

and socially but also emotionally ... they need a high level of both legal and general advice.[71]

Similarly, someone with a lot of complex wealth-related issues is not just an ordinary person with money. They may need advice about, for example, tax avoidance. Doctrinal legal advice would be valuable, but so would political advice, for whether it is worth engaging in aggressive tax avoidance schemes may depend on the degree of public exposure to which one would be subject, and what harm that exposure would do. As to why the case for teaching social awareness is at least as strong as that of commercial awareness: part of the reason for the alienation of most poor people from law and from most lawyers is that so many of the latter lack social awareness (particularly in the sense of empathising with the socially marginal). Further, law and lawyers cater far more for the wealthy (tax avoidance schemes, and lawyers and accountants to advise on them are legion) than for the poor (I doubt there are many bedroom tax avoidance schemes).

This is all important for those (increasingly few) people who practise poor law, which is essential to maintain 'an independent, strong, diverse and effective legal profession'; and equally important for law students who ought to be taught how and why there is a gap between the majority of society on the one hand, and lawyers and the law on the other. Let us return to the regulatory objectives that are conveniently ignored by the LSB: the public interest, access to justice and the rule of law. The teaching of social awareness as broadly conceived in this section is clearly vital to the first two. The rule of law is a more complex issue.

One cannot study public law without studying the rule of law, so the foundation subjects ensure this is covered even though the other regulatory objectives are not. But most teaching of the rule of law is formalistic. It rarely touches on the gap between 'law in the books' and 'law in action' or between most people in marginalised sections of society and most lawyers. But there is a strong argument that these issues go to the root of the rule of law. Richard Young and I argue that, if we look at the real power (in contrast with formal powers) held by the police in relation to the socially marginalised, the rule of law is only partially applicable to pre-trial criminal justice.[72] For insofar as the rule of law is about control of state agencies, we need to understand how far police powers, for example, actually control the police. The answer is that they do so only to some extent, in some ways and differently in relation to different sections of society. And this is, in part, because of the way most lawyers conceive their role and their clients. The lack of social awareness and unwillingness to challenge authority of many

---

[71] Sommerlad, 'Socio-Legal Studies' (n 68) 195.

[72] A Sanders and R Young, 'The Rule of Law, Due Process and Pre-Trial Criminal Justice' (1994) 47 *Current Legal Problems* 125.

lawyers will only be reinforced if the LETR approach—or, worse, that of Huxley-Binns—is adopted. We cannot rely on the radical instincts of 'activist' lawyers to ensure that the state, its agencies and its powerful corporations are held to account. Students need to be taught how power works and why it needs to be controlled.

For students to understand, and to reach, these kinds of conclusions, they need to be taught socio-legal skills and sociological substance. The fact that most respondents to the LETR Report did not know, or perhaps did not care, about any of this is irrelevant. If a socio-legal approach is needed to understand the rule of law regulatory objective, then legal education and training must include it, whatever professional lawyers may think. As Twining points out, 'The LETR Report is incoherent in its treatment of jurisprudence and socio-legal studies'.[73] Its failure is, first, in not analysing what the regulatory objectives require (as distinct from what professionals think is wanted or needed). Second, it fails by not distinguishing socio-legal studies as a discrete subject from socio-legal approaches to substantive subjects.

V. THE CENTRALITY OF SOCIO-LEGAL APPROACHES

We have seen that the legal skills that are generally advocated are concerned almost solely with the doctrinal approach to law: finding the law (primarily through case law and statute), understanding what the law is, applying the law to problem situations, identifying the coverage of the law. Occasionally evaluative skills are identified: whether the law is good or bad, succeeds or fails in its objectives, what reforms would be valuable. But one needs criteria for evaluating the quality of law, its success or failure, and what kinds of changes are necessary or desirable. Identification of these criteria cannot be found within the details of the law itself. In this section I explore two extended examples from my own area of criminal law/justice to show why context and socio-legalism are equally important, and that non-doctrinal skills are needed to engage in this work. I then briefly look more generally at the central contribution socio-legalism can make.

A. The Problem with Subjective Tests: 'Intention' and the Law of Murder

To be guilty of murder, D must 'intend' to kill or inflict GBH. We may work out that if someone plants a bomb in a building and gives a warning in advance then they are unlikely to 'intend' anyone to die, even if the

---

[73] Twining, 'LETR: The Role of Academics' (n 5) 102.

warning is given only shortly before detonation is due. Thus, if an occupant of the building does die, and if the jury decides, as it is entitled to do, that the bomber intended all occupants to escape, he or she would be guilty of manslaughter but not of murder—even under the extended meaning of 'intention' in *R v Woollin*.[74] However, is this good or bad? No amount of doctrinal analysis can tell us the answer. It all depends on how wide we want the scope of murder to be, and what the purpose is of having separate offences of 'murder' and 'manslaughter'.

To answer these questions we need to know something 'about law' which goes beyond a doctrinal understanding of 'intention'. Understanding the values underlying law, undervalued in most QLDs according to the LETR Report, would take us a long way towards understanding the symbolic significance of separate murder and manslaughter offences. But symbolism does not exist for the sake of itself; if we value the symbolic function of law it is because we think it serves a purpose. In this case we want to mark out only the most serious cases for what is generally perceived as the worst crime on the statute book. But is this bomber's action really regarded by 'public opinion' as less heinous than, say, the person who deliberately inflicts GBH on someone who unfortunately dies? This is an empirical matter, and one that cannot be answered either by doctrinal analysis or by analysis of legal values. It is a socio-legal question; it can be answered only by using social science skills (surveys, questionnaires, statistical and interview analysis etc). Undergraduate students do not need to collect such data, but they need these skills at a very basic level in order to interpret the data and to critically appraise others' interpretations of it.

The problem goes further. We said before that whether or not the bomber would be guilty of murder depends on whether he or she intended anyone to die or suffer GBH. What if the bomber's intention is unknown?[75] The law is clear on this: every element of an offence—including mens rea (in this instance, intention)—has to be proven 'beyond reasonable doubt'. The issue of principle is identical for all subjective tests. Lord Diplock identified the problem in the context of recklessness in *R v Caldwell*:

> The only person who knows what the accused's mental processes were is the accused himself ... If the accused gives evidence that because of his rage, excitement or drunkenness the risk of particular harmful consequences of his acts simply did not occur to him, a jury would find it hard to be satisfied beyond reasonable doubt that his true mental process was not that.[76]

We do not need to agree with everything Diplock says (accused people cannot always reconstruct their mental processes following dramatic events,

---

[74] *R v Woollin* [1999] AC 82 (HL).
[75] A Pedain, 'Intention and the Terrorist Example' (2003) *Criminal Law Review* 579.
[76] *R v Caldwell* [1982] AC 341.

and his 'Caldwell solution' raised as many problems as it solved) in order to accept that mental processes are often difficult to establish beyond reasonable doubt. But this concern—fear of wrongful acquittals—has never been taken seriously by commentators. In *R v G & R* Lord Bingham stated:

> I cannot accept that ... [the subjective test] ... would lead to the acquittal of those whom public policy would require to be convicted. There is nothing to suggest that this was seen as a problem before *R v Caldwell* ... There is no reason to doubt the common sense which tribunals of fact bring to their task. In a contested case based on intention, the defendant rarely admits intending the injurious result in question, but the tribunal of fact will readily infer such an intention, in a proper case, from all the circumstances and probabilities and evidence of what the defendant did and said at the time. Similarly with recklessness.[77]

Proving subjective elements is hardly tackled in the legal literature. It is probably true that, as Lord Bingham said; no one suggested it was a problem before *Caldwell*. No one has suggested it is a problem since, either. I cannot find any discussion of the issue at all in any of the textbooks, even where this passage is quoted.[78] But that does not mean that the problem does not exist. Whether 'tribunals of fact' do 'readily infer' the state of mind required 'in proper cases' is an empirical question. It cannot be answered by appeal to doctrinal method or legal values. We know that most contested cases end in conviction, and it may be that this is as true of cases where intention (and subjective mens rea more generally) is disputed as where actus reus issues are disputed. Equally, it may not be so. Empirical socio-legal research is needed to find this out and also to discover why and how magistrates and juries reach their decisions: the extent to which they go through the process outlined by Lord Bingham, or make inferences in the absence of strong evidence (as one might think likely on the basis of Lord Diplock's remarks) or simply find defendants guilty without making such inferences because they think that such defendants 'deserve' to be convicted on a general basis.

In the absence of research, the following case is illuminating.[79] A young man (D) got into a fight in a pub. He came off badly, left and drove off. A short while later he drove back near the pub. He saw the man with whom he had fought (V1) walking down the road with the friends with whom he had been drinking. D drove towards them, killing one of the friends (V2). D was charged with murder, on the basis that he drove at his adversaries. His defence was that he had no intent to kill or commit GBH. He said that he drove towards the group of young men—not at them—and did so in order to get close enough to get out of his car and continue the fight. The main

---

[77] *R v G & R* [2003] 3 WLR (HL), para 39.
[78] For an example see D Ormerod (ed), *Smith and Hogan's Criminal Law: Cases and Materials*, 10th edn (Oxford, Oxford University Press, 2009) 152.
[79] This was a case I dealt with as a member of the Parole Board in the 1990s.

evidence in his favour was that it was not V1 who was killed, but V2, a man with whom he had no argument.

How should the jury have tackled the problem? In *Stephens*[80] the trial judge directed the jury that 'the standard of proof is this: before you can convict the defendant you must be satisfied that you feel sure of his guilt. That's the same thing as being satisfied beyond reasonable doubt of his guilt. Nothing less will do'. The jury sent a number of notes to the judge from their deliberation room, one of which asked 'What constitutes reasonable doubt? How certain do you have to be?' The judge responded to the first question that 'a reasonable doubt is the sort that might affect the mind of a person dealing with matters of importance in his own affairs'. So the jury could only convict D of murder if they had no reasonable doubt in the *Stephens* sense about his intention or understanding of the risk he was taking when he drove towards V1 or V2. The jury did convict D of murder. But we will never know whether it was 'sure' in the *Stephens* sense, whether it was not 'sure' but made the inference anyway, or whether it simply thought someone behaving like this was morally deserving of conviction regardless. It is certainly not as obvious as Lord Bingham suggests.

It seems that both Lord Diplock and Lord Bingham could be correct in one respect. Juries and magistrates may convict many people of crimes despite essential elements of their crimes not being proven beyond reasonable doubt. Sociologically, the subjective test gives no trouble. But this is not because subjective states of mind are transparent to courts and juries; it is because the rooms in which juries and magistrates deliberate are hidden from view. Juries and magistrates can, in practice, decide on any basis they wish, because their verdicts are closed to virtually all questioning.[81] As Lady Hale DP puts it in relation to jurors disobeying instructions concerning internet searches, 'jurors do not always understand the judge's directions and even if they do understand them they do not always follow them ... [But] the courts have to go on trusting the jury otherwise the whole system will collapse'.[82] It may be that inferences are as often not drawn 'properly' as jurors illicitly consult the web about characters in the cases they are trying.

---

[80] *Stephens* [2002] All ER (D) 34.

[81] Research on jury and magistrate decision-making is complex and nuanced, but usually indirect as we cannot literally listen to deliberations. But to summarise it baldly, juries rarely ignore judicial guidance, but nor do they always follow it slavishly. They tend to follow a broad notion of 'justice' which for many would lead to conviction in cases where they think someone had a requisite mental element that could not be proven either way. Even less is known about magistrates, but there are good reasons to doubt the quality of many aspects of their justice. See generally, A Sanders, R Young and M Burton, *Criminal Justice*, 4th edn (Oxford, Oxford University Press, 2010) chs 9 and 10.

[82] B Hale, 'Connections Between Academic and Practical Legal Work' (City University lecture, July 2013) 8.

This story shows that, in any rational world, understanding the internal logic of the rule in *R v Woollin*—the doctrine—could only ever be part of the discussion about subjective mens rea. An equally important part of that discussion surely has to be how subjective mens rea is interpreted in the courts by magistrates and juries. Yet traditional legal skills and doctrinal analysis, and even discussion of legal values, do not provide the tools with which to have that discussion. Further, the requirement of subjective mens rea for serious crime is traditionally seen as protecting freedom and restricting the ambit of the criminal law, but this is generally asserted rather than discussed at any length in criminal law texts and journals.[83] In reality, there are relatively few disputes about subjective mens rea in the courts because the police do their best to secure evidence of culpability. The best evidence of this is confession evidence:

> Police: 'Did you intend to smash the windscreen?'
> Suspect: 'No'
> Police: 'So you just swung your hand out in a reckless manner?'
> Suspect: 'Yes, that's it, just arguing … Just arguing, reckless, it wasn't intentional'.[84]

The problem is that police interrogation, the involuntary custody that goes with it and the anxiety, humiliation and incalculable knock-on effects that go along with custody extends the ambit of police authority and is the very antithesis of freedom.[85] We see nothing of this discussion, nor the problem of proving mens rea in the courts, in the criminal law textbooks and in hardly any criminal law courses. Yet if the values underlying criminal law include freedom, and if we are to spend more time on this—as the LETR Report rightly urges us to—it only makes sense to do so if we see how successful the policy (subjective mens rea) is in achieving its objective (restriction of state power). Only socio-legal work as outlined in this paragraph can do this.

B. Reform of the Law of Prostitution

The criminal law relating to prostitution in the United Kingdom has remained largely unchanged since the Sexual Offences Act 2003. Prostitution itself is

---

[83] See, eg, J Herring, *Criminal Law: Text, Cases and Materials* (Oxford, Oxford University Press, 2012) 171–73.

[84] M McConville, A Sanders and R Leng, *The Case for the Prosecution* (London, Routledge, 1991) 70.

[85] This is not to suggest that the only reason for police interrogation is to establish subjective mens rea. But it is a major reason, and it is likely that it would be easier to restrict if mens rea were objective. On police custody and interrogation in general, see Sanders, Young and Burton, *Criminal Justice* (n 81) chs 4 and 5.

not criminal, nor is buying sexual services. But much behaviour associated with sex work is criminal. This includes soliciting, loitering, living off its earnings and maintaining premises for its purpose. Only relatively recently has some behaviour of clients been criminalised: kerb crawling, and buying sexual services from trafficked women. Criminalisation is aimed more at sex workers than their clients. In the past few years arguments have been increasingly put forward for moving towards the 'Nordic model', which criminalises clients, not sex workers. Other alternatives include complete decriminalisation or forms of regulation such as licensing systems.[86]

There are two main ways in which we can evaluate these different models. First, by looking at 'legal values': what symbolic messages do we want the law to convey? Arguably the current law embodies Victorian values: that selling sex is morally bad, and thus 'fallen women' are morally bad and deserving of condemnation; and that men are weak and thus should not be condemned, but should simply have temptation removed.[87] A law based on modern Western values would be very different. One strand would argue that treating women as sex objects for sale is grossly demeaning to women (and, arguably, to male purchasers too). The law should not condone—or, worse, encourage—behaviour that is grossly demeaning, particularly as it is women in general, not just sex workers, who are tarnished. The purchase of sex should therefore be criminalised (the Nordic model). Arguably, its sale should too. Licensing would be the worst solution of all as it would be state encouragement of sex work. A second strand would argue that selling sex is a choice that some women make, and is no more demeaning than cleaning people's toilets or undergoing cosmetic surgery in order to command high modelling fees. Sex work and the purchase of sex should therefore be decriminalised and/or licensed.[88]

Much of the current discussion in public life is on these lines.[89] The LETR approach, unlike the purely black letter approach, would equip students to engage in, and evaluate such arguments. However, neither approach would

---

[86] N Westmarland, 'From the Personal to the Political: Shifting Perspectives on Street Prostitution in England and Wales' in G Gangoli and N Westmarland (eds), *International Approaches to Prostitution—Law and Policy in Europe and Asia* (Bristol, Policy Press, 2006); M-L Skilbrei and C Holmström, 'Is there a Nordic Prostitution Regime?' (2011) 40 *Crime and Justice* 479.

[87] See T Sanders, 'Blinded by Morality: Prostitution Policy in the UK' (2005) 86 *Capital & Class* 9; M Whowell, 'Male Sex Work: Exploring Regulation in England and Wales' (2010) 37 *Journal of Law and Society* 125.

[88] This formulation assumes that all sex workers are women and clients are men. In reality, of course, all other biologically possible forms of prostitution exist, although they are not as common. Since sex work is used here simply to illustrate a more general point, these other forms of prostitution will not be discussed in this chapter.

[89] A Topping, 'UK Urged to Follow Nordic Model of Criminalising Prostitution Clients' *The Guardian* (London, 11 December 2013), available at: www.theguardian.com/global-development/2013/dec/11/uk-nordic-model-prostitution-clients-buyer-sex; R Matthews, 'Policing Prostitution: Ten Years On' (2005) 45 *British Journal of Criminology* 877;

equip students to engage in, and evaluate arguments on the lines of the second way of evaluating these models: the instrumental approach.

When the Wolfenden Report recommended decriminalisation of the act of prostitution, but continued criminalisation of public manifestations of it, its argument was that, though people should not be forced to witness public immorality, private immorality was not the law's business. We have seen that the law reflects a very skewed view of where responsibility for this 'immorality' lies. But the instrumental element (eliminating public manifestation of prostitution) was equally important to the Wolfenden Committee and, presumably, to the legislators who enacted its main recommendations, even though this instrumental element was not successfully operationalised for many years.

In more recent years a number of other potential instrumental objectives have presented themselves. In particular, what harm does sex work do or facilitate? The main harms are violence against sex workers by clients, and exploitation and/or trafficking of sex workers by pimps.[90] A 'values' approach is needed initially to decide which harms the law should most strenuously aim to deal with, but an extended socio-legal analysis is needed to identify the best way of dealing with whatever harms are prioritised—for, as is obvious from the prevalence of 'red light' areas in most cities for many years, simply criminalising an activity does not mean that it necessarily goes away. And, as we know from the prohibition experiment in the United States in the 1920s and 1930s, the unintended effects of criminalising goods and activities for which there is a seemingly unstoppable demand are sometimes worse than the harms that were the initial spur to the legislation in the first place. Arguably this is the situation with drugs laws, for example, in the United Kingdom and other Western societies.[91]

Few in the twenty-first century would argue that violence and exploitation are of less concern than involuntary sightings of sex workers and their clients. But would criminalising clients best reduce violence and exploitation, or would licensing or complete decriminalisation be more effective? These are socio-legal questions that are not answerable using 'internal' legal logic; so the idea that any meaningful discussion of the law of prostitution and possible reforms can take place using traditional legal sources and skills is simply untenable.

J West, 'Prostitution: Collectives and the Politics of Regulation' (2000) 7 *Gender, Work & Organization* 106.

[90] See T Sanders and R Campbell, 'Designing Out Vulnerability, Building in Respect: Violence, Safety and Sex Work Policy' (2007) 58 *British Journal of Sociology* 1.

[91] See, eg, the research summarised in F Measham and N South, 'Drugs, Alcohol and Crime' in M Maguire, R Morgan and R Reiner (eds), *Oxford Handbook of Criminology* (Oxford, Oxford University Press, 2012).

C. Socio-Legalism in the Round

Other criminal law examples could include medical manslaughter and assisted suicide, where in both cases most legal discussions touch on the 'socio' aspects but cannot deal with them adequately using only doctrinal and 'values' skills and substance, and where not dealing with the 'socio' thoroughly distorts all understanding.[92] All these criminal law examples illustrate Matthew Weait's point that doctrinal material alone cannot even provide 'a comprehensive account of how or why that decision was reached'.[93] He argues, using the extended example of a GBH through HIV infection case, that engagement with the trial process is necessary to ensure that students understand how case law is a distillation of a complex process (as with the motor murder case discussed earlier).

We can do the same kind of exercise with any subject—for example, the 'rule of law' example discussed in section IV, Karen Devine's discussion of tort, Charlotte O'Brien's discussion of EU law and Rosemary Auchmuty's discussion of equity, trusts and land law.[94] Doctrine is based on certainty and the primacy of legal rules. This implicit endorsement of legal positivism is dishonest unless books and curricula acknowledge the implicit rejection of, say, Dworkin's approach or that of the realists. Linda Mulcahy and Sally Wheeler show that positivism is thoroughly misleading in many aspects of contract law as many business relationships are premised on flexibility and bypassing the rules of 'offer and acceptance'.[95] In many law degrees this type of material is only incorporated into options, largely haphazardly.[96] So, as argued in section I, the view that 'we are all socio-legal now'[97] is really not tenable. Evidence for this is the fact that even PhDs in law are

---

[92] For examples of the kind of discussion I have in mind see: A Sanders, 'Victims' Voices, Victims' Interests and Criminal Justice in the Health Care Setting' in D Griffiths and A Sanders (eds), *Bioethics, Medicine and the Criminal Law, Volume 2: Medicine, Crime and Society* (Cambridge, Cambridge University Press, 2013) 81, ch 5; D Griffiths and A Sanders, 'The Road to the Dock: Prosecution Decision-Making in Medical Manslaughter Cases' in D Griffiths and A Sanders (eds), *Bioethics, Medicine and the Criminal Law, Volume 2: Medicine, Crime and Society* (Cambridge, Cambridge University Press, 2013) 117, ch 7.

[93] M Weait, 'Criminal Law: Thinking about Criminal Law from a Trial Perspective' in C Hunter (ed), *Integrating Socio-Legal Studies into the Law Curriculum* (Basingstoke, Palgrave Macmillan, 2012) 163.

[94] Hunter, *Integrating Socio-Legal Studies* (n 26) chs in Part II.

[95] S Wheeler, 'Contract Law: Socio-Legal Accounts of the Lived World of Contract' in C Hunter (ed), *Integrating Socio-Legal Studies into the Law Curriculum* (Basingstoke, Palgrave Macmillan, 2012) 104.

[96] See P Vincent-Jones and S Blandy, 'Applied Research Methods and Law Reform: The Leeds Experience' in C Hunter (ed), *Integrating Socio-Legal Studies into the Law Curriculum* (Basingstoke, Palgrave Macmillan, 2012) for the difficulties created by 'foundation' subjects being predominantly taught doctrinally.

[97] Cownie, *Legal Academics* (n 21) 198.

not disproportionately socio-legal; in fact the reverse seems to be true.[98] Students need some understanding not just of the substantive socio-legal material, but of methods too: not to carry out empirical research themselves, but to become 'critical consumers of empirical legal research'.[99] This is true not least because some students are future judges. The insight of one of our most distinguished judges[100] would be shared more widely if more had a socio-legal background.

> I find it (socio-legal work) helpful in informing me about how the real world works. So, for example, I have referred to the research of Gillian Douglas and others[101] to support a statement that people tend not to have a full understanding of the legal effect of the choices they make as to property ownership;[102] to the research of Anne Barlow and others on why people live together without marrying to support the view that they are not necessarily rejecting the legal consequences of marriage;[103] and to the findings of Sue Arthur and others on the financial arrangements which people make after divorce or separation.[104]

But the socio-legal approach should be central to legal education not just to ensure that the judges of the future can do their jobs. While this approach may not be necessary for lawyers who see their jobs as merely technical or money making, it is necessary to mould the truly 'professional' lawyer, as described earlier.

VI. CONCLUSION

I have argued in this chapter that the most important regulatory objectives in the LSA that relate to education are to: ensure an independent, strong, diverse and effective legal profession; protect and promote the public interest; support the constitutional principle of the rule of law; and improve access to justice. Little or none of this will be the subject of vocational or workplace training, so legal regulation must ensure that academic legal education does reference it substantially. In other words, the subjects studied, and skills acquired, need to instil in students an understanding of 'the

---

[98] Genn, Partington and Wheeler, *Law in the Real World* (n 23) para 87.

[99] Hunter, *Integrating Socio-Legal Studies* (n 26) 13.

[100] Hale, 'Connections' (n 82) 6. She is not entirely alone in this respect. For similar views see P Austin, 'Academics, Practitioners and Judges' (2004) 26 *Sydney Law Review* 463. But I had to go to the other side of the globe to find this similar view!

[101] G Douglas, 'Dealing with Property Issues on Co-Habitation Breakdown' (2007) 36 *Family Law* 67.

[102] *Stack v Dowden* [2007] UKHL 17; [2007] 2 AC 432.

[103] A Barlow, 'Just a Piece of Paper? Marriage and Co-Habitation' in A Park (ed), *British Social Attitudes: Public Policy, Social Ties: The 18th Report* (London, Sage Publications, 2001) 45.

[104] *Miller v Miller* [2006] UKHL 24, [2006] 2 AC 618, 128.

public interest', 'the rule of law', the significance of (and barriers to) 'access to justice', and what is meant by an 'independent' and 'effective' legal profession. The education required goes far beyond the technocratic kind of education required of technical trades and warned against by Thornton; it requires an intellectual and critical education, albeit one that is about law and legally related topics.

Doctrinal study alone cannot do this. The LETR Report acknowledges some of the deficiencies of the doctrinal approach that dominates twenty-first century UK law schools, but seems to think that simply adding more emphasis on legal values and 'black letter' skills will remedy the problem. It also considers that the current foundation subjects are an adequate proxy for what is needed as a foundation for vocational study, without considering what the regulatory objectives require. The LETR team asked respondents the value they placed on the range of legal and legally related subjects, and relied on a consensus that does not value socio-legal studies without helping respondents to understand the difference between socio-legal studies as a subject and socio-legal approaches to subjects. The Report therefore failed to achieve its objective of identifying what newly trained lawyers need to know and understand. The materials were available yet not consulted—whether, for example, the edited collection by Caroline Hunter[105] or the speech by Lady Hale DP. We have seen that a meaningful understanding of 'core' subjects themselves requires at least some kind of socio-legal perspective (in addition to other perspectives). We have also seen that students need to know 'about' law as well as knowing law itself. The particular example chosen, in the shape of section IV, was 'about' the relationship of law to class, but knowing 'about' the relationship of law to gender and ethnicity is equally important.[106]

One way of summarising the argument is that traditionally students learn 'knowledge' and the legal skills to use that knowledge; the LETR Report takes this a step further, making the case for students to understand the values needed to use that knowledge well. It should, however, have taken a third step, by arguing that students should be equipped with the knowledge and skills to assess when it is (and is not) indeed used well (ie, what the impact is of law in general and of particular laws, something assessable only socio-legally). The LETR Report should therefore have identified three ways in which law degrees (and law conversion courses) at present fail to comply with the LSA:

1. The regulatory objectives require less than is currently mandated in the sense that there is no reason why all intending legal professionals

---

[105] See Hunter, *Integrating Socio-Legal Studies* (n 26) and accompanying text.
[106] See, eg, Bradney, *Conversations, Choices and Chances* (n 42) 91.

should have to study the foundation subjects at all; or, at least, in the depth currently required.

2. The regulatory objectives require more than is currently mandated in the sense that understanding of, for example, inequality and its relationship to law is not obvious to all practitioners but is crucial for many socially marginalised individuals and groups. Further, to understand what rules are (the doctrinal approach, as with, for example, the meaning of 'intention') is insufficient; it is also essential to understand how rules are (or are not) applied, what their purpose is and whether they achieve those purposes. In order to become true professionals, students need to know 'about law' as well as to know 'law'.

3. In order to understand much of the material that is 'about law' above, socio-legal skills are needed.

If QLDs and law conversion courses are reformed to comply with regulation on these lines, graduates would enter the professions far better equipped to be thinking, compassionate and effective lawyers. Their 'employability' in respect of all professions and sectors of society would also be enhanced. As Black points out, these graduates will be more amenable to principles-based and outcomes-focused regulation than graduates educated primarily in rules-based doctrinalism.[107] And they would also be intellectually better educated. QLDs and law conversion courses are already commodified and corporatist. If we heed the calls to take them further down this line, students, the professions and our wider society will be ill served, and the stranglehold of the power elite will be strengthened. Instead, a new 'Joint Statement' for QLDs and law conversion courses could specify that:

a. A range of foundational law subjects be covered in some way, and individual law schools (or law students) would have freedom to choose any of these to cover in depth.

b. At least some of these subjects should be tackled doctrinally, socio-legally and with respect to legal values.

c. A full range of skills be instilled and assessed, including socio-legal skills.

d. All the regulatory objectives be addressed in the course of the degree in ways that law schools see fit.

There would be no need to specify how much of a degree need be occupied with these elements. But it might be prudent to specify that at least 50 per cent of a QLD should consist of modules that 'are' or are 'about' law. This would enable the identical specifications to be set for QLDs and conversion courses. And what of the SRA's wish to abolish graduate entry

---

[107] Black, 'Regulation, Education and Training' (n 43) 3. Contrast the 2014 version of the BSB Handbook with the previous rules-based versions.

as the main route into the solicitors' profession? If lawyering were a trade like plumbing, this might be fine. But it is not. The liberal values-oriented approach half advocated by the LETR Report, and the socio-legal approach advocated here, require graduate style education. Lawyering is a profession, not a trade: it requires the deployment of skills and knowledge with a sense of values and a sense of what can realistically and justly be achieved. This is set out in the regulatory objectives of the LSA. If graduate education is abolished as the main route for trainee solicitors it will have to be reinvented as the 'public service' elements of the regulatory objectives will not be taught in vocational colleges or in apprenticeships. Doubtless the SRA's policy reflects its frustration with the low-level education and training provided by doctrinalism, but the answer is not to despair of legal education but to reform it.

The socio-legal approach is one way of saying that students should do subjects that are 'about law' as well as subjects that 'are' law, and is one way of looking critically at how law works. It is not the only skill and subject matter that students should learn. But the time has surely come for us to realise that it is an essential part of the mix.

8

Creating a More Flexible Approach to Education and Training

ALEX ROY

THE REGULATION OF legal services has undergone something of a revolution in the past five years: starting with the Legal Services Act 2007 (LSA) and followed by the creation of independent legal services regulators and the Legal Services Board (LSB) as oversight regulator in 2009.[1] Since then further reforms have led to the licensing of Alternative Business Structures (legal firms that are not solely lawyer owned and managed),[2] 'outcomes-focused regulation'[3] and most recently the Legal Education and Training Review (LETR), commissioned by the Solicitors Regulation Authority (SRA), Bar Standards Board (BSB) and ILEX Professional Standards.[4]

The pace of change in legal services regulation has been fast. Yet this is a market where one in three people do not get the legal help they need,[5] fewer than one in five small businesses get legal advice when they have a

---

[1] There are eight professions and eight approved regulators under the Legal Services Act 2007. For a list, see www.legalservicesboard.org.uk/can_we_help/approved_regulators.

[2] Legal Services Board, 'Alternative Business Structures: Research Review' (LSB, 2011), available at: research.legalservicesboard.org.uk/wp-content/media/2011-ABS-research-note. pdf. For an empirical review of how ABS have fared in another jurisdiction, see C Parker, T Gordon and S Mark, 'Regulating Law Firm Ethics Management: An Empirical Assessment of an Innovation in Regulation of the Legal Profession in New South Wales' (2010) 37 *Journal of Law and Society* 466.

[3] Outcomes-focused regulation is part of a new governance shift away from traditional, detailed command and control regulation towards a model in which high-level principles and outcomes are set, but the means of achieving those outcomes is left to the regulated community/entity. For some thoughts on this shift in the context of legal services, see J Flood, 'The Re-Landscaping of the Legal Profession: Large Law Firms and Professional Re-Regulation' (2011) 59 *Current Sociology* 507.

[4] See Legal Education and Training Review, 'Setting Standards: The Future of Legal Services Education and Training Regulation in England and Wales' (SRA, BSB and CILEX, 2013), available at: www.letr.org.uk.

[5] See G Williams, 'Legal Services Benchmarking Report' (BDRC Continental, 2012), available at: research.legalservicesboard.org.uk/wp-content/media/2012-Individual-consumers-legal-needs-report.pdf.

problem and only 13 per cent of small businesses see legal advice as value for money.[6] The legal profession has for centuries espoused the benefit of self-regulation in maintaining quality and ethics. However, in the desire to promote professionalism, too often the underlying basis of consumer need—the need of individuals and businesses to solve their legal problems—gets lost. For this, affordable legal advice is essential. Affordability can, and should, be supported by greater flexibility both for providers and their consumers.

The LSB calls for flexibility,[7] but not for a decline in standards or quality of service. Instead, it is seeking to open the market to new ideas and new practices that in turn will encourage the development of new services to meet the needs of a wider consumer base—that is, the one in three people or four in five small businesses not currently getting the legal help they need. More people should be able to access legal services, not fewer. There is an opportunity to create greater flexibility for: educational providers; individuals pursuing a career in legal services; firms offering legal services, through the market responding to consumer needs. To support the legal services regulators the LSB published guidance following the publication of the LETR Research Report outlining how we will hold them to account in ensuring the delivery of a modern, flexible education and training environment.[8]

This chapter first examines the problems that exist with the current model; it then turns to consider what flexibility in legal education might look like in practice.

I. REGULATION THROUGH EDUCATION AND TRAINING STANDARDS

Primarily this chapter is about regulation. In fact, it is about the role of education and training within regulation, rather than a discussion about education and training within a wider framework of professionalism.[9] Indeed, the first thing to note about the role of education and training within a regulatory framework is the extent to which it acts as a proxy rather than a measure of quality. Legal services regulators have few tools to

---

[6] See P Pleasence and NJ Balmer, 'In Need of Advice? Findings of a Small Business Legal Needs Benchmarking Survey' (PPSR, 2013), available at: research.legalservicesboard.org.uk/wp-content/media/In-Need-of-Advice-report.pdf.

[7] Legal Services Board, 'Increasing Flexibility in Legal Education and Training' (LSB, 2013), available at: www.legalservicesboard.org.uk/what_we_do/consultations/closed/pdf/20130918_consultation_paper_on_guidance_for_education_and_training_FINAL_for_publication.pdf. Hereafter, 'the LSB Guidance'.

[8] ibid.

[9] For discussion on the relevance of education and training to legal professionalism, see RL Abel, *The Making of the English Legal Profession* (Oxford, Basil Blackwell Books, 1998); and RL Abel, *American Lawyers* (Oxford, Oxford University Press, 1989).

track the quality of legal services (an issue that, when studied, has revealed causes for concern).[10] Instead, they primarily rely on broad-based training at the start of a professional's legal career. This high entry barrier is supported by an acknowledgement that laws and processes change over time, so a further system of continuing professional development (CPD) is imposed to maintain and update knowledge. Regulators then apply supervision (including monitoring and discipline) to ensure behaviour in practice reflects these learnt skills.

Such an approach to regulation has many benefits. These include being easy to track, providing controls over who offers services and being measurable. But equally, this approach has many disadvantages. The most obvious disadvantage is that actual learning may not be targeted at the area of legal advice in which the individual offers services, not least as the bulk of learning is concentrated at the start of a career that may last 40 years or more. This approach may also have an excessive focus on knowledge with too little attention paid to skills and attributes. While focusing on regulated legal professionals, we should not forget that of a total legal workforce of 315,000 only around half are from the regulated professions.[11] The rest are not required to have any qualifications other than those stipulated by their employers.[12] In order to provide the small number of reserved legal activities,[13] people who are not regulated by a legal services regulator can only work under the supervision of someone who is legally qualified and regulated. Providers may offer non-reserved activities (for example, the writing of wills and the buying and selling of bodies corporate) completely outside the scope of regulation.

Existing training arrangements can have a potentially negative impact on the market. The LSB has concerns in particular about the impact the high barriers to entering the market—to provide reserved legal services—have on diversity.[14] Inevitably, requiring entrants to study for a degree followed by a

---

[10] For a summary assessment of quality literature see R Sullivan, 'Quality in Legal Services: A Literature Review' (LSB, 2011), available at: research.legalservicesboard.org.uk/wp-content/media/2011-Quality-and-the-legal-profession.pdf.

[11] Office for National Statistics, 'Annual Business Inquiry' (ONS, 2013) Section M, compared with numbers of regulated legal practitioners.

[12] Here, see the workforce review and projections created by Warwick University as part of the Legal Education and Training Review: Legal Education and Training Review, 'Setting Standards' (n 4), available at: letr.org.uk/the-report/chapter-3/workforce-projections-and-implications/index.html.

[13] These are the six activities that only a provider authorised by a legal services regulator can offer. They are: the exercise of rights of audience; the conduct of litigation; reserved instrument activities; probate activities; notarial activities; and the administration of oaths. See Legal Services Act 2007, s 12.

[14] For a review of these barriers, see H Sommerlad et al, 'Diversity in the Legal Profession in England and Wales: A Qualitative Study of Barriers and Individual Choices' (LSB, 2010), available at: www.legalservicesboard.org.uk/what_we_do/Research/Publications/pdf/lsb_diversity_in_the_legal_profession_final_rev.pdf.

year-long postgraduate course will impose significant costs on them. While other options exist, such as the Chartered Institute of Legal Executives (CILEx) training route or legal apprenticeships, the solicitor route remains most common in practice. The socio-economic bias built into the profession should concern us. It has not yet been addressed, even while other changes have improved access to the profession for women and those from an ethnic minority background. Diversity will enable those offering legal services to better understand their clients and represent the whole of society, not just the narrow section that can afford intensive and costly training.

The final report from the LETR team challenges regulators to look again at the way they require lawyers to be trained.[15] This gives regulators an opportunity to think about the risks they seek to manage using education and training, as opposed to using other regulatory approaches. This method of identifying risks and choosing tools to best tackle them sits at the heart of the modern approach to regulation, which is best summarised in the Principles of Better Regulation.[16] If, for example, there is a risk of low quality legal advice then there are a range of approaches available to regulators. These include requiring specific qualifications, monitoring management information systems, sanctioning and remedial training and ensuring compensation schemes are in place where other measures fail.

With legal activities such as criminal advocacy, concerns about the impact of poor quality service or the suitability of compensation as an effective remedy, are very real. However, few argue that problems of quality are solely the result of educational standards. Instead, they concern a much wider set of behaviours. 'Before the event' qualifications are likely to be suitable for addressing the risk of poor quality service perhaps most commonly in situations where monetary compensation simply would not be an effective remedy for errors.[17] Equally, as I will return to later, ongoing re-accreditation may be appropriate to supplement a one-off qualification gained at the start of a career.

Other triggers can lead to a desire to specify entry qualifications. These triggers might include the type of consumer or the extent to which individuals are able to judge whether the advice they have received has truly met their needs. While a large corporate client with in-house counsel may be happy to rely on reputation and their own experience, an individual with no legal experience challenging a benefits decision is more likely to desire clear educational attainments. This difference in needs is already reflected in the

[15] Legal Education and Training Review, 'Setting Standards' (n 4).

[16] See Better Regulation Taskforce, 'Principles of Good Regulation' (Better Regulation Taskforce, 2003), available at: www.webarchive.nationalarchives.gov.uk/20100407162704; www.archive.cabinetoffice.gov.uk/brc/upload/assets; www.brc.gov.uk/principlesleaflet.pdf.

[17] On the topic of quality and criminal advocacy, see A Devereux et al, 'Legal Services Commission: Quality Assurance for Advocates' (Centre for Professional Legal Studies, Cardiff Law School, 2009), available at: www.law.cf.ac.uk/research/pubs/repository/2269.pdf.

restrictions on complaints redress available from the Legal Ombudsman,[18] and could be further recognised by front line regulators through the use of education and training standards. Regulators should carefully consider the question of when requiring knowledge prior to working in a legal environment is necessary for dealing with the risks inherent in the services being provided. In some areas, knowledge-based criteria could potentially be replaced with a choice of knowledge or systems. In others, initial knowledge will remain essential in order to deliver services.

Perhaps the biggest challenge created by the LSA's regulatory settlement is the relationship between the independent regulators and their parent professional bodies.[19] It seems reasonable for any professional club to want to set entry barriers (which could include education and training). But how can this be squared with the LSA's regulatory objectives (in particular, the obligation to improve access to justice),[20] or responsibilities inherent in the state given monopoly bestowed on the profession?[21] It appears inevitable that at some stage the symbiotic relationship between regulators and professional bodies will be broken.

Regulators must regulate against risks. How could this obligation be met in future? One course could be for regulators to set 'day one outcomes' for activities they consider high risk, with any provider wishing to offer these activities requiring licensing by the regulator as meeting those outcomes. At the same time, professional bodies may regain control over the title attached to their branch of the profession, and set standards they see fit to the attainment of that title. It would then be open to regulators and professional bodies to reach agreement that people meeting the standards attached to a given title also meet the day one outcomes set by regulators for one or more high risk activities. In this way, holding a professional title would be one, but not the only, route to authorisation to offer a reserved activity. However, until the market develops further, the tension between professional desire for excellence, and regulatory desire to minimise unnecessary barriers and so achieve good service at a minimum cost, will remain.

Even within the framework of the LSA there is scope for regulators to offer greater flexibility to the market while they continue meeting their

---

[18] See Legal Ombudsman, 'Scheme Rules' (Legal Ombudsman, 2013) s 2.1 a-f, available at: www.legalombudsman.org.uk/downloads/documents/publications/Scheme-Rules.pdf.

[19] Out of the approved regulators listed in the Act only the Council for Licensed Conveyancers and the Master of the Faculties do not also have representative functions. See Legal Services Board, 'Approved Regulators' (LSB, 2009), available at: www.legalservices-board.org.uk/can_we_help/approved_regulators/index.htm.

[20] Legal Services Act 2007, s 1.

[21] The issue of monopolies and professions has been of concern to the Office of Fair Trading. See Office of Fair Trading, 'Competition in Professions' (OFT, 2001), available at: www.webarchive.nationalarchives.gov.uk/20140402142426; www.oft.gov.uk/shared_oft/reports/professional_bodies/oft328.pdf.

regulatory objectives. In the following sections I will consider the range of challenges for regulators considering greater flexibility.

II. FLEXIBILITY OVER A CAREER

For too long regulators (and before them the professional bodies) have limited the provision of reserved legal services to those who have studied in a set way for a specified amount of time. As noted earlier, this is not only potentially harmful to the diversity of the legal market, but it may also fail to deliver the knowledge and skills required by those aiming to practise non-reserved activities. Increasingly, the concept of competency frameworks (capturing applied knowledge or skills)[22] has replaced the idea of prescribed learning format (dictating where/how long learning should take place). Competency frameworks allow regulators to prescribe a range of outcomes that are linked to specific risks, and target the level of intervention to the level of risk and suitability of that type of intervention. A competency framework would set out what a competent member of a profession should know and be able to do, but would not necessarily prescribe how those skills, attributes or knowledge should be attained. This concept was captured in the LSB guidance to the approved regulators on the LETR when it stated, 'education and training requirements [should] focus on what an individual must know, understand and be able to do at the point of authorisation'.[23]

Introducing greater flexibility, by removing prescription on the way required knowledge and skills are gained, allows the development of a wider range of training routes. We have already seen the adoption of apprenticeships within law firms offering non-graduate entry to the profession. These, in particular, offer a potentially valuable tool to address a relative lack of socio-economic diversity. Such opportunities are part of a broader range of training options rather than being a single 'silver bullet'.

Perhaps the single biggest contribution that flexibility could make to the quality and accessibility of legal services would be through offering more restricted authorisations to provide legal services, as opposed to the broader solicitor qualification. In developing the range of providers able to offer reserved activities (for example, the introduction of licensed conveyancers) the market, and government, have accepted the case that affordable high quality legal services can be provided by specialists alongside generalists. As

---

[22] For a general introduction to competency frameworks, see J Burke, *Competency Based Education and Training* (London, Falmer, 1995).

[23] Legal Services Board, 'Guidance on Regulatory Arrangements for Education and Training Issued under Section 162 of the Legal Services Act 2007' (LSB, 2014), available at: www.legalservicesboard.org.uk/what_we_do/regulation/pdf/20140304_LSB_Education_And_Training_Guidance.pdf.

discussed earlier, this could be possibly resolved by regulators authorising specific activities separate from professional titles. These activities could themselves be linked with different competencies. Regulators could regulate a set of activities being offered by a range of different types of legal professionals. Competencies would be set by regulators. A mixture of professional bodies and educational providers could then seek to develop routes for individuals wishing to offer these activities.

Training of lawyers could in future be transformed into a series of knowledge packages, underpinned by a common ethical and reasoning framework. Existing differences between types of authorised persons illustrate that there is no common knowledge base needed for all lawyers. This could allow much greater flexibility for individuals within a career; for example, training perhaps as a probate specialist and adding further authorisations at a later date. Individuals would have the opportunity to transfer between different regulators. Or perhaps one day we could see a single regulator for all legal services?

Inevitably, thinking about accreditation for specific legal activities, be they an area of law or a type of work, leads to consideration of re-accreditation. The need for re-accreditation depends on the risk posed by the activities undertaken. For example, criminal advocacy has been deemed worthy of a re-accreditation scheme (Quality Assurance Scheme for Advocates or QASA) as a result of both the nature of the risks to individuals engaging in these services and the wider public interest.[24] As regulation becomes linked more directly with activities, rather than professions, regulators may identify more areas where such risks are clear and where re-accreditation would deliver real benefits. The LSB's LETR guidance stated that, 'standards [should be] set that find the right balance between what is required at entry and what can be fulfilled through ongoing competency requirements'.[25]

Opening more training routes, however, poses the danger of creating a second class of lawyers, redefining the existing range of paralegal roles with new titles that hold little sway with consumers. This, in a world where the professions are generally held in high regard by consumers,[26] is certainly a risk to those qualifying via new routes. But surely we must, in providing a regulatory framework for lawyers to compete within, trust the market to reward those providers that can demonstrate the value they offer and so get more consumers—whether through repeat customers or general market reputation?

---

[24] See Quality Assurance Scheme for Advocates, 'About QASA' (QASA, 2013), available at: www.qasa.org.uk/about-qasa.html.

[25] Legal Services Board, 'Guidance' (n 23).

[26] See, eg, the research on consumer experiences of legal services by the Legal Services Board: Legal Services Board, 'Consumer Experiences of Legal Services' (LSB, 2013), available at: research.legalservicesboard.org.uk/reports/consumer-experience-of-legal-services.

It seems likely that in many areas corporate brands will emerge and provide a reassuring mark of quality, while in others, individuals, subject to the brand of professionalism, will still hold sway. The market will decide where consumers trust firms and where they look for wider brands of professionalism. The prize is opening up the market so more people can receive legal services at an affordable price for an agreed service, from people that are regulated to provide the service, with regulation proportionate to the risks. In many cases optimum regulation may simply mean access to an ombudsman with no educational entry barriers.

III. FLEXIBILITY FOR FIRMS

The reality for modern law firms is that they employ a range of individuals both from, and outside, the legal profession. Legal businesses already have, and use, the flexibility to employ the range of people they need to deliver legal services. They already take responsibility for ensuring the quality of advice irrespective of who within a firm does the work.[27] The way such division of labour works within a law firm will in part be a consequence of regulation, most notably the reserved activities, and in part a matter of routine economic and personnel decisions taken by the firm.

It is important that, when designing the educational system of the future, we build on the flexibility already offered, most notably after the academic stage. Education and training requirements must make sense when firms are increasingly using technology to support legal drafting and many other tasks. Regulators are likely to feel a growing pressure to monitor the software employed by firms as much as the individuals using the software. The skills firms require from their employees will also have to change, as Richard Susskind sets out in detail in his book *Tomorrow's Lawyers*.[28] While Susskind's focus is primarily on the delivery of corporate law in large legal practices, similar changes are equally plausible for individual lawyers—will systematisation of legal areas such as wills, conveyancing, divorce and so on lead to a major demand for legal IT technicians? If so, how will they be trained and would legal regulators be competent to judge the validity of their training or CPD?

There is already a growing realisation among regulators in England and Wales that the model adopted to maintain technical knowledge—hours-based

---

[27] This responsibility is broadly captured within the SRA Handbook Principle 5—'provide a proper standard of services to your clients': Solicitors Regulation Authority, 'Solicitors Regulation Authority Handbook' (SRA, 2011) Principle 5.

[28] R Susskind, *Tomorrow's Lawyers: An Introduction to Your Future* (Oxford, Oxford University Press, 2013).

CPD—is not fit for purpose.[29] New models are being considered: encouraging individuals to take responsibility for their training needs; encouraging reflective learning; and moving away from hours-based compliance. A range of options is currently under consideration by the SRA for how to take forward their regulation of solicitors' continuing competence.[30] Few should doubt that as firms are given greater responsibilities by regulators to ensure that their staff have the necessary skills for the roles they perform, they will make certain their employees receive the right training and development.

The requirement on firms to consider the skills present within their workforce is reflected in the LSB's LETR guidance, which says that, 'Obligations in respect of education and training [should be] balanced appropriately between the individual and entity, both at the point of entry and ongoing'.[31] This recognises the existing primacy of the firm in determining the types and skills of people they employ. While legal regulators have traditionally focused principally on the professionals they employ, the new outcomes-focused regulatory world recognises that authorised persons only make up a fraction of the workforce. While it would be impossible for regulators to interfere in each individual employment and working decision, they should perhaps have some grip on the entities they regulate and assurance from those entities that they understand the risks they face and the skills required of their workforce.

IV. FLEXIBILITY FOR EDUCATIONAL PROVIDERS

Just as firms who provide legal services are operating in a global market, the same is true of educational providers, whether delivering undergraduate, postgraduate, vocational or academic education. Legal education is a global market, as a result both of the education of international students in England and Wales and, increasingly, through the desire of educators from England and Wales to set up legal education centres overseas.[32] This competition is both based on the robustness and validity of different legal qualifications and also on the system of law adopted itself. English and Welsh law continues to enjoy many advantages. These are reflected in the

---

[29] See, eg, SRA's consultation: Solicitors Regulation Authority, 'Open Consultations: Training for Tomorrow: A New Approach to Continuing Competence' (SRA, 2014), available at: www.sra.org.uk/sra/consultations/t4t-continuing-competence.page#download.
[30] ibid.
[31] Legal Services Board, 'Guidance' (n 23).
[32] The Legal Services Board commissioned work in this area. See J Flood, 'Legal Education in the Global Context: Challenges from Globalization, Technology and Changes in Government Regulation' (Legal Services Board, 2011), available at: www.legalservicesboard. org.uk/news_publications/latest_news/pdf/lsb_legal_education_report_flood.pdf.

continued strength of commercial courts settling international disputes in London and the prevalence of common law jurisdictions across the globe. But equally, the commercial, cultural and entrepreneurial dominance of the United States has caused a shift towards the American Juris Doctor qualification in many countries.[33]

International competition for legal services education poses challenges for the positioning of legal education in this country. As regulators increasingly start to look at day one outcomes and competencies, the potential for greater innovation from educational providers can be realised. For those educational providers who wish to innovate, greater regulatory flexibility will allow them to look at different, improved ways of ensuring students achieve the desired outcomes. For those educational providers who do not seek, or have any desire, to innovate, nothing should change as long as their course ensures students meet the outcomes set.

Many educational providers, particularly at undergraduate level, may choose not to change the courses they offer. Others will see innovation of legal education as an opportunity to differentiate their offering at both undergraduate and postgraduate level, making themselves more attractive to students who are keen to enter legal practice. There is perhaps also a role for professional bodies to work with educational providers to develop courses that meet the needs of mid and small-sized firms looking to diversify the skills of their recruits.

As the education market seeks to develop a wider set of options for those aspiring to work in the legal sector, regulators will be challenged to develop sufficiently robust approaches to assuring day one competencies. This could involve looking at course or assessment frameworks. Educational providers and regulators will share an interest in not stifling the development of flexibility in education that delivers the skills needed by the market, while at the same time maintaining the quality and brand value of existing legal education qualifications.

V. FLEXIBILITY FOR THE MARKET

A major concern of many commentators is that there are simply too many students studying law. These students, it is argued, are wasting money on qualifications that give little hope of ever delivering an acceptable return on their investment. The traditional response from the profession has been to seek to restrict numbers entering the profession through the professional

---

[33] eg, see University of British Columbia, 'UBC Board of Governors Approves Request FOR LLB (Bachelor of Laws) Degree to be Renamed JD (Juris Doctor)' (UBC, 2008), available at: www.law.ubc.ca/news-events/news-room/ubc-board-governors-approves-request-llb-bachelor-laws-degree-be-renamed-jd.

training routes.[34] This very question is being explored in the case of criminal barristers by Sir Bill Jeffrey's review of independent criminal advocacy, which he is conducting for the Ministry of Justice.[35]

In any market there is competition for scarce resources. In this case, would-be lawyers compete for scarce training contracts/pupillages, and later on, for jobs. This process of competition ensures that the very best candidates emerge successfully in the market. Three particular issues tend to dominate here:

1. Are there too many lawyers coming through the system?
2. Are the fixed costs of training too high?
3. What happens to those who are unsuccessful?

In practice I would argue that while complex, the responses to each of these issues are related.

In terms of numbers of lawyers, evidence of a continued lack of access to legal services tends to support the view that there is not an excess of people qualifying as lawyers.[36] It may be that, given the demand for legal services, the current system is not training the right types of lawyer and that the cost of training may be too high given the likely returns. Which leads to the third issue: is the training flexible enough to allow individuals trained as lawyers, but who do not get their first choice of job, to find other jobs within the legal sector?

Greater flexibility in training routes could lower the cost of training and allow training provided to be more closely tailored to the varied needs of the market. The question that training providers must ask is: how can they better understand the needs of the market and tailor their courses accordingly? And then: how can they sell their courses to individuals who may not be aware of the need to seek more flexible education opportunities? Such changes are important for individuals seeking to work in legal services but must also meet the needs of firms.

VI. CONCLUSIONS

The legal services market is changing rapidly. New services envisaged by far-sighted commentators such as Susskind are starting to emerge and with

---

[34] A Aldridge, 'Why it Doesn't Mean Much When the Chair of the Bar Council says they Want to Cap BPTC Numbers' *Legal Cheek* (21 January 2014), available at: www.legalcheek.com/2014/01/why-it-means-nothing-when-the-chair-of-the-bar-council-says-they-want-to-cap-bptc-numbers.

[35] Ministry of Justice, 'Review of Provision of Independent Criminal Advocacy' (MOJ, 2013), available at: www.justice.gov.uk/legal-aid/newslatest-updates/crime-news/review-of-provision-of-independent-criminal-advocacy.

[36] See Pleasence and Balmer, 'In Need of Advice' (n 6).

them the need for different types of lawyers. Regulators are beginning to look again at the way they have traditionally imposed education and training requirements, and to question whether these restrictions are necessary or perhaps harmful to the interests of consumers or even lawyers.

In future, regulators will have to focus more on risk and the range of interventions they can make to tackle risk where necessary. These include, but are not limited to, education and training requirements. This is likely to see providers of legal education rewarded with more freedom to innovate and create courses that better meet the needs of the market and individuals seeking to work in the market. Some providers will want to continue providing legal education as they always have. That will be their choice and, for many students, exactly what they want. Others will spy an opportunity and may find themselves at the forefront of a revolution in the training of the lawyers of tomorrow.

9

The Future of Legal Education from the Profession's Viewpoint: A Brave New World?

TONY KING

THE LEGAL SERVICES sector (covering all providers of legal services from solicitors and barristers to will writers and licensed conveyancers) is a major employer (with approximately 350,000 people working in the sector) and a significant contributor to the country's GDP.[1] Furthermore, law is at the heart of society. It is therefore essential that both the law and the sector are able to adapt to meet society's needs. Recent years have seen a range of developments (such as the current economic situation, new entrants coming into the sector and the Legal Education and Training Review (LETR)),[2] which have generated considerable change. However, in order to fulfil its societal role and to ensure the provision of access to justice for all, the legal sector needs to attract quality entrants and then train them throughout their careers to ensure they deliver excellent service in their chosen fields.

Over the years, the profession has been very successful in attracting well qualified and talented entrants. However, will that continue in the light of the current economic situation and recent legislative changes? It is dangerous to make sweeping generalisations. Nevertheless, and at the risk of oversimplifying the issues, the branch of the profession handling substantial commercial work, while not untouched by the current economic situation, continues to perform relatively strongly. In contrast, those branches of the profession which are heavily reliant on public funding are facing more

---

[1] R Wilson, 'Future Workforce Demand in the Legal Services Sector' (LETR, 2012), available at: www.letr.org.uk/wp-content/uploads/The-Changing-Demand-for-Skills-in-the-Legal-Services-Sector-Full-v2-2.pdf.

[2] Legal Education and Training Review, 'Setting Standards: The Future of Legal Services Education and Training Regulation in England and Wales' (SRA, BSB and CILEX, 2013), available at: www.letr.org.uk.

significant economic challenges.[3] These economic challenges are making it difficult for at least some practitioners in those branches to be able to attract and retain expert practitioners with the resultant risk of adverse consequences for access to justice.

This situation may be compounded by the recent changes to university funding.[4] Gaining a degree is still a very attractive proposition for many school leavers. However, the prospect of emerging from their academic training with debts which could be anything up to £50,000 will give some school leavers reason for pause. Some may opt out of tertiary education altogether. For others, their choice of career path may be influenced by the wish to ensure that they will be able to service that debt relatively easily and so they opt for the higher paying branches of the profession.

This chapter is in two parts. The first part is a review of the profession looking at what individuals and entities make up the profession, the nature of the work they do and the changes and challenges they face. The second part considers possible solutions to the challenges including the government's reliance on the market, the roles of the regulators in facilitating access, mobility and transferability as well as the roles of the academy and the practising profession.

I. THE ISSUES FACING THE PROFESSION

An entire book would be needed to cover this comprehensively and so this chapter will look at issues selectively. The legal profession has existed for centuries and was stable in terms of structure and approach for much of that time.[5] However, the profession has seen considerable change over the last quarter of a century with the pace of change accelerating in a range of areas—the economy, the client base, the service deliverers, technology, to name but a few. The following section considers these issues in more detail.

A. What is the 'Profession'?

In order to consider the issues affecting the profession, we need to be clear on what we should be looking at. If it is the profession (or professions)

---

[3] RL Abel, 'Law Without Politics: Legal Aid Under Advanced Capitalism' (1985) 32 *University of California at Los Angeles Law Review* 474; P Sanderson and H Sommerlad, 'Colonising Law for the Poor: Reconfiguring Legal Advice in the New Regulatory State' in V Bryson and P Fisher (eds), *Redefining Social Justice* (Manchester, Manchester University Press, 2011).

[4] Higher Education Act 2004, s 24.

[5] For an overview of the history of the legal profession, see J Baker, *An Introduction to English Legal History* (London, Butterworths, 2002) ch 10.

in the relatively narrow 'traditional' sense, it means looking at solicitors, barristers and legal executives. However, they are not the only providers of legal services. Therefore, the chapter looks at issues affecting the providers of legal services in the widest sense and so perhaps a more accurate question would be: 'What is the legal services sector?'

When looked at in that way, it is the sector which provides all types of legal services whether provided by members of the traditional legal professions (solicitors, barristers and legal executives) or not and through whatever organisational structure those 'legal service providers' deliver their services.

Therefore, in addition to the traditional legal professions, the sector includes:

— Paralegals
— Licensed conveyancers
— Will writers
— Immigration advisers, and so on.

While most of the providers working in the sector are regulated (by the Solicitors Regulation Authority (SRA), the Bar Standards Board (BSB), ILEX Professional Standards (IPS) and so on), some are not. The mere fact that a particular provider is not regulated does not of itself call into question the professionalism, effectiveness or efficiency of that provider. However, for the sake of the protection of the public, it may be appropriate for all providers working in the sector to be subject to regulation. As the introduction to this chapter made plain, the sector is a substantial one with some 350,000 people working in it and producing billions in contributions to GDP.[6]

B. What Services Does the Sector Provide?

Fairly obviously, it is legal services of all kinds. The titles of some of the service deliverers given in the previous section make clear the nature of the service they provide to the public. It is not the purpose of this chapter to provide a comprehensive list of all the work which legal service providers deliver but a simple categorisation of their work could be:

— Private client contentious work
— Private client non-contentious work
— Commercial contentious work
— Commercial non-contentious work.

---

[6] See Legal Education and Training Review, 'Setting Standards' (n 2) ch 1.

While the 'private client/commercial' distinction may be clear to insiders in the sector, it may not be self-evident to the average lay person. 'Private client' work would cover anything affecting individuals in their personal capacity from wills, probate and conveyancing through to divorce, personal injury and crime. 'Commercial' work will cover anything with a business aspect from setting up companies and mergers and acquisitions work through finance work to major civil litigation actions.

C. What Entities Provide the Services?

Just as the range of service providers working within the sector has changed in recent years, so have the entities delivering those services. Much of the legal work done in England and Wales continues to be provided by solicitors and legal executives working in law firms and barristers working in chambers. However, those traditional entities now face a wide range of competition. The larger traditional law firms doing commercial work face competition from international firms. For example, a member of the 'magic circle' of law firms will regard itself as being in competition with the other members of that elite group (as well as with other English law firms). It will also see itself in competition with the local offices of a number of substantial US-origin law firms.

A law firm focusing on private client work may now find itself in competition with a range of entities—firms of legal executives, licensed conveyancers, will writers and Alternative Business Structures (ABS) authorised by the SRA. The last were introduced by the Legal Services Act 2007 (LSA) and are perhaps one of the most significant changes affecting the legal services sector.[7] A variety of organisations have gained authorisation and some are rapidly becoming major players in their chosen market.

While the spread of entities may lead to healthy competition in the sector, the positive consequences of that competition can be balanced by the negative ones. Greater efficiency and so more cost-effective services may be encouraged but some entities may be driven out of business. This last result may have to be accepted as a natural consequence of the free market but it is undesirable if it adversely impacts on access to justice. For example, if a small private client firm which (aside from any other services it may offer) is the only firm offering mental health advice in its area is driven out of business, its clients may lose access to the vital support they need.

---

[7] ABS are firms where either a non-lawyer is a manager of the firm, or has an ownership-type interest in the firm.

Other aspects of the entities offering legal services which have changed in recent times are their structures and geographical reach. The last few years have seen the growth of associations of law firms and the creation of 'virtual' law firms. The former are individual law firms which group together, short of full merger, to share certain common services (training, technology etc).[8] The latter are firms which make use of technology and can be made up of individual lawyers who may be physically separated but who join together in fluid groups tailored to the needs of particular clients' work.[9]

Turning to the geographical spread of the entities in the sector, the last two or three decades have seen some dramatic changes. Focusing on law firms, for many years most would service the needs of their immediate locality with a small number based in the big cities operating on a wider national or international stage. Nowadays, the geographical spread of law firms can be much greater. Some continue to service the needs of their immediate locality but others operate on a regional, national, international or even global scale.[10] There are a variety of possible ways of defining 'international' or 'global' law firms. Some may provide English law advice to international clients often through both English and international offices. Others may operate on a truly global scale through an extensive network of offices around the world which offer both English and local law advice by virtue of having lawyers qualified in a number of jurisdictions working in them.

When looking at the 'players' in the legal services sector, this chapter has so far focused on the service providers who deliver the services to the public (whatever their legal needs). An important and very influential group which must not be overlooked is the 'in-house lawyers' (those working for, usually but not always, substantial organisations).[11] This group will both provide legal advice to their employers and also manage the external legal advice their employing organisations buy. The impact of this group is looked at in the next section.

D. The Challenges Affecting the Legal Services Sector

Inevitably, different branches of the sector and the different players in the sector will face challenges which, in detail, are very different. However, they

---

[8] Eg, Quality Solicitors. See: www.qualitysolicitors.com.

[9] Eg, Everyman Legal. See: www.everymanlegal.co.uk.

[10] See J Flood, 'Institutional Bridging: How Large Firms Engage in Globalization' (2013) 54 *Boston College Law Review* 1, available at: www.johnflood.com/pdfs/SSRN-id2257291.pdf.

[11] In-housers have been the subject of a recent report by the SRA. There are now 25,600 solicitors working in-house, twice the number in 2000 and representing 18% of the solicitor population. See: Solicitors Regulation Authority, 'Research on the Role of In House Solicitors' (SRA, 2014), available at: www.sra.org.uk/reports.

all face two broad challenges—first, competition in the light of the economic and regulatory environment in which they operate and, second, the need to ensure that they recruit and retain the right people to maintain and grow their businesses. This section will look at those two broad challenges.

i. Competition and the Economy

This topic could, of course, be subdivided into its constituent parts but here will be taken together, as combined they drive a significant challenge for the sector—price. The extent to which competition and the economy can impact on an organisation's business will depend, to some extent, on its business strategy. While not using quite those terms, we have touched on this issue already when looking at the different kinds of legal services organisations in the sector offered in different geographical locations. For example, private client non-contentious work in the organisation's immediate locality or substantial non-contentious commercial work offered in a range of jurisdictions as part of the business of a global firm. Whatever the organisation's business strategy, a very useful way of looking at the specific services the organisation offers is by reference to Furlong's Breakdown of Law Firm Work.

Furlong's Breakdown of Law Firm Work

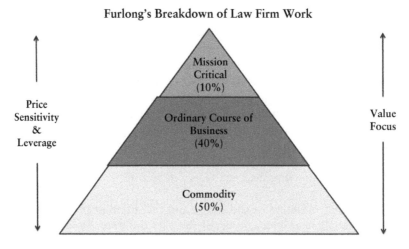

Source: Jordon Furlong, *The rise of the super-boutique*, August 19, 2011 Hildebrandt Baker Robbins, *Process Management and Process Improvement Workshop* (June 2010)

Furlong's 'Breakdown' helps in understanding the impact of 'price sensitivity' (how much can the lawyer charge for the work) and 'leverage' (how many people at what level of expertise are needed to do the work). To give illustrations of how the Breakdown might work in practice, a multinational corporate organisation embarking on a transformative merger or acquisition may be prepared to pay significant fees to get advice from an expert practitioner in the field. Equally, an entity facing a litigation action which will bring it to its knees if the case is lost will be prepared to pay much higher fees for advice on its defence from an expert than for, say, routine debt collection work. This type of 'mission critical' advice may be given by a small team or even by an individual. The detailed management of the merger or acquisition or the day to day running of the litigation case can be seen as 'ordinary course of business' needing a larger team of experienced people. In contrast, the handling of an entity's debt collection work can be 'commoditised' (ie, managed through a routine process) and is done profitably by being done by a large number of people who follow the process and who may not need to be highly qualified.

Picking up the point that legal work can straddle the divisions in the Breakdown, while the structuring of a cross-border merger and acquisition (M&A) transaction may require a small number of highly specialised experts, the more routine 'due diligence' or 'document review' could be done by following a process and so requires a larger number of less specialised workers. Some firms 'outsource' that type of work (that is, they pass it onto other firms which can do the work to the right quality level but at a lower price) or 'offshore' it (that is, have the work done in another jurisdiction where lawyers' fees are lower but where again the work can be done to the right quality level).[12]

In the current economic environment all clients, big and small, commercial or private, are price sensitive and that is where competition between entities offering the same services comes into play. The most obvious illustration of this is the trend to move away from charging by the hour for some work and the increasing use of capped or fixed fees. The organisations offering the services may continue to use the hourly charge-out rate for internal financial management purposes. However, clients looking for certainty in their legal spend may negotiate a fixed fee (for example, £5000) or a capped fee (not more that £10,000). At the risk of oversimplification, the hourly rate may be appropriate for 'mission critical' work while a fixed fee may be suitable for commoditised work.

Looking at large commercial clients, price may be only one of the factors taken into account when choosing a law firm. However, it is a significant one, as evidenced by the involvement of procurement teams who will work with the client organisation's in-house legal team to identify law firms which can supply the service to the right quality standard at the right price. Turning to private clients, most individuals do not have the buying power to be able to drive down the cost of legal services on their own. However, many private clients want legal services which could be described

---

[12] For a review of these practices, see AM Kadzik, 'Current Trend to Outsource Legal Work Abroad and the Ethical Issues Related to Such Practices' (2006) 19 *Legal Ethics* 731.

as 'volume services'. This means work which is not highly specialised and can be done by following a process, in other words, commoditised. Personal injury or domestic conveyancing can, in certain circumstances, fall into this category and the fact that there may be a number of firms in a locality competing for the work can also drive down the cost.

Whatever the business strategy of the organisation, it is fair to say that the vast majority of lawyers have seen an increase in competition with the entry into their markets of new players, whether ABS following the LSA or international law firms moving into the English market. While all organisations face pricing pressures, for some government policy has added additional challenges with the changes to legal aid putting some smaller firms offering that service under financial strain.

Pricing pressures (whether as a result of legal aid changes or not) have led to events which were unheard of in the legal services market only a couple of decades ago: redundancies, even in substantial commercial firms, and failures of law firms (such as Halliwells).[13] Another dramatic development which emerged in the latter half of the twentieth century is law firm merger.[14] There have been a number of high profile mergers of both national and cross-border law firms. While the concept is often associated with the larger commercial firms, it is a strategic technique used across the sector to achieve economies of scale, increased market share, comprehensive service offerings and so on. This may imply that 'size is king' but a better way of looking at it is 'efficiency is king'. Any organisation, large or small, needs to deliver its services in the most efficient and cost-effective way which delivers value to its clients and so ensures fees are paid which deliver the desired margin. The competition/price concept is an obvious business issue but so is legal education.

To state the obvious, the organisation providing the services, whatever services they may be, needs people working for it who are capable of delivering those services to the right standard of quality. Legal education has, therefore, a significant and obvious role to play. By 'legal education' I refer both to learning substantive law in the course of studying for a law degree and also learning legal practice through the acquisition of knowledge on courses leading to professional qualifications and the experience of working for a legal services provider.

The majority of entities which provide legal services are businesses which need to be managed effectively if they are to produce profit. Some providers

---

[13] See A Aldridge, 'Corporate Law Firm Undone by Boom Time Success' *The Guardian* (London, 22 October 2010), available at: www.theguardian.com/law/2010/oct/22/corporate-law-firms-boom-era-excess.

[14] See BE Aronson, 'Elite Law Firm Mergers and Reputational Competition: Is Bigger Really Better?—An International Comparison' (2007) 40 *Vanderbilt Journal of International Law* 763.

are 'not-for-profit' organisations, but of course they also need to be managed effectively. Therefore, the people working in those entities need to possess the right level of 'managerial' skills to perform their particular tasks or roles. The managerial training needed is additional (and complementary) to the knowledge of law and practice covered by the term 'legal education'.

Employing organisations operating in the sector collectively provide a significant amount of training to their people (whether through in-house training provision and/or sending their people on external training programmes). All this costs money and the expense will be factored into the organisations' overheads. 'Formal' education programmes are one method of training an entity's workforce but learning 'on the job' is an equally powerful training method. However, in cost conscious times, clients will be reluctant to pay for the training of their lawyers. Therefore, either the organisation has to absorb the cost or it has to recruit a workforce which already possesses the knowledge and skills. Who those people are and what knowledge and skills they need will depend on the nature of the organisation's business strategy and so we now turn to the 'people challenge'.

ii. The People

We have seen that the people working in the legal services sector can have a range of qualifications (as solicitors, barristers, legal executives and so on) and will perform a range of roles. The organisation's business strategy will determine the 'mix' of those people. Let us now look at the key 'people' issues for the sector.

a. The 'People Profile' of the Sector

A significant proportion of people who work in the legal services sector hold the 'traditional' qualifications—that of solicitor, barrister or legal executive.[15] However, the holders of a range of 'new' qualifications are active in the sector, such as will writers and licensed conveyancers. Furthermore, economic pressures coupled with developments in technology have led to the emergence of a range of new roles, such as paralegals, legal process analysts, legal project managers and so on.[16]

Looking at the entrants to the sector, many will have followed one of the traditional paths to qualification (as solicitor, barrister or legal executive). Most will expect to specialise in a particular branch of the law and so will move from a relatively broad-based educational foundation at the start of their careers to, for some, a highly specialised area of work as their career

---

[15] See Wilson, 'Future Workforce Demand' (n 1).
[16] R Susskind, *Tomorrow's Lawyers: An Introduction to Your Future* (Oxford, Oxford University Press, 2013).

progresses. Furthermore (and as has already been covered), given that law is a business sector, many will need to develop managerial skills (the ability to manage a business including its finances, its clients and its people). While the holders of each of the three traditional qualifications will follow similar paths to gaining those qualifications, increasingly their training will reflect (so far as the relevant Training Regulations allow)[17] the branch of the sector in which the entrant will work. To take but one example: there are Legal Practice Courses (LPC) which are tailored to the future work of trainee solicitors taking up training contracts in commercial firms. Such tailoring quite rightly does not aim to over-specialise the trainees too early in their careers and so their employing organisations will support them in their development as both expert practitioners and business managers. However, the pricing pressures that many of those employers face (particularly their clients' reluctance to pay to train their advisers) means that many employers will want their recruits to possess as broad a range of knowledge and skills as is feasible at that stage in their career. This will give the employers a solid foundation on which they can build a developmental structure.

These issues will apply equally to the holders of new qualifications, such as will writers and licensed conveyancers. For some in this group, a challenge will be the transferability of their current qualification. What credit will a licensed conveyancer get for his or her existing qualification should he or she wish to qualify as a solicitor? This issue of transferability was touched on by the LETR and the three regulators which launched that review will look at that issue over the coming years.[18]

Furlong's Breakdown, discussed above, reflects the fact that many of the tasks handled by workers in the legal services sector can be commoditised. The people carrying on those tasks may not need to hold one of the traditional qualifications (albeit that many employing organisations may appoint holders of those qualifications to oversee the handling of the work). The people who handle the commoditised elements of legal practice can have a variety of qualifications and titles. The term 'paralegal' is becoming common currency in the legal services sector, but people who may hold that role can come from a range of backgrounds: some may be graduates who have completed the LPC but have been unable to secure a training contract to qualify as a solicitor; some may hold a degree but have not yet embarked on further professional qualifications; some may hold few formal qualifications; some may be on full-time contracts, others may be on fixed-term contracts. An issue for the sector is to define what paralegal means and to determine what training or qualifications, if any, are needed.[19]

---

[17] Solicitors Regulation Authority, 'SRA Training Regulations 2011' (SRA, 2011), available at: www.sra.org.uk/solicitors/handbook/qualificationregs/content.page.

[18] See Legal Education and Training Review, 'Setting Standards' (n 2) chs 6 and 7.

[19] ibid, in particular ch 6.

Recently, legal 'apprenticeships' have come into the picture with the development of programmes leading to Level 4 qualifications.[20] It is early days for this scheme but it is a route to legal qualification which school leavers can follow by combining work with study. This route may be attractive to aspiring lawyers who do not want to take on the burden of significant student debt. However, it is vital that the qualification process is seen as producing fully-qualified lawyers who are equivalent to any who have followed the traditional qualification routes. For this reason, it is essential that the educational standards of the training of apprentices are the same as for other routes to the qualification. Furthermore, if an apprentice can become, say, a solicitor, giving the apprentice the opportunity to gain a degree should avoid any questioning of the quality of the qualification. Of course, the apprenticeship-type model is not new; it is similar to the one which has been open to aspiring legal executives for many years, and was a common direct route into, for example, the solicitors' profession until the 1980s.

All the people we have looked at so far in this section will perform tasks which would probably have been recognisable to someone working in the sector 25 or even 50 years' ago. However, the increased use of technology in the profession coupled with the drive for efficiency is leading to the creation of a range of roles previously unknown in the sector. Richard Susskind identified in his book *Tomorrow's Lawyers*, a range of new jobs for lawyers.[21] These include:

— Legal Knowledge Engineer (computer-based knowledge)
— Legal Technologist (combining IT skills with legal training)
— Legal Hybrid (a lawyer with other formally acquired skills such as organisational development)
— Legal Process Analyst
— Legal Fees Analyst
— Legal Project Manager
— Online Dispute Resolution Practitioner
— Legal Management Consultant
— Legal Risk Manager.

Not every entity in the sector will have (or need) people performing these types of role, but they are increasingly common. The teams of Professional Support Lawyers which many law firms employ perform the tasks of Legal Knowledge Engineers. The drive (and need) for efficiency has led some firms to employ Legal Process Analysts (whatever title the individual firm

---

[20] See: www.cilex.org.uk/study/legal_apprenticeships.aspx.
[21] Susskind, *Tomorrow's Lawyers* (n 16).

may give them) whose role is to apply process re-engineering techniques to improve firms' internal processes. The list could go on.

Some of these roles may be performed by lawyers who have moved into a new function or acquired a new skill; others may be specialists who have gained these skills while working in other sectors and who have been recruited to perform these tasks in the law firm.

b. 'Generation Y'

Much is made of the different attitudes to work of the entrants into the sector who have been badged as 'Generation Y'.[22] It is dangerous to over-generalise, but at the risk of falling into that trap, many of the new entrants to the sector may have different expectations as to how they will manage their careers than did the current seniors in the sector. The 'Generation Y-ers' may expect to move employers several times and even have serial careers. For some, the traditional 'carrot' of 'partnership' in a law firm may hold little attraction, especially if the consequence of the current economy is to reduce the number of partnership places and lengthen the time it takes to reach that level.[23] This group represents a two-fold challenge. First, the Generation Y-ers need to think how best to prepare themselves for their perhaps more flexible career aspirations (and be given support to do so). Second, their employers need to give thought as to how to manage them and their development in a way which meets the aspirations of the individual while meeting the business requirements of the organisation.

c. Inclusion and Diversity

Employers in the sector are facing increasing demands for inclusion and diversity from government, the regulators, society and their clients.[24] This is not to say that employers are reluctant to accede to this demand as doing so can have significant business benefits.[25] Given the multicultural nature of society as well as the increasing globalisation of law, a diverse workforce will support many businesses' objectives.

---

[22] For a wide review, see the 2008 Special Issue of the *Journal of Managerial Psychology*: V Williams, 'Generational Differences at Work' (2008) 8 *Journal of Managerial Psychology* 857.

[23] M Galanter and T Palay, *Tournament of Lawyers: The Transformation of the Large Law Firm* (Chicago, University of Chicago Press, 1994); M Galanter and W Henderson, 'The Elastic Tournament: A Second Transformation of the Big Law Firm' (2008) 60 *Stanford Law Review* 1867.

[24] J Braithwaite, 'The Strategic Use of Demand Side Diversity Pressure on the Solicitors' Profession' (2010) 37 *Journal of Law and Society* 442.

[25] For an overview of the 'business case' for diversity, see: Department for Innovation & Skills, 'The Business Case for Equality and Diversity' BIS Occasional Paper No 4 (Government Equality Office, 2013), available at: www.gov.uk/government/uploads/system/uploads/attach-ment_data/file/49638/the_business_case_for_equality_and_diversity.pdf.

While the aim of achieving inclusivity and diversity may be applauded across the sector, it is not necessarily easy to achieve. The law is seen as a stable career and so is an attractive proposition in the recruitment market. Many employers are, therefore, privileged in terms of being able to choose the best applicants. While that makes business sense, who are the 'best' applicants? The cost of qualifying as a lawyer may put very good potential applicants off starting the process at all. If there is a perception that a particular employer or group of employers only select recruits with a particular academic profile, good potential recruits may self-select out of that market. The challenge is, therefore, one of finding ways of opening the sector to as wide a range of talented would-be entrants as possible while recognising the business need of employers to recruit a workforce able to do the work to the required quality standards.[26]

Ensuring diversity in recruitment is one thing. Maintaining diversity among the workforce is another. Many parts of the sector are demanding, for example, in terms of the hours which need to be worked. Criminal defence lawyers may have to visit a police station in the middle of the night; transactional lawyers may have to work very long hours to complete the deal within a tight deadline. These time demands may cause tension with workers' caring obligations. The challenge for the sector is to find ways of achieving an appropriate work–life balance for the workforce while servicing the needs of the public. If a lawyer leaves the sector because his or her work–life balance is out of kilter or if the lawyer 'burns out', this is a significant loss to both parties—the individual and the employer. There is no simple answer to this though there is a range of options open: flexible working, project working, the use of technology and so on.

II. THE RANGE OF SOLUTIONS TO THE CHALLENGES FACING THE SECTOR

First, how can the challenges be summarised? The legal services sector covers all aspects of law nationally and in the case of some players in the sector, internationally or even globally. It should not be overlooked that the English legal qualification is one of the two leading global qualifications (along with that of a New York attorney). This is a consequence of the global dominance of UK and US-origin business enterprises which value working within a legal structure with which they are familiar and which they trust. To be clear, this is not to imply any criticism of other legal systems.

---

[26] See H Sommerlad et al, 'Diversity in the Legal Profession in England and Wales: A Qualitative Study of Barriers and Individual Choices' (LSB, 2010), available at: www.legalservicesboard. org.uk/what_we_do/Research/Publications/pdf/lsb_diversity_in_the_legal_profession_final_rev.pdf.

Therefore, maintaining the strength of the 'brand' globally is essential to 'UK Plc' as well as to the health of the individual players who provide those services. This complexity of 'subject matter' poses a challenge as regards the 'shape' of the training continuum for individuals entering the various branches of the sector.

The nature of the economy and the business environment in which players in the sector operate has meant there have been changes in the way legal businesses structure themselves and how they resource their workforce. A range of new qualifications and roles have been added to the three traditional qualifications for workers in this sector. The business models of the various types of employers in the sector have driven the creation of many of the new roles. This has been matched to some extent by the economy reducing the number of places for would-be entrants to the traditional qualifications and also increasing the number of people who wish to enter the sector but who are either unwilling or unable to meet the cost of the traditional qualification routes.

Linked to that is the issue of inclusion and diversity. If the upper echelons (however they may be defined) become the preserve of 'rich kids' only, that is, to say the least, undesirable. Therefore, the sector needs to ensure it is open to all would-be entrants of the right calibre and that it ensures diversity at all levels across all branches of the sector, including facilitating transferability between the branches where appropriate. How are these challenges going to be met? I would argue by all the players in the sector (the academy, the employing organisations, the regulators and so on) working together.

A. The Qualification Routes

The first challenge is to ensure that the various routes to qualification (which for the purpose of this section covers both formal qualification as a solicitor, legal executive or whatever, as well as preparation for a role, for example as a debt collection process handler) are 'fit for purpose'. Focusing on the qualifying law degree part of the training continuum for solicitors or barristers, there is the issue of the contents of the Joint Statement. The Joint Statement, agreed by the SRA and the BSB, determines which topics must be covered for a law degree to satisfy the requirements for the so-called 'Academic Stage' of training.[27] It is perfectly legitimate for the academy to say that the law degree is a liberal arts degree, not a practical preparation for practice (especially given that approximately only 50 per cent of law graduates enter the practising profession) and so resist

---

[27] See Solicitors Regulation Authority, 'Joint Statement on the Academic Stage of Training' (SRA, 2002), available at: www.sra.org.uk/students/academic-stage-joint-statement-bsb-law-society.page.

suggestions as regards detailed content from the practising profession. It is equally legitimate for the practising profession to say that the law degree is the foundation of future careers of aspiring solicitors and barristers and so the practitioners are entitled to comment on the contents of those degrees.

The way forward is for both groups to work together to find solutions which work for all sides. Practitioners from some branches of the profession have called for the addition of the law of organisations and the philosophy of ethics to be added, in some form, to the required contents of a qualifying law degree.[28] The law of organisations (company law, partnership law and so on) is a long-established academic subject and one which is relevant (to a greater or lesser extent) to virtually every part of the legal services sector, both to the entities providing the services and to their clients. The ethical obligations of a lawyer are a key element in the 'selling proposition' of the legal profession. Ensuring all future lawyers have a sound academic underpinning to their knowledge of the codes of conduct (which can be taught later in the training continuum) to which they will be subject in future is important for the future 'health' of the sector and for the protection of the public. If the focus is on the teaching of the philosophy of ethics rather than on the contents of the relevant codes of conduct, it is a course of study which will be valuable whatever career a law student follows. Ethics are certainly important to lawyers but they are also important in every other work sector. Some parts of the academy have pointed out that these changes may cause significant resource problems and that is fair comment.[29] However, could the resource gaps be filled by combining with other relevant faculties? Some practitioners may want their recruits to have a broader-based foundation of legal knowledge to help them cope with the inevitable changes in legislation and legal 'fashion' over an individual's career. Members of the academy can say that a law degree teaches students to 'think like a lawyer' and so gives them the tools to cope with any changes which Parliament or the economy may throw at them.[30]

The solution is not simple or obvious; it will come out of discussion between the academy and the practitioners. The range of employability initiatives which many universities have in place are positive proof of how well the two sides can work together. To be clear, this section is neither supporting nor criticising any particular position taken by the academy

---

[28] See, eg, the submissions made by the City of London Law Society to the LETR: City of London Law Society, 'Response to the Call for Evidence by the Executive of the Legal Education and Training Review' (City of London Law Society, 2012), available at: www.letr. org.uk/wp-content/uploads/CLLS-Response.pdf.

[29] See the response to the LETR call for evidence from the Society of Legal Scholars: Society of Legal Scholars, 'Discussion Paper 01/2012: Response from the Society of Legal Scholars' (LETR, 2012), available at: www.letr.org.uk/wp-content/uploads/SLS-Response1.pdf.

[30] See A Boon and J Webb, 'Legal Education and Training in England and Wales: Back to the Future?' (2008) 58 *Journal of Legal Education* 79; A Bradney, 'Aristocratic Values, the Liberal Law School and the Modern Lawyer' (2011) 17 *Web Journal of Current Legal Issues* 1.

or the practitioners. It is merely advocating that both sides work together to find solutions appropriate to their differing needs and objectives. That said—and especially in the light of the economic challenges which many would-be entrants to the profession face—the innovative structures which many academic institutions have developed is to be applauded.

There is most certainly a place for traditional academic law degrees run over the standard three years. However, different models equally have their place. Part-time degrees, whether face to face or mixed media, will suit students for whom a three-year full-time study degree may not be suitable, whether for financial or personal reasons. A two-year 'condensed' degree may have similar attractions. 'Pure' academic degrees (whatever the structure) have considerable value, as do those with a more practical tilt, whether by virtue of the subjects taught or the experience gained in parallel with the academic study (for example, through clinical education). Given that law is a business, giving students an appreciation of that as they follow the training continuum to qualification will help them in the long run. Therefore, including 'business' topics (such as strategy, finance, leadership) in the 'formal' part of the qualification training continuum may be beneficial. However, there will inevitably be constraints on what can be covered, whether that is resourcing issues for the teaching institution, the cost to the student or the stage at which the student will use the knowledge gained. A student may use his or her knowledge of contract from the first day in the office of their employer. However, that student may not use at least some parts of a full MBA programme until some years into his or her practising career.

We should not overlook the fact that the training continuum for solicitors and barristers includes two academic elements—the academic stage (the degree or the graduate diploma in law) and the professional training courses (the LPC or the Bar Professional Training Course). These two elements must be looked at together and the latter should form a true bridge between the former and the training contract or pupillage. That in itself may mean that fruitful discussions are to be had between practitioners, the providers of the professional training courses and the academy about what is required at each step. The employing organisations in the sector will obviously be interested in preparing their recruits to work in their particular organisations. However, what a law business requires of its new entrants will have some commonalities with the requirements of employers in many other sectors. For example, a knowledge of contract or company law is of benefit to a wide range of business sectors and the ability to think like a lawyer could be of use in an even wider range. Therefore, the academy and the practising profession working together on these issues could benefit the 50 per cent or so of students who do not enter the practising profession as much as the group which do.

It would be wrong to ignore the entrants to the sector who are not following the path to qualification as solicitors or barristers. Clearly practitioners with other qualifications who work in the sector should have similar discussions with the providers of their training (whether that is an educational establishment, a training organisation or their employers) to ensure their business needs are met in an appropriate way.

Finally, what of the members of the workforce who need training to perform a role rather than necessarily to gain a qualification? Their training may take the form of in-house or on the job training in the particular process but the academy is made up of educational specialists who may, therefore, have a significant contribution to make in terms of designing and delivering the most effective form of such training.

B. Post-Qualification Continuing Professional Development or 'Continuing Competence'?

Some of the groups which work in the sector will have to meet continuing education obligations imposed on them by their regulators (for example, the CPD obligations of solicitors which were recently under review by the SRA).[31] All workers in the sector will need to keep up to date with developments in their particular area and there is considerable support already available for that. There are many continuing education providers offering a range of courses on topics which meet most if not all the needs of the sector. Many of the larger organisations will have in-house training functions which meet the particular requirements of the organisation. Again there is an opportunity for greater cooperation between the practitioners in the sector and the academy. One obvious area for cooperation between the practising profession and the academy (which already happens to a considerable extent) is to ensure that workers in the sector are up to date with recent developments. This is not the only area of cooperation which currently takes place—many members of the academy are experts in particular areas of practice and the exchanges between them and practitioners working in the same field through publications, conferences and so on can be of considerable benefit to both sides.

It is not just in the field of law that the academy and practitioners can benefit from each other. This chapter has made the point a number of times that law is a business and the workers in the sector need to be effective managers as well as legal experts. Many lawyers have gone on executive education programmes run by law schools as well as management training courses run by continuing education providers. This is an area of activity

---

[31] Solicitors Regulation Authority, 'Training for Tomorrow: A New Approach to Continuing Competence' (SRA, 2014), available at: www.sra.org.uk/sra/consultations/t4t-continuing-competence.page.

which could expand as the managerial challenges which many lawyers face become increasingly complex.

The LETR recommended a review of the existing continuing education requirements which some of the regulators have put in place and, for example, the SRA has recently considered the existing CPD obligations to ensure the continuing competence of solicitors.[32] This leads us to the role which the regulators have to play.

C. The Role of the Regulators

The regulators of the various regulated groups which work within the legal services sector (the SRA, the BSB, IPS being the main but not only ones) will take steps to ensure the holders of their respective qualifications have met appropriate standards at the point of qualification and maintain those standards post-qualification.

This means that the regulators will have an interest in the various stages which the holders of their qualifications go through prior to qualifying and so they need to be part of the discussions between the academy and the relevant practitioners to ensure each qualification's training continuum is fit for purpose. This has many aspects which are beyond the scope of this chapter but there is one particular point in relation to diversity which is worth making. In the recent past, the professions of solicitor and barrister have become predominately graduate only. A very important exception to that is that legal executives can qualify as solicitors even if they do not have a degree. If there are new routes to qualification for non-graduates (such as the apprenticeship route), the regulators must ensure that those routes are comparable to the equivalent 'graduate route' so as to avoid any risk of a two-tier qualification. This is a matter of setting (high) standards for all entrants to the profession (and for ongoing continuing education). This will make it clear that all individuals holding the qualification have achieved the same standard on gaining the title (and afterwards) irrespective of the route followed.

Inclusion and diversity can only be good for the sector, so while the regulators must ensure appropriate quality standards for all entrants, they should facilitate both entrants coming into the sector and also mobility within the sector. On the latter point, this means giving appropriate credit for previous qualifications for someone working in one branch of the sector who wants to move into another. For example, it is only right that a licensed conveyancer who wishes to qualify as a solicitor should be given credit for his or her relevant studies to date.

---

[32] ibid.

A different issue is where someone holding a particular regulator's qualification wishes either to prove a specialism or to move into a new area of work. This leads us into the issue of post-qualification accreditation which exists for some areas of practice.[33] Whether it is feasible or indeed desirable for all areas of practice is up for debate. However, where it is a feasible option it carries with it the benefit of objective assessment following well structured training (in which the academy could participate) giving a benefit to the holder of the accreditation as well as protection and/or reassurance to the public using his or her services.

D. Communication Channels

This chapter has already covered a number of communication channels—between the academy, the practitioners in the sector and the relevant regulators. One other very important communication channel is between the sector (including the academy) and the would-be entrants to the sector. However much effort the various stakeholders in the sector (the regulators, the teaching institutions, the employers and so on) may currently be putting into ensuring that would-be entrants are aware of the opportunities within the various branches of the sector and the routes to entry, more can surely be done.

Some students may not be fully aware of the cost of going through their chosen qualification route: for example, what is the combined cost of their degree and the professional qualification exams? They may not be aware of the employment prospects within their chosen branch: for example, what are their chances of getting a training contract or pupillage? They may not be aware of the alternative employment options within the sector: for example, could they follow the legal executive route or the apprenticeship route? What is the full range of employing organisations operating in the sector? It is probably not realistic to ensure all the information which every would-be entrant to a sector could conceivably want or need will reach the entire potential target audience. However, the sector should continue to work on this and make use of all communication channels open to them (for example, via the internet, university careers services and even into schools).

III. CONCLUSION

The legal services sector is facing a range of challenges in this time of change—legislative, financial, organisational and regulatory. The sector is dynamic and vibrant, as are the workers within it and all those who support

---

[33] Eg, solicitor advocates.

it (the academy and so on). All those players need to work together to be clear on the challenges the sector faces and find innovative solutions to them which work for everyone.

The participants and stakeholders in the sector are already engaged in a wide range of initiatives which will ensure the sector continues to go from strength to strength. That said, the following 'boxes' need to be ticked. First, the sector must attract the right quality of entrants. This is a communication issue, a matter of standards and an access issue. The benefits and challenges of a career in the law need to be communicated to would-be entrants to minimise the risk of suitable entrants being put off and to ensure that all entrants embark on the career in possession of the facts. There is a considerable volume of information available online, but understandably it can be confusing. Is it all objective? Is it comprehensive? Does it reach everyone? This is perhaps a role for the regulators and there may be scope for wider use of social media.

There must be clarity on what is required in the various parts of the sector. One size cannot fit all but, for example, there should be a statement of the common standard which all solicitors should achieve on qualification even if their subsequent careers may take them into a wide variety of specialist areas. The SRA's work on a Competency Statement is a step in the right direction and will permit appropriate mobility across the sector (by allowing credit for pre-existing qualifications or experience towards meeting the competence requirements). There must be no unnecessary barriers to entry but equally there must be no compromise on quality. The range of options for study (full-time, part-time, online etc) should ensure any student can find a study format to suit his or her circumstances.

Second, the training continuum needs to reflect the needs of the various parts of the sector. This means the teaching institutions and the employers must communicate so that each side knows what the other needs and can deliver. Requests to include the philosophy of ethics in the qualifying law degree being balanced by an understanding of how that can be resourced is an illustration of this. Developing apprenticeship training models which lead to a degree might be another.

Thirdly, all parts of the sector must continue to work together to ensure the 'continuing competence' of the entire workforce for the benefit of the providers of legal services and their clients. This will need to be tailored to suit the needs of the different parts of the sector. However, the academy, the practitioners and the regulators working together to produce tailored and relevant solutions will benefit all the stakeholders.

10

An Agenda for Research on the Legal Profession and Legal Education: One American's Perspective

RICHARD L ABEL[1]

I T IS AN honour to contribute to this book arising from the Centre for Professional Legal Education and Research (CEPLER) conference on the 'Futures of Legal Education and the Legal Profession'. I was struck by the serendipity that CEPLER is a near anagram for CLEPR, the Council on Legal Education for Professional Responsibility, launched by the Ford Foundation in 1969 to encourage clinical legal education in order to address two central social problems: unequal access to law and unethical behaviour by lawyers. I will return to those issues later.

I offer a 'US' perspective on lawyers and legal education with some diffidence—certainly not because the United States is a model to be imitated, but rather because comparative research unsettles accepted notions. I have repeatedly been forced to question basic assumptions: first, by studying African law in London and Kenya;[2] then, by Phil Thomas's invitation to comment on the 1979 Report of the Royal Commission on Legal Services;[3] next, by joining Philip Lewis in the Working Group for

[1] I am grateful to Hilary Sommerlad and Steven Vaughan for providing comments on this chapter and pointing out similarities and differences between the United States and United Kingdom.
[2] RL Abel, 'Law in Context, the Sociology of Legal Institutions, Litigation in Society: Phases in the Conception of Research Questions about the Legal System of Kenya' in R Luckham (ed), *Law and Social Enquiry: Case Histories of Research* (Uppsala, Scandinavian Institute of African Studies; New York: International Center for Law in Development, 1981).
[3] RL Abel, 'The Politics of the Market for Legal Services' in PA Thomas (ed), *Law in the Balance: Legal Services in the Eighties* (Oxford, Martin Robertson, 1982).

Comparative Study of Legal Professions;[4] and finally, by exploring the role of law in the struggle against apartheid in South Africa.[5]

I am going to discuss four interconnected topics: the profession's relationship to the economy and its implications for legal education; the causes of and remedies for ethical misconduct by lawyers; how legal education can ameliorate the chronic problem of unequal access to justice; and the defence of the rule of law in moments of crisis.

I. THE LEGAL PROFESSION AND THE ECONOMY

Recently, academic journals and popular media in the United States have raised alarms about the alleged overproduction of lawyers.[6] The belief that changes in the market for lawyers' services may dramatically influence the profession's future is inherent in the chapters in this collection by Julia Evetts, and by James Faulconbridge and Daniel Muzio.[7] What is the right number of lawyers? A historical perspective may be illuminating. Until well after the Second World War, the legal professions in the United States and England and Wales, deliberately limited entry: in the United States, by raising pre-law requirements and reducing law school places; in England and Wales through the cost and number of apprenticeships, limited first positions in solicitors' firms and seats in chambers, and the scarcity of briefs for newly qualified barristers; both jurisdictions manipulated pass rates on professional examinations.[8] The ratio of population to lawyers in the United States remained relatively constant for six decades (1890–1950) despite rapid economic growth and expanding government (especially during the New Deal and the Second World War). There were no more law students in 1960 than there had been in 1930. Then the floodgates opened: the number of US law students tripled in just two decades, halving the ratio of population to lawyers. Expansion of university law departments throughout the United Kingdom during that period was even more dramatic: from 3000 places to 14,500, nearly fivefold. Law schools also proliferated rapidly in

---

[4] RL Abel and PSC Lewis (eds), *Lawyers in Society* (3 vols) (Berkeley, University of California Press, 1988–89).

[5] RL Abel, *Politics by Other Means: Law in the Struggle against Apartheid, 1980–1994* (New York, Routledge, 1995).

[6] BZ Tamanaha, *Failing Law Schools* (Chicago, University of Chicago Press, 2012); RN Jonakait, 'The Two Hemispheres of Legal Education and the Rise and Fall of Local Law Schools' (2006–07) 51 *New York Law School Law Review* 862; RM Zahorsky, 'Law Job Stagnation May Have Started before the Recession—And It May Be a Sign of Lasting Change' (2011) *American Bar Association Journal* (1 July); P Campos, 'The Crisis of the American Law School' (2012) 46 *University of Michigan Journal of Law Reform* 177.

[7] See ch 2 by Evetts and ch 3 by Faulconbridge and Muzio in this collection.

[8] RL Abel, *The Legal Profession in England and Wales* (Oxford, Basil Blackwell Books, 1988) chs 2, 10; RL Abel, *American Lawyers* (Oxford, Oxford University Press, 1989) ch 3.

countries as diverse as Australia and Israel;[9] and Japan opened new graduate law departments, whose students were exempted from the arduous examination to become *bengoshi*.[10]

Many factors contributed to this expansion. Exemplifying the second wave of feminism, the number of women law students in the United States grew more than tenfold, from under 5000 in 1969 to 50,000 in 1986, constituting almost the entire increase in enrolment.[11] In both countries the democratisation of higher education coincided with the post-war economic boom.[12] Many US law students were inspired by the rights revolution: the civil rights and anti-war movements, feminism, environmentalism, consumerism, and the 'War on Poverty'. The post-war legal aid scheme in England and Wales greatly increased the demand for lawyers, assuring a steady income to fledgling barristers. Law firms expanded and globalised, as size and visibility in the world's financial capitals became surrogate measures of quality and prestige.

This rapid growth eventually encountered several obstacles. The number of women law students reached parity with men. The conservative reaction—Reagan and the Bushes in the United States; Thatcher, Major and Cameron in the United Kingdom—attacked legal aid and government regulation. Affirmative action in the United States, which greatly increased the number of minority law students, provoked a backlash, which is still being felt.[13] 'Big Law' in the United States and 'magic circle' firms in England recruited an increasing proportion of graduates from a broader range of law departments, and their dramatically higher salaries strongly shaped the aspirations of a generation of law students.[14] US firms with over a hundred

---

[9] L Zer-Gutman, 'Effects of the Acceleration in the Number of Lawyers in Israel' (2012) 19 *International Journal of the Legal Profession* 247; M Thornton, 'The New Knowledge Economy and the Transformation of the Law Discipline' (2012) 19 *International Journal of the Legal Profession* 265; HM Kritzer, 'It's the Law Schools Stupid! Explaining the Continuing Increase in the Number of Lawyers' (2012) 19 *International Journal of the Legal Profession* 209.

[10] KW Chan, 'Setting the Limits: Who Controls the Size of the Legal Profession in Japan?' (2012) 19 *International Journal of the Legal Profession* 321; S Miyazawa, KW Chan and I Lee, 'The Reform of Legal Education in East Asia' (2008) 4 *Annual Review of Law and Social Science* 333.

[11] C Menkel-Meadow, 'Feminization of the Legal Profession: The Comparative Sociology of Women Lawyers' in RL Abel and PSC Lewis (eds), *Lawyers in Society Volume 3: Comparative Theories* (Berkeley, University of California Press, 1989) ch 5.

[12] G Neave, 'From the Other End of the Telescope: De-Professionalisation, Re-Professionalisation, and the Development of Higher Education, 1950–1986' in RL Abel and PSC Lewis (eds), *Lawyers in Society Volume 3: Comparative Theories* (Berkeley, University of California Press, 1989) ch 4.

[13] *Gratz v Bollinger* [2003] 539 US 244; *Grutter v Bollinger* [2003] 539 US 306; *Parents Involved v Seattle School District* [2007] 551 US 701; *Schuette v Coalition to Defend Affirmative Action* [2014] 572 US.

[14] TP Seto, 'Where Do Partners Come From?' (2012) 62 *Journal of Legal Education* 242 (graduates from bottom-tier Chicago law schools hired by the largest Chicago firms). This was less true in the United Kingdom, where 80% of all 'magic circle' trainees came from

lawyers hired just 15 per cent of graduates entering private practice in 1982 but 41 per cent in 2008, almost a threefold increase.[15] City firms employed 29 per cent of trainee solicitors in 2009.[16] But the housing bubble, combined with the marketing of sub-prime mortgages, together with the sovereign debt crisis and consequent global economic contraction and rising unemployment, caused a dramatic collapse in the large firm sector. (We saw this movie before, when Silicon Valley's dot.com bubble burst in 2000.) Trainee contracts for solicitors declined from a peak of 6000 to about 4800 in 2012. Large American firms hired 8462 graduates in 2008 but little more than half as many (4757) three years later.[17] Dewey & LeBoeuf (with over 1400 lawyers at its peak) declared bankruptcy in 2012.[18] Weil, Gotshal & Manges, one of the most profitable firms in the United States, laid off 60 associates and 110 non-lawyers and cut compensation for about 10 per cent of its partners.[19] Cost-cutting corporate clients refused to pay exorbitant hourly rates to train new lawyers and brought work in-house. Firms replaced lawyers on the partnership track with cheaper contract lawyers, outsourced work to countries like India, and delegated it to para-professionals. Just as we have seen information technology drastically reduce demand for occupations like bank teller, travel agent, petrol station attendant and retail salesperson, so IT has made lawyers more productive and let firms substitute capital for labour in more routine tasks (document review, drafting, legal research, even brief writing). Each of these trends is core to chapter nine in this collection by Tony King.[20] Accountants and management consultants have invaded lawyers' markets; 'alternative business structures' may do so in the United Kingdom.[21] We need to understand the factors that influence demand for lawyers and how it might fluctuate in the future.

Contraction of the large firm sector has led some to warn that there are too many lawyers.[22] A social constructivist would ask: who is raising the alarm, what are their interests and why are they doing so now? There is a troubling parallel with those who railed against the alleged 'litigation crisis'

Russell Group universities: http://www.legalweek.com/legal-week/analysis/2354461/the-oxbridge-conveyor-belt-a-progress-report-on-law-firms-efforts-to-widen-the-graduate-recruitment-pool

[15] I developed these figures from annual reports by the National Association for Law Placement, 'Trends in Graduate Employment' (NALP, 2013), available at: www.nalp.org/trends.

[16] Law Society, 'Annual Statistical Report 2009' (Law Society, 2009).

[17] See 'Trends in Graduate Unemployment' (n 15).

[18] JB Stewart, 'The Collapse' *The New Yorker* (New York, 14 October 2013) 80.

[19] P Lattman, 'Mass Layoffs at a Top-Flight Firm' *New York Times* (24 June 2013).

[20] See ch 9 by King in this collection.

[21] The Legal Services Act 2007 made possible this form of legal services organisation in England and Wales, and the Legal Services (Scotland) Act 2010 allows them in Scotland (where they are known as licensed legal services providers).

[22] See Abel, *Politics by Other Means* (n 5).

or 'compensation culture'.[23] For decades American insurance companies and repeat-player defendants—employers, product manufacturers, organisations representing doctors—have spent huge sums to convince the public and legislators that personal injury lawyers file large numbers of frivolous claims and have sought to pack state courts with judges sympathetic to that belief. The British have been even more contemptuous of American 'cowboys' who chase ambulances.[24] Such behaviour is often blamed on the alleged overproduction of lawyers. But there is no litigation crisis. The Oxford Socio-Legal Centre's landmark 'misfortunate study' showed that only about 1 in 10 accident victims suffering serious disability recovered tort damages.[25] The Rand Corporation found a similar proportion in the United States.[26] Michael Saks, Marc Galanter, Michael McCann and William Haltom have debunked the myth of litigiousness in the United States, demonstrating that any increase in civil litigation is attributable to 'business' plaintiffs, not individuals.[27]

The assertion that there are too many lawyers requires us to ask: who should decide that number and by what criteria?[28] Let me briefly review the alternatives. Many professions historically enjoyed a *numerus clausus*, keeping the total number of members constant; French *notaires* still do.[29] Other occupations jealously defend similar privileges: London's black cabs and New York's yellow taxis (now against ride-sharing apps);[30] pubs and off licences; gambling casinos; hotels resisting competition from Airbnb and

---

[23] A Morris, 'The "Compensation Culture" and the Politics of Tort' in TT Arvind and J Steele (eds), *Tort Law and the Legislature: Common Law, Statute and the Dynamics of Legal Change* (Oxford, Hart Publishing, 2013).

[24] RL Abel, 'An American Hamburger Stand in St Paul's Cathedral: Replacing Legal Aid with Conditional Fees in English Personal Injury Litigation' (2002) 51 *DePaul Law Review* 253; R Verkaik, 'Scandal of "No Win No Fee" Cowboys' *The Independent* (London, 1 January 2009).

[25] D Harris et al, *Compensation and Support for Illness and Injury* (Oxford, Oxford University Press, 1984).

[26] DR Hensler et al, *Costs and Compensation for Accidental Injury in the United States* (Santa Monica, Rand Corporation, 1991).

[27] MJ Saks, 'Do We Really Know Anything about the Behavior of the Tort Litigation System—And Why Not?' (1992) 140 *University of Pennsylvania Law Review* 1147; M Galanter, 'Reading the Landscape of Disputes: What We Know and Don't Know (and Think We Know) About Our Allegedly Contentious and Litigious Society' (1983) 31 UCLA 4; W Haltom and M McCann, *Distorting the Law: Politics, Media, and the Litigation Crisis* (Chicago, University of Chicago Press, 2004).

[28] RL Abel, 'What *Does* and *Should* Influence the Number of Lawyers?' (2012) 19 *International Journal of the Legal Profession* 131.

[29] A Boigeol, 'The French Bar: The Difficulties of Unifying a Divided Profession' in RL Abel and PSC Lewis (eds), *Lawyers in Society Volume 2: The Civil Law World* (Berkeley, University of California Press, 1988) ch 7.

[30] Two medallions for NYC yellow cabs sold for more than $2.5 million in November 2013; the average price for an individual medallion has risen from less than $550,000 in 2008 to more than $1 million: M Flegenheimer, '$1 Million Medallions Stifling the Dreams of Cabdrivers' *New York Times* (New York, 14 November 2013). A variety of websites let private car owners offer to drive passengers, eg: www.lyft.me; www.side.cr; www.uber.com.

similar sites.[31] But limiting numbers increases prices without necessarily ensuring quality (or reducing alcoholism or compulsive gambling). Many professions historically used ascribed characteristics—class, gender, race, religion—to limit numbers and raise status. Some of the resistance to the proliferation of private law schools in Israel is Ashkenazi animus against Sephardic Jews (ironic, given the historic barriers to Jews entering the legal profession and other desirable occupations in Europe and the United States).[32] However, in both the United States and United Kingdom today, the legal profession's legitimacy depends on paying lip service to representativeness, even if the demographics (other than gender) have not changed that much.[33]

Although formal education now occupies the core of every profession's self-conception, it became essential for US lawyers only in the early twentieth century and for English lawyers 50 years later, well after the Second World War. The American Bar Association (ABA) deliberately controlled the number and backgrounds of lawyers by cutting part-time law school places from 31,000 in 1928 to just 12,000 in 1953, drastically reducing entry by students who had to work during the day.[34] I used to say, only half facetiously, that the American Medical Association (AMA) was responsible for the 1983 invasion of Grenada, which Reagan justified as necessary to 'save' the Americans who were studying medicine there because the AMA had limited the number of places in US medical schools. Examinations and medical residencies still prevent a large proportion of the foreign educated doctors living in the United States from qualifying to practise.[35]

Educational qualifications often have tenuous connections to the positions for which they qualify, for instance, the requirement of an 'Oxbridge' honours degree in classics in order to serve in the nineteenth-century British or colonial civil service.[36] We know almost nothing about the use lawyers

---

[31] W Gellhorn, *Individual Freedom and Governmental Restraint* (Baton Rouge, Louisiana State University Press, 1956); W Gellhorn, 'The Abuse of Occupational Licensing' (1976) 44 *University of Chicago Law Review* 6; LM Friedman, 'Freedom of Contract and Occupational Licensing, 1890–1910: A Legal and Social Study' (1965) 53 *California Law Review* 487.

[32] N Ziv, 'Unauthorized Practice of Law and the Production of Lawyers' (2012) 19 *International Journal of the Legal Profession* 175.

[33] RL Abel, *English Lawyers between Market and State: The Politics of Professionalism* (Oxford, Oxford University Press, 2003) ch 4. On the covert role of ascribed characteristics in law firm hiring, see HL Sommerlad, 'The Commercialisation of Law and the Enterprising Legal Practitioner: Continuity and Change' (2011) 18 *International Journal of the Legal Profession* 73.

[34] Abel, *American Lawyers* (n 8) Table 5.

[35] C Rampell, 'Path to United States Practice is Long Slog to Foreign Doctors' *New York Times* (New York, 11 August 2013). On the doctor shortage, see 'Letters to the Editor' *New York Times* (11 December 2013) in response to S Gottlieb and EJ Emanuel, 'No, There Won't Be A Doctor Shortage' *New York Times* (4 December 2013).

[36] P Vasunia, 'Greek, Latin and the Indian Civil Service' (2005) 51 *The Cambridge Classic Journal* 35.

make of the knowledge and skills they acquire as law students.[37] I once met an anthropologist studying the maths people deployed in daily life; not surprisingly, no one used the long division he or she had struggled to master in primary school (much less hand calculation of square roots). Law graduates often disparage the worth of their own education while simultaneously insisting that succeeding cohorts undergo the same *rite de passage*. But there is enormous national variation in the timing, length, content and pedagogy of legal education and no reason to believe there is one best system.[38] This may be an opportune time for innovation. In response to rising educational indebtedness, some US law schools are joining with undergraduate colleges to reduce the length of the combined course from seven years to six. In August 2013 President Obama casually said 'law schools would be wise to think about being two years instead of three years'.[39] By contrast, countries as diverse as Australia, Japan and South Africa have moved law from a first to a postgraduate degree. We should compare the knowledge and skills of law graduates across educational institutions, both within and between countries.

In the United States, scepticism about the value of formal legal education (often expressed by employers and judges),[40] and concern about its rising cost, have revived interest in apprenticeship.[41] Unfortunately, its advocates are poorly informed about the experience of other countries. In England and Wales, articles and pupillage required payment of a premium that could equal a year's average income. Solicitor apprentices served unpaid for up to five years, barristers for up to two. Masters influenced numbers by their willingness to accept apprentices and freely indulged biases in selecting them. Training contracts rose from 4826 in 1996/97 to 6303 in 2007/08; even so, there was a shortfall of 1797 contracts in the latter year compared with those passing the Legal Practice Course.[42] The limited empirical research on apprenticeship has raised serious doubt about its educational value. That is hardly surprising: if universities subordinate teaching to research, solicitors firms and barristers chambers necessarily elevate profit above instruction.

---

[37] But see CM Campbell, 'Lawyers and their Public' (1976) *Juridical Review* 20; J Carlin, *Lawyers on their Own* (New Brunswick, New Jersey, Rutgers University Press, 1962) 41, 77.

[38] D Tyack, *The One Best System: A History of American Urban Education* (Cambridge, Harvard University Press, 1974); D Ravitch, *The Great School Wars: New York City, 1805–1973* (New York, Basic Books, 1974).

[39] J Sink, 'Obama: Make Law School Two Years' *The Hill* (23 August 2013), available at: thehill.com/homenews/administration/318523-obama-make-law-school-two-years.

[40] HT Edwards, 'The Growing Disjunction between Legal Education and the Legal Profession' (1992) 91 *Michigan Law Review* 34.

[41] The incentives of master and apprentice are more closely aligned where the master is training the apprentice to become an employee. N Schwartz, 'Where Factory Apprenticeship is Latest Model from Germany' *New York Times* (30 November 2013).

[42] Lawyer Watch, 'A History of LPC Numbers' (*Lawyer Watch*, 2010), available at: www.lawyerwatch.wordpress.com/2010/11/09/a-history-of-lpc-numbers.

All contemporary legal professions require examinations. Here again one can see the all too visible hand of the ABA, which reduced the number of jurisdictions granting in-state law students a diploma privilege (ie, exemption from the Bar exam) from 32 to just one or two.[43] But few, if any, occupational examinations have ever been validated, ie, compared examinees' results to professional performance. Is 'the knowledge' a necessary and sufficient prerequisite for driving a black cab? Even France is reconsidering its revered *baccalauréat*.[44] There is persuasive evidence that legal professions use examinations to regulate numbers. The Japanese Institute for Legal Training and Research—the only path to becoming a *bengoshi*—long admitted just 2 per cent of those who took its notoriously difficult entrance examination, often after having spent years cramming for it following completion of a university law degree.[45] When Japan decided it needed more lawyers it relaxed the examination and exempted those who studied law as a postgraduate degree.[46] In 1923, 25 per cent passed the Bar exam in Texas but 100 per cent did so in North Dakota—differences that cannot reflect relative competence.[47] The pass rate for the English Bar Finals rose to a high of 87 per cent just before the Crash of 1929, only to plummet to 50 per cent the following year and remain that low or lower for decades.[48] The pass rate for the Law Society's Final reached an astonishing 97 per cent in 1920, presumably to compensate for catastrophic losses in the First World War, averaging 87 per cent between 1918 and 1930, only to decline steadily during the Depression to just 54 per cent in 1939.[49]

If all these barriers raise interesting empirical and policy questions, what about the default position of capitalist economies: let the market control? Law is hardly the only occupational category that has experienced a mismatch between supply and demand. US graduate schools have seen cycles of boom and bust in jobs for PhDs in English, history, the social sciences and engineering.[50] Just when pet ownership is decreasing, the United States is producing more veterinarians, who are encumbered with more educational debt than

---

[43] Abel, *American Lawyers* (n 8) Table 13.

[44] S Sayare, 'Rite of Passage for French Students Receives Poor Grade' *New York Times* (27 June 2013).

[45] K Rokumoto, 'The Present State of Japanese Practicing Attorneys: On the Way to Full Professionalization?' in RL Abel and PSC Lewis (eds), *Lawyers in Society Volume 2: The Civil Law World* (Berkeley, University of California Press, 1988).

[46] Chan, 'Setting the Limits' (n 10).

[47] Abel, *American Lawyers* (n 8) Table 16.

[48] Abel, *The Legal Profession* (n 8) Table 1.1.

[49] ibid, Table 2.10.

[50] EK Abel, *Terminal Degrees: The Job Crisis in Higher Education* (New York, Praeger, 1984).

law graduates.[51] Credential inflation[52] has led aspiring chefs to incur huge debts to obtain a BA at the four-year Culinary Institute of America rather than work their way up in restaurant kitchens—only to find there are no jobs.[53]

None of this should be surprising. A century and a half ago Karl Marx showed that labour, although commodified by capitalism, remains qualitatively different from other commodities.[54] Despite Joseph Schumpeter's enthusiasm for capitalism's 'creative destruction',[55] few would willingly change places with those forced to sell their labour in the 'freest' markets: gardening, casualised construction work, care for the dependent (children, the elderly and disabled), food service, office cleaning. It is no coincidence that these positions are filled by immigrants, women and people of colour, who have no choice. Almost 40 years ago a Harvard economist demonstrated that professions often exhibit worse imbalances between supply and demand than other labour markets because they require a greater investment in human capital.[56] But market forces are powerful if not inexorable. Like other jobs, legal work is becoming increasingly contingent and part-time, especially for women raising children and those from less privileged backgrounds.[57] We urgently need to study their legal careers, whose trajectories will become more common in the future and more divergent from the professional elite.

II. THE 'CRISIS' IN LEGAL EDUCATION

Legal education has been experiencing its own crises, related to the job market changes sketched above but also attributable to other causes.[58] In the United Kingdom, the Legal Education and Training Review addresses an overlapping set of issues.[59] In the United States, an ABA Task Force recently

---

[51] D Segal, 'High Debt and Falling Demand Trap New Vets' *New York Times* (23 February 2013).

[52] R Collins, *The Credential Society: An Historical Sociology of Education and Stratification* (New York, Academic Press, 1979).

[53] J Moskin and G Collins, 'Students Protest at Culinary Institute' *New York Times* (23 April 2013).

[54] K Marx, *Capital* (London, JM Dent & Sons, 1934).

[55] J Schumpeter, *Capitalism, Socialism and Democracy* (New York, Harper, 1942).

[56] RB Freeman, 'Legal Cobwebs: A Recursive Model of the Market for Lawyers' (1975) 57 *The Review of Economics and Statistics* 179.

[57] H Sommerlad et al, *Diversity in the Legal Profession in England and Wales: A Qualitative Study of Barriers and Individual Choices* (London, Legal Services Board, 2010); H Sommerlad and P Sanderson; 'Professionalism, Discrimination, Difference and Choice in Women's Experience of Law Jobs' in P Thomas (ed), *Discriminating Lawyers* (London, Cavendish, 2000).

[58] Tamanaha, *Failing Law Schools* (n 6).

[59] Legal Education and Training Review, 'Setting Standards: The Future of Legal Services Education and Training Regulation in England and Wales' (SRA, BSB and CILEX, 2013), available at: www.letr.org.uk.

published a draft report raising fundamental questions about how lawyers should be trained and whether non-lawyers can provide legal services.[60]

In October 2013 the number taking the Law School Aptitude Test (LSAT: a prerequisite for applicants) was down 11 per cent from a year earlier and down 45 per cent from its peak in 2009.[61] US law school tuition fees have risen faster than either inflation or the costs of higher education generally. Public universities have suffered a steady decline in government funding, forcing them to rely increasingly on contract research (for government and industry) and alumni donations, whose preferences shape research and pedagogy (as EP Thompson warned more than 40 years ago).[62] Students have paid the rising costs by borrowing, hoping to land a 'Big Law' job paying an outsized salary. But like inner city boys hoping to become professional basketball players or girls aspiring to be models or pop singers, few will succeed.[63] The salary distribution for the class of 2011 was bimodal, with a small peak around $165,000 and a much larger bulge around $45,000.[64] The same salary distribution is also seen in the United Kingdom.[65] US law schools have been seduced by the scramble for *US News* rankings. But whereas market competition can increase productivity (and thus everyone's well-being), Lester Thurow showed 30 years ago that positional scarcity makes competition for status a zero-sum game.[66] Wendy Espeland and Michael Sauder have carefully analysed how *US News* rankings distort law school applications, admissions, transfers, financial aid, faculty recruitment and compensation, curricula, pedagogy, graduate placement, even law firm hiring.[67] Schools constrict access (sometimes eliminating part-time programmes that provided access to disadvantaged students), lavish scholarships on students who least need them and pay astronomical salaries to so-called superstar faculty members. They shift resources from pedagogy to research, whose value is measured by citation indices, which can reward

---

[60] American Bar Association Task Force on the Future of Legal Education, 'Draft Report on Proposed Reforms to Pricing, Accrediting and Licensing' (ABA, 2013).

[61] J Schwartz, 'Drop in LSAT Takers Shows Legal Field's Slump' *New York Times* (31 October 2013).

[62] EP Thompson, *Warwick University Ltd: Industry, Management and the Universities* (Harmondsworth, Penguin, 1970).

[63] S James, 'Hoop Dreams' documentary film (FineLine Features, 1994).

[64] National Association for Law Placement, 'Class of 2012 Salary Distribution Curve' (NALP, 2013).

[65] Solicitors Regulation Authority, 'Review of the Minimum Salary Requirement for Trainee Solicitors' (SRA, 2012), available at: www.sra.org.uk/minimum-salary.

[66] LC Thurow, *The Zero-Sum Society: Distribution and the Possibilities for Economic Change* (New York, Basic Books, 1980).

[67] W Espeland and M Sauder, 'Rankings and Reactivity: How Public Measures Recreate Social Worlds' (2007) 113 *American Journal of Sociology* 1; M Sauder and W Espeland, 'The Discipline of Rankings: Tight Coupling and Organizational Change' (2009) 74 *American Sociological Review* 63; W Espeland and M Sauder, 'Rating the Rankings' (2009) 2 *Contexts* 16; W Espeland and M Sauder, *Fear of Falling: How Media Rankings Changed Legal Education in America* (New York, Russell Sage Foundation, forthcoming).

egregious methodology or erroneous findings—for instance the 2010 Carmen Reinhart/Kenneth Rogoff paper asserting that any country whose debt reached 90 per cent of GNP was in imminent danger of default.[68] Perhaps emulating the ranking of corporate law firms in terms of profits per equity partner (PEP),[69] the PayScale College Salary Report ranks colleges by the starting salaries of their graduates and average return on investment (ignoring differences in the cultural capital of entrants).[70] Two months after resigning as Obama's Secretary of Homeland Security to become president of the University of California, Janet Napolitano said she was 'deeply skeptical' of the administration's recent proposal to rate undergraduate education by measures like average tuition and graduates' debt burden.[71] We need similar research into the perverse effects of the Research Assessment Exercise (RAE) and Research Excellence Framework (REF) in higher education in the UK.

Despite the scepticism just expressed, however, I believe one should never waste the opportunities offered by a good crisis—especially given the resistance of legal education to change. I suggest we explore three questions:

1. What should be taught, how and where? We need better information about the knowledge and skills lawyers deploy in practice. Given the constantly increasing division of labour within the legal profession, law departments cannot be the exclusive—perhaps not even the principal—locus of pedagogy. We need to discover what students learn in university but never use; what lawyers learn during apprenticeship and on the job; how to make such learning more effective and efficient; and how the cumulative acquisition of human capital shapes lawyers' careers.

2. Who learns where? Universities also function as a sorting mechanism—a role at least as important as imparting knowledge—by deciding whom to admit, assessing student performance and allocating graduates to places across the legal profession's hierarchy. Forty years ago, German law faculties were said to enjoy equal status; students attended the closest one so they could live at home.[72] Half a century ago, most Americans attended law schools and practised law in their home states. Now, however, the status differences among law departments in most common law countries are extreme and notorious, as documented by Jerome Carlin and John Heinz and Edward Laumann in the United States.[73]

---

[68] CM Reinhart and KS Rogoff, 'Growth in a Time of Debt' (2010) 100 *American Economic Review* 573.

[69] See ch 3 by Faulconbridge and Muzio in this collection.

[70] www.payscale.com. See JB Stewart, 'New Metric for Colleges: Graduates' Salaries' *New York Times* (13 September 2013).

[71] N Anderson, 'Napolitano, University of California President, "Deeply Skeptical" of Obama College Rating Plan' *Washington Post* (6 December 2013).

[72] E Klausa, *Deutsche und Amerikanische Rechtslehrer* (Berlin, Nomos, 1981).

[73] Carlin, *Lawyers on their Own* (n 37); JP Heinz and EO Laumann, *Chicago Lawyers: The Social Structure of the Bar*, rev edn (Chicago, Northwestern University Press and Chicago

Departments compete for status by seeking to enrol students with the most human capital, thereby reproducing unequal endowments. The rising cost of legal education intensifies this process. Echoing a proposal advanced nearly a century ago,[74] some observers have argued for formally bifurcating legal education: offering cheaper training for lawyers dealing with the allegedly simpler problems of individuals and a more expensive course for those serving corporations and the wealthy.[75] But that would further entrench unequal justice. And Gary Bellow taught us more than 35 years ago that the legal problems of the poor are, if anything, more challenging than those of the rich because the deck is stacked against them.[76]

3. How much should legal education cost, and how should it be financed? Panic about rising costs has provoked a variety of proposals. Law is a postgraduate degree in the United States, Canada, Australia, South Africa and increasingly in Japan, but not in any of the various jurisdictions which make up the UK. Civil law universities often combine law with philosophy, economics, political science and history over six or more years. Should lawyers study law exclusively, or does a liberal education confer benefits on society as well as the individual? Law often has been taught by practitioners—paid far less than full-time academics—who bring extensive practical experience but lack theoretical perspective. The University of London used to offer an external degree by correspondence; will MOOCs (massive open online courses) revive this, and would that be desirable? How should legal education be financed: by the state, alumni, family resources, or need or merit-based scholarships (funded by those paying full freight)? If the human capital that education confers pays significant returns to the individual, why should it be subsidised by others? If students borrow to finance their education, should repayment be forgiven for those who do public service? How should that be defined? Should repayment be a function of income? Should private investors be able to purchase an equity interest in another person's human capital and share the return from future income?[77]

ABA, 1982); JP Heinz et al, *Urban Lawyers: The New Social Structure of the Bar* (Chicago, University of Chicago Press, 2005).

[74] AZ Reed, *Training for the Public Profession of Law* (New York, Carnegie Foundation 1921).

[75] See Abel, *Politics by Other Means* (n 5); but see B Garth, 'Crises: Crisis Rhetoric and Competition in Legal Education: A Sociological Perspective on the (Latest) Crisis of the Legal Profession and Legal Education' (2013) 24 *Stanford Law & Policy Review* 503, available at: www.ssrn.com/abstract=2166441; E Chambliss, 'It's Not About Us: Beyond the Job Market Critique of US Law Schools' (2013) 26 *Georgetown Journal of Legal Ethics* 423.

[76] G Bellow, 'Turning Solutions into Problems: The Legal Aid Experience' (August 1977) 34 *NLADA Briefcase*.

[77] T Siegel Bernard, 'Frayed Prospects, Despite a Degree: Unusual Programs Link Student Loans to Future Earnings' *New York Times* (20 July 2013).

III. THE CAUSES AND CURES OF LAWYER MISCONDUCT

In addition to asking how many lawyers we need and how to produce them, we should think about what lawyers do and how they do it. When I joined UCLA 40 years ago I was asked to teach a course on the legal profession. In the aftermath of Watergate—whose primary perpetrators from Nixon on down all were lawyers—the ABA decided that the best way to prevent such unethical behaviour was to compel law schools to require a course on legal ethics. However, convinced that the decisions of individual lawyers are powerfully shaped by institutions, I taught the course as a sociology of the legal profession, devoting half the semester to the profession's core ethical problem: unequal access to law.[78] I will return to that below. Ten years ago I decided to look at the ethical problems that preoccupy virtually all other American law teachers and researchers: the dilemmas individual lawyers face in their daily practice. Legal academics focus almost exclusively on clarifying the philosophical foundations of ethical rules and refining and applying them to new situations. Socio-legal scholars, by contrast, seek to describe and explain the behaviour to which the rules apply because one cannot effectively change behaviour without understanding it. In other substantive areas socio-legal scholars study deviance, family interaction, compliance with tax law and other regulatory regimes, how businesses form and enforce contracts and responses to accidental injury. I decided to examine the behaviour of lawyers who violated ethical rules. I also hoped to address a pedagogic problem. US law students resent the compulsory course on professional responsibility.[79] Law school teaches students to view law positivistically, like Holmes's 'bad man', cynically interpreting every rule in the client's interest and taking advantage of systemic under-enforcement.[80] Legal ethics, by contrast, asks students to view law as an end rather than a means, to honour its spirit and not just follow the letter. I hoped that case studies of disciplined lawyers would help students see how they might behave unethically and say to themselves: 'there but for the grace of God go I'.

We insist that lawyers behave ethically because the division of labour compels clients, adversaries, fora and society to trust them. Ethical misconduct presents a paradigmatic instance of white-collar crime: not a 'who-done-it', since the facts are rarely disputed, but rather a question of whether the behaviour was unethical and why it occurred. I studied lawyer deviance by reading disciplinary cases in New York and California—the two largest jurisdictions in the United States, which together contain 275,000

---

[78] RL Abel (ed), *Lawyers: A Critical Reader* (New York, New Press, 1997).

[79] RM Pipkin, 'Law School Instruction in Professional Responsibility: A Curricular Paradox' (1979) *American Bar Foundation Research Journal* 1109; FK Zemans and VG Rosenblum, *The Making of a Public Profession* (Chicago, American Bar Foundation, 1981).

[80] E Mertz, *The Language of Law School: Learning to "Think Like a Lawyer"* (Oxford, Oxford University Press, 2007).

lawyers.[81] Because respondents rightly treat prosecutions as matters of professional life or death, trials are unusually thorough, and convicted lawyers are strongly motivated to disclose biographical detail during the penalty phase. Because discipline relies almost exclusively on client complaints, most cases involve allegations of excessive fees and neglect.[82] I deliberately included overzealous lawyers, about whom clients understandably do not complain. I also looked at ambulance chasing, fraud and conflict of interest. Almost all respondents were solo or small firm practitioners: large firms, house counsel and government lawyers were virtually absent, as were women, even though their numbers are approaching half the profession.[83]

Although many lawyers seek psychic rewards from grateful clients,[84] money, not surprisingly, lies at the root of most lawyer misbehaviour, which is prompted by greed or need. Lawyers feel entitled to be paid handsomely for their expertise, dedication and hard work. Most misconduct is not a product of ignorance: disciplined lawyers tend to be older and more experienced. They are committed to their misconduct, rarely expressing remorse (even strategically, to reduce the penalty);[85] many are recidivists who have disregarded prior fines and private reprimands.

My research left me sceptical about existing efforts to prevent misconduct. Clarifying, modifying or extending ethical rules will have little effect because the wrongfulness of the conduct rarely is ambiguous. Law school courses and continuing education are unlikely to help since ignorance of the rules is not the problem. Rather, lawyers learn to engage in unethical behaviour by watching or talking to other lawyers.[86] Nor are disciplinary bodies excessively lenient: those convicted of serious misconduct tend to be punished severely. The real problem is that the system is reactive and unsuited to most misconduct. First, it depends on complaints by clients, who are unaware of ethical rules, poorly situated to observe much misconduct, unmotivated to complain, and often emotionally attached to their lawyers. Clients might be

---

[81] RL Abel, *Lawyers in the Dock: Learning from Attorney Disciplinary Proceedings* (Oxford, Oxford University Press, 2008); RL Abel, *Lawyers on Trial: Understanding Ethical Misconduct* (Oxford, Oxford University Press, 2010).

[82] I excluded cases where the respondent had committed a felony because these are really an adjunct of the criminal process.

[83] In the United Kingdom, black and minority ethnic solicitors are overrepresented: H Ouseley, *Independent Review into Disproportionate Regulatory Outcomes for Black and Minority Ethnic Solicitors* (Birmingham, SRA, 2008); P Kandola, 'Solicitors Regulation Authority Commissioned Research into Issues of Disproportionality' (Birmingham, SRA, 2010).

[84] A Sarat and WLF Felstiner, *Divorce Lawyers and their Clients: Power and Meaning in the Legal Process* (Oxford, Oxford University Press, 1995).

[85] Lawyers, of course, are not unique in this, as Dante suggests in *Inferno*. See RP Harrison, 'Dante: The Most Vivid Version' *New York Review of Books* (New York, 24 October 2013) 41, 42.

[86] JE Carlin, *Lawyers' Ethics: A Survey of the New York City Bar* (Russell Sage Foundation, 1966); LC Levin, 'The Ethical World of Solo and Small Law Firm Practitioners' (2004–05) 41 *Houston Law Review* 309.

encouraged to complain if disciplinary bodies acted promptly and offered material incentives. How effective is the British system of compensation for inadequate professional service? Second, the remedies are inappropriate for the most common complaints: excessive fees, neglect, and incompetence. That is one reason why the disciplinary system sifts out most complaints, dismissing them as outside its jurisdiction or imposing trivial penalties in secret, confirming lawyers' beliefs they can get away with it. The system might publicise all complaints, but that would expose lawyers to the cost of false positives (ie, reputational damage from unfounded complaints).

My research also suggested other responses. Solicitors' firms must have an internal mechanism for handling client complaints.[87] Which clients invoke it, how often and with what consequences? The Law Society could promulgate a client's bill of rights and require solicitors to provide it with every retainer. Would this change the relationship between lawyers and clients? What has been the effect on fees of the requirement to provide advance cost estimates and inform clients if these are exceeded? The bill of rights could offer clients the option of a second opinion and cost estimate before they sign a retainer. How does the possibility of a judicial assessment of costs after the fact influence fees? Do audits of client accounts by the Solicitors Regulation Authority make misappropriation of client funds less common than in the United States? Would mandatory computerised tickler systems reduce the incidence of missed deadlines? Solo practitioners are over-represented among disciplined lawyers; should partnerships be mandatory, so that at least one other lawyer is financially responsible for misconduct in the firm? Malpractice insurance premiums are experience rated (if at all) by crude specialisation categories.[88] How costly and effective would it be to use more refined behavioural criteria? What if insurers competed in price, motivating them to regulate their insureds to reduce malpractice? Information asymmetries create both the need for trust and opportunities for betrayal. Could those asymmetries be reduced by for-profit referral sources (with a reputational stake in their ability to assess the quality and integrity of lawyers)? By third-party payers (though these might be more concerned about price than quality)? Or by aggregating one-off clients (for instance, through trade unions or consumer groups)? Restrictive practices could be relaxed in the hope that freer competition would boost quality and lower prices. Should lawyers be able to solicit clients? Should the lawyers' monopoly be constricted to allow para-professionals to compete? To perform what functions? Or would this just require another layer of regulation? Will Alternative Business Structures maintain quality while reducing

---

[87] C Christensen, S Day and J Worthington, '"Learned Profession?—The Stuff of Sherry Talk": The Response to Practice Rule 15?' (1999) 6 *International Journal of the Legal Profession* 27.

[88] FL Goldfein, 'Legal Malpractice Insurance' (1998) 61 *Temple Law Review* 1285.

price? Will allowing clients to trade-off quality for price amplify existing inequalities within the legal system? Would de-legalising areas of social life do so? How does mediation affect the balance of power between divorcing spouses? If no-fault compensation were an alternative to tort, would it be chosen disproportionately by the less advantaged?

Inspired by an earlier project with the Working Group for Comparative Study of Legal Professions,[89] I sought to interest its members in conducting case studies of lawyer deviance and discipline in their own countries. The journal *Legal Ethics* published accounts from England, Canada, Australia, New Zealand and the Netherlands, with an analysis by Leslie Levin.[90] I hope researchers in other countries will be inspired to explore a range of questions. What is the effect on lawyer behaviour of the structure of the profession: size, composition, homogeneity, geographic distribution, stratification, division? What about structures of practice, for example, the size and longevity of productive units? Do national differences in legal education make a difference? What about modes of client referral, pricing and intensity of competition? How does relaxing particular restrictive practices affect conduct? What about differences in how lawyers are compensated: private clients versus public and private third-party payers; hourly rates, contingent fees, percentages of deals, competitive bids? What about differences in clienteles: individuals and organisations, monetary and cultural resources? Are disciplinary processes and remedies in other countries more or less effective? Is excessive zeal a problem unique to the common law's adversary system?

IV. EQUALISING THE SCALES OF JUSTICE

The greatest ethical dilemma confronting the legal profession is the unequal distribution of legal services. Tony King's chapter in this collection addresses this issue.[91] The wealthy do not harm the poor by indulging in lavish housing, expensive restaurants, luxury goods, first-class travel or superior health care. Mansions do not cause homelessness, three-star Michelin restaurants do not cause starvation, first-class sleeper seats did not rob me of a night's sleep crossing the Atlantic and Harley Street doctors do not impoverish the NHS. But unequal justice is not lesser justice; it is injustice. An adversarial legal system can produce fair processes and just outcomes only when there is equality of arms. This poses a structural problem for professional associations, law departments and other institutional players. Individual lawyers resolve it by calling themselves hired guns. But this 'adversary system

---

[89] Abel and Lewis, *Lawyers in Society* (n 4).

[90] RL Abel (ed), 'Comparative Studies of Lawyer Deviance and Discipline' (2012) 15 *Legal Ethics* (special issue).

[91] See ch 9 by King in this collection.

excuse', as David Luban called it, is a hypocritical evasion when we know the deck is stacked.[92]

The British Labour government after the Second World War and the Democratic Party's War on Poverty in the United States in the 1960s, committed public funds to redress the imbalance. But legal aid budgets peaked decades ago, and there is no prospect of recovering those earlier levels, much less of government equalising the scales of justice.[93] That compels us to consider other ways to redistribute legal services. In the United States (which has always privileged the private sector over the state), the principal mechanisms have been public interest law firms supported by private philanthropy (foundations and fundraising), small private firms committed to public interest work and pro bono contributions by large firms. Quantitatively, these contributions greatly overshadow legal aid. We need to evaluate the kind and quality of work done by each category of provider in the United Kingdom as well as the United States.[94] Public interest law, which began in the United States with civil liberties (the American Civil Liberties Union) and civil rights (the National Association for the Advancement of Coloured People) and expanded to feminism, environmentalism, consumerism and poverty in the 1960s, has since addressed an ever widening range of issues: privacy, national security, education, housing, nutrition, animal rights, low-wage work, health care, disability, sexual orientation and information technology. And public interest law has globalised, with organisations burgeoning in the global south, American and European lawyers working throughout the world and NGOs like Amnesty International and regional governments like the European Union becoming more active in the United States and Europe.[95]

We need to increase such efforts and improve their quality. How have professional associations fostered such work? What is the effect of non-material incentives, such as awards to lawyers and firms? Why do some firms and lawyers produce more pro bono services than others? A few US law schools require pro bono activity for graduation; should that be universal? New York's chief judge recently required 50 hours of pro bono work as a condition for admission to the Bar. What are the long-term consequences

---

[92] D Luban, 'The Adversary System Excuse' in D Luban (ed), *The Good Lawyer* (Totowa, New Jersey, Rowman & Allanheld, 1984).

[93] H Sommerlad and P Sanderson, 'Social Justice on the Margins: The Future of the Not-For-Profit Sector as Providers of Legal Advice in England and Wales' (2013) 35 *Journal of Social Welfare and Family Law* 305; Z Tillman, 'Legal Aid Demand Outpaces Program Growth, Providers Say' *National Law Journal* (Washington DC, 20 January 2014).

[94] RL Abel, 'State, Market, Philanthropy, and Self-Help as Legal Services Delivery Mechanisms' in R Granfield and L Mather (eds), *Private Lawyers and the Public Interest: The Evolving Role of Pro Bono in the Legal Profession* (Oxford, Oxford University Press, 2009).

[95] A Sarat and S Scheingold (eds), *Cause Lawyering and the State in a Global Era* (Oxford, Oxford University Press, 2001).

of such mandates? He also authorised corporate counsel who were not members of the New York Bar (because they did not appear in court) to offer pro bono services in the state.[96] How do law schools encourage—or discourage—public interest commitment among graduates? A significant proportion of US law students—more than half in the 1970s—claim they want to promote social justice.[97] But most graduates end up in commercial firms. There is vigorous debate about whether this 'public interest drift' reflects a more realistic appraisal of employment opportunities, the burden of educational debt, stark differences in pay and prestige, or beliefs about the intrinsic rewards of the work and opportunities for training, advancement and lateral movement. With colleagues at UCLA and Berkeley, I am beginning such a study of graduates of six California law schools to determine the influence on careers of endowment (what students bring to law school), education (what they do at law school) and experience (in each postgraduate position). This was inspired by UCLA's Program in Public Interest Law and Policy, which since 1997 has admitted 25 students to the law school each year and offered them financial aid, peer support, special courses, guest lectures, summer internships, mentoring, career placement and postgraduate fellowships.[98] We want to determine the influence of each component on long-term public interest commitment, including pro bono services by those in private firms. Although all this may express US exceptionalism—the by-product of a written constitution with a Bill of Rights, two centuries of judicial review, the rights revolution and the weakness of trade unions and political parties—I would urge a comparative study of the political orientations and career expectations of entering law students in the United Kingdom, how law departments differ in student demographics and pedagogy, and the influence of both sets of variables on subsequent careers.

Coming of age in the United States at the end of 1950s, I learned only later about such tragic betrayals of the rule of law as the war time internment of Japanese Americans and Senator Joseph McCarthy's red-baiting. The civil rights struggle inspired me to become a lawyer. After graduating from law school in 1965, I spent the summer in Jackson, Mississippi with the Lawyers Committee for Civil Rights under Law. The courage of black and white activists made an indelible impression. Twenty-five years later, moved by those memories, I began research in South Africa, leading to a book on the role of law in the struggle against apartheid.[99] When Abu Ghraib was exposed in April 2004 I knew I had to understand the American

---

[96] JC McKinley, 'Rule Change Could Ease "Justice Gap" for the Poor' *New York Times* (2 December 2013).

[97] HS Erlanger and DA Klegon, 'Socialization Effects of Professional School' (1978) 12 *Law & Society Review* 11.

[98] RL Abel, 'Choosing, Nurturing, Training and Placing Public Interest Law Students (2002) 70 *Fordham Law Review* 1563.

[99] Abel, *Politics by Other Means* (n 5).

response to 9/11—the greatest challenge to the rule of law in my adult life. I expected law to be at least as successful in opposing executive and legislative overreaching in the United States as it had been in the struggle against apartheid. South Africa had no written constitution; the US Constitution has contained a Bill of Rights for more than 200 years. South Africa had no tradition of judicial review; the United States had two centuries of experience. The South African judiciary had been appointed exclusively by the National Party; roughly equal numbers of US federal judges have been appointed by each of the two parties. For more than four decades the National Party controlled a parliament in which Helen Suzman was the sole opposition voice for 13 years; Republicans and Democrats regularly handed control of the American government to each other. South African newspapers operated under stringent censorship, and the government controlled radio and television. The First Amendment ensures broad freedom for American media. The South African legal profession was almost all white, and only a handful of lawyers opposed apartheid. The US legal profession had begun to integrate in the 1960s, and both individual lawyers and professional associations had a long tradition of challenging the government.

And yet the rule of law has suffered grievously in the United States since 9/11. Only foot soldiers were punished for Abu Ghraib, not the superiors who ordered or encouraged the abuses. The CIA held detainees in secret prisons, subjecting them to waterboarding and other harsh interrogation practices authorised by Justice Department lawyers. It rendered them to countries known to torture prisoners. Civilian contractors engaged in abuse with impunity. Psychologists were complicit in designing and conducting harsh interrogations.[100] The United States created Guantanamo Bay prison to obstruct judicial scrutiny. The United States engaged in assassinations, even of its own citizens, and conducted drone attacks killing and wounding thousands of civilians. The United States violated the sovereignty of Iraq, Afghanistan, Pakistan, Yemen and Somalia, disregarding or frustrating oversight by international organisations. Congress has been complicit in many of the worst abuses, blocking transfers of detainees from Guantanamo, which are essential to its closure. Congress stripped federal courts of habeas corpus jurisdiction; and judges who found ways to exercise it were reversed on appeal. Courts martial exonerated many charged with abuses and displayed lenience towards those found guilty. Both the Bush and the Obama administrations successfully invoked the state secrets doctrine to block judicial scrutiny of their abuses and frustrate damage claims. After nearly 13 years the military commissions have not conducted a single full-scale

---

[100] RL Abel, 'Professional Integrity' in M Freeman and D Napier (eds), *Law and Anthropology, Volume 12: Current Legal Issues* (Oxford, Oxford University Press, 2009) 430.

trial.[101] The civil liberties of US citizens and residents have been massively violated. Criminal prosecutions of alleged terrorists have been based on informants, whose actions verge on entrapment. Edward Snowden's leaks are only the latest instalment of revelations about National Security Agency (NSA) eavesdropping in the United States and around the world. The electorate has done little to rein in its representatives. Bush effectively played the fear card in 2004. And though Democrats won control of the House in 2006 and both the Senate and Presidency in 2008 and 2012 (while losing the House in 2010), Obama ended only some abuses—secret prisons and enhanced interrogation techniques—while intensifying others—targeted killings and eavesdropping—and dropping federal prosecutions of high value detainees and keeping Guantanamo open.

How effective has law been in exposing, halting, and correcting these abuses? Disappointingly little, despite the enormous resources and dedication of highly expert lawyers in NGOs (including the American Civil Liberties Union, Amnesty International, Human Rights First, Human Rights Watch, and the Center for Constitutional Rights); the pro bono contributions of solo and small firm practitioners, public defenders, and large firm associates and partners representing Guantanamo detainees; and the courage of military lawyers. The most powerful counterweights have been investigative reporting and leaks by brave government officials, WikiLeaks, Chelsea Manning and Edward Snowden, which forced public debate of Abu Ghraib, the CIA's secret prisons and renditions, enhanced interrogation techniques and NSA eavesdropping on telephone conversations and internet communications. Nevertheless, I am trying to identify the limited circumstances in which law has successfully opposed abuses by the executive and legislature in the hope that this will help future champions of the rule of law make the best use of their scarce material and political resources. Although I have looked only at the United States, this is a global problem, making it essential to conduct comparative research on the ways in which different legal and political institutions, civil societies and cultures have defended core rule of law concepts at moments of crisis.

I am confident that, inspired by other Keplers (the German mathematician and scientist who discovered the laws of planetary motion and the eponymous spacecraft searching for exoplanets), this CEPLER will continue to chart the contributions of law and lawyers to the ideals of justice.

---

[101] RL Abel, 'Law Under Stress: The Struggle Against Apartheid in South Africa, 1980–94 and the Defense of Legality in the United States after 9/11' (2011) 26 *South African Journal on Human Rights* 217.

Index